Lovely Lady Dressed in Blue

Lovely Lady dressed in blue—
Teach me how to pray!
God was just your little Boy,
Tell me what to say!

Did you lift Him up, sometimes,
Gently, on your knee?
Did you sing to Him the way
Mother does to me?

Did you hold His hand at night?
Did you ever try
Telling stories of the world?
O! And did He cry!

Do you really think He cares
If I tell Him things—
Little things that happen? And
Do the Angels' wings

Make a noise? And can He hear
Me if I speak low?
Does He understand me now?
Tell me—for you know?

Lovely Lady dressed in blue—
Teach me how to pray!
God was just your little Boy,
And you know the way.

Joe Kotcka

The Christian Pursuit

THE CHRISTIAN PURSUIT

by

HENRI MARDUEL

With a Foreword by the Rev.
FRANCIS J. RIPLEY

*Fear wist not to evade as Love
wist to pursue.*

Francis Thompson: *The Hound of Heaven*

P. J. KENEDY & SONS

NEW YORK

This translation of Perspectives Spirituelles
(*Editions Xavier Mappus, Paris*) *was made by*
Daphne Knott-Bower and Angela de Hartog

NIHIL OBSTAT : JOANNES M. T. BARTON, S.T.D., L.S.S.
CENSOR DEPUTATUS
IMPRIMATUR : PATRITIUS CASEY
VICARIUS GENERALIS
WESTMONASTERII : DIE 20 JUNII 1964

The Nihil obstat *and* Imprimatur *are a declaration that*
a book or pamphlet is considered to be free from doctrinal
or moral error. It is not implied that those who have
granted the Nihil obstat *and* Imprimatur *agree with the*
contents, opinions or statements expressed.

Contents

Foreword

How many of the Catholic laity of today take the spiritual life seriously? I have the impression that the percentage is far lower than it was a century ago. This opinion is confirmed when one examines the catalogues of, say, the firm of Burns & Oates, then operating at 28, Orchard Street, London. No doubt the increased tempo of life makes spirituality more difficult; but has the Catholic community surrendered too easily to the spirit of the world? As I write I have before me a book called *The Golden Manual: a Guide To Catholic Devotion, Public and Private*. Published by Burns & Oates it bears the *Imprimatur* of Nicholas, Bishop of Melipotamus, dated January 1st, 1850. It contains 821 pages. All of them are well thumbed.

It is not difficult for me to imagine my great-grandparents spending the evenings in the Lancashire farmhouse where they lived sitting at the fireside and quietly going through and absorbing the contents of books like this *Golden Manual*. Of course, the modern Catholic will say that the people of 1850 had no television, no radio, no cheap paper-backed novels, no popular glossy magazines and no demanding social life to distract them nor any aeroplanes or motor cars to take them away from their homes. We grant all this. Still the question must be faced: have Catholics in general surrendered too easily to the demands of this modern world? Are priests as insistent as they used to be in giving instruction on the need and methods of prayer? Can it be said that as a community we really love God when so lamentably few of us are prepared to attend popular devotions, hear sermons and receive Christ's Eucharistic Benediction? In my own archdiocese of Liverpool, traditionally one of the most fervent in the country, the attendance at Sunday Benediction has fallen from 50,856 in 1952 to 25,111 in 1963. The estimated Catholic population of the archdiocese is 512,087. Figures like these speak for themselves.

Think, if you will, of the organizations of the Catholic laity which require and give training in a definite way of spirituality. There are very few of them indeed and their membership is pitifully small. Our Retreat Houses are few in number and they are struggling to survive. How many of our Catholic people spend some definite time every day in mental prayer? How many have a set time for spiritual reading or in any way make a practice of it? How many visit the Blessed Sacrament regularly? How many undertake definite practices of mortification? If one's own powers of observation are to be trusted the answer to all these questions seems to be the same: hardly any.

Yet the words of Our Saviour still ring through the centuries: "Be you therefore perfect, as also your Heavenly Father is perfect" (Matt. 5. 48). He was speaking to a crowd of ordinary people assembled on a hillside. He was reminding them that as God's children by grace and adoption they must far exceed pagans and publicans in the practice of virtue. Instead of "perfect", St Luke, in the parallel passage, has "merciful". Our Lord in the context was exhorting his hearers to exercise mercy towards the unfortunate and the miserable but also benevolence and beneficence towards all, enemies included. Note the example our Lord gave to those people. Their perfection is to resemble in some way that of God himself. There can be no equality between the finite and the infinite. God is infinite in all perfection; man can only, in a limited degree, imitate and resemble him in the practice of perfection. The Greek text of St Luke makes it clear that our Lord was gently commanding. His words are partly perceptive and of obligation, partly of counsel. All Christians are bound to strive to acquire the perfection necessary for their state, so far as the precepts of God bearing on that state, and the duties of their state are concerned. All must keep God's commandments; all must love even their enemies. But all are counselled to strive after perfection according to their capacity. As God is filled with perfection to his infinite capacity so each of us should strive to be as perfect as our limited capacity permits. We are perfect as our heavenly Father is perfect if we sincerely strive to attain the degree of perfection he wills for us.

I have been reading through the pages which follow, by Fr Henri Marduel. Solidly based on the word of God, the writings of the Popes and the works of St Thomas Aquinas, they are eminently practical. The chapters, which are generally short and therefore suitable for busy people, stress the basic principles of the spiritual life and apply them to the matter of daily living in this twentieth century. I hope the book will be widely read. May I offer the reader a word of advice? Do not try to cover ground in this book. Take it slowly. Read with a pencil ready. Underline the sentences which particularly appeal to you. If you do not like marking the book then make practical notes on each chapter. You will rarely find a page in which there is absolutely nothing of interest. Remember that these chapters are meant to provide food for thought. Linger over each paragraph trying to draw spiritual nourishment from each as the busy bee does from each of the flowers in the garden. Superficial reading of a book like this will be useless. The disease of "headlineitis" is so prevalent today that many of us have lost the art of serious reading. We expect to take everything in rather as we absorb the morning paper. It is grossly unfair to do that with a spiritual book as excellent as this. It deserves to be read prayerfully and carefully. Those who take the trouble will be richly rewarded.

FRANCIS J. RIPLEY

Introduction

It is not without a great deal of hesitation and even a certain reluctance that I have undertaken the writing of this book. It is an attempt to sum up the contents of the retreats I have preached at the Foyer de Charité in Chateauneuf de Galaure, as well as in other places in France, in Belgium and in Switzerland. However, many competent persons whom I have consulted have urged me so strongly to go ahead that any further misgivings on my part would show a lack of trust in Providence.

It has in fact turned out to be a difficult task, because the rules of the written word are very different from those of the spoken word. The speaker can establish a personal contact with his audience, especially when he spends a whole week with them. His language can be more conversational, even light-hearted on occasion; he can sense the mood of his listeners and use an anecdote to illustrate a point in a way which might seem laboured in print. For this reason I have had to take my notes and start again from the beginning, in order to make a rather more literary and cohesive whole. At the same time I had to keep within the framework familiar to my listeners, and see that the original points were clearly made; this could only result in a compromise, which was only arrived at after a series of difficult and sometimes painful decisions.

This book is intended for lay people of average religious and secular education, and, as its title suggests, it aims at giving a picture of Christianity as a whole, rather than examining any of its aspects in detail. Consequently this is not a kind of catechism; still less is it an essay in apologetics. It is a study of the interaction between life and religion. It goes without saying that the doctrine is not only orthodox but entirely classical: in the realms of spiritual guidance no one has the right to steer into unknown waters. It is for this reason that I have quoted extensively from the Bible, the Acts of the Popes and the works of St Thomas Aquinas. It would not have been difficult to give many additional references, but this might have lent the book a somewhat forbidding air of erudition.

I am glad to have this opportunity to express my thanks to all those who have given me so much help and encouragement, and who in many ways are more the authors of this book than I am. It is not possible to mention all of them, but I would like to name at least Canon Babolat, Père Livragne of the Congregation of the Oratory, and Père Monier of the Society of Jesus, who will, I hope, find in these pages an undistorted echo of their ideas. And above all—Père Finet,[1] whom we all hold in such great affection, and whom I have had the joy and privilege of knowing for over thirty years. It was he who collected and sifted so much of the material for these retreats in the fundamentals of Christianity, and who worked out a way of preaching for a total of about six hours a day for the better part of a week, without losing his listeners' interest and attention. I would like to assure all of them of my prayers and gratitude.

———————

Quotations from the Bible are taken from the Knox translation, unless otherwise stated, and all references are also numbered according to this version, i.e. according to the Vulgate numbering.

[1] Canon Finet is the head of the Foyer de Charité at Chateauneuf de Galaure.

Preface to the English Edition

By way of preface to this book, I have been asked to tell my English readers something about what are known in France as "Retreats in Christianity". These retreats are given in the Foyers de Charité.[1]

The first Foyer de Charité, which is the mother-house of all the others, was founded in 1937, at Chateauneuf de Galaure, about 50 miles south of Lyons, not far from the valley of the Rhône. There are many original concepts in this foundation which make it different from other forms of Christian community. It is impossible to understand what life in a Foyer is really like without having lived it, but I will outline its main characteristics.

It is a Christian community modelled on the original community in Jerusalem and undertaking some form of work which varies from Foyer to Foyer and depends on the needs of the region and the abilities of the members of the community. Particular emphasis is laid on education, for the Foyers must be a source of light as well as of love.

At the head of each Foyer is a priest, who is the father of the household, and who is ultimately responsible for both the spiritual and the material welfare of the community. He may be assisted by one or more other priests, and the rest of the community is made up of lay people, both men and women, who make a promise of celibacy, and consecrate themselves to God through our Lady.

At the Chateauneuf Foyer there are at the moment three priests and about a hundred lay people, who run a retreat-house, two boarding-schools, one for boys and one for girls, and a farm, also courses in domestic science and various other

[1] As yet there is no Foyer de Charité in any English-speaking country, and so no English name has been decided upon. In French the word "foyer" means, originally, focus or hearth, fire-place; from this derive the further meanings of home, family, and, more recently, a centre, "focal" point from which a movement derives inspiration and on which it converges.

services for the local villages. Materially each Foyer and the various activities within that Foyer aim at being self-supporting.

As we all know, from the time the Church became firmly established under the Roman Empire, some of its members began to feel that the majority of Christians were no longer living as Christ wanted them to, and so they left the comforts and distractions of their surroundings and went away into the desert to meet the devil face to face and do battle with him. It was not long before these solitary hermits came to group themselves together in communities, and so the first monasteries were formed; but they still continued to live very much apart from the mass of Christians. Then came the mendicant orders, whose members spent most of their lives away from their monasteries, preaching. After the more contemplative orders came the first active orders, the nursing nuns and later the men's orders such as the "clerics regular", who even more than the mendicant orders lived in close contact with the people. Lastly, in our own time, we have the secular institutes, whose members live in the world, and can often be distinguished from their neighbours only by a more spontaneous and self-forgetting spirit of service. Thus we can see that God is calling Christians of today to new states of perfection, which separate them less and less from the rest of the world, for whom he has asked them to be the light and the leaven.

Today there are sixteen Foyers de Charité scattered over several continents: in France and Belgium, in Togo, in Colombia and Mexico; and there are plans for opening further Foyers in Switzerland, in Canada and in the West Indies. All these Foyers are linked to the mother-house in Chateauneuf in rather the same way as the different Benedictine abbeys are linked with each other. In all the Foyers, retreats are given which are known as "retreats in Christianity", because they are preached to a cross-section of the Christian community: secular priests and members of religious orders, doctors and housewives, intellectuals and farm labourers, artists and social workers, elderly couples and young students. They are not only for Catholics; for example at Chateauneuf de Galaure a Buddhist, a Muslim, a Rabbi and of course quite a number of non-Catholic Christians have all made retreats. This is enough to show that the retreats never have a specialized approach designed for a

particular group, but concentrate on giving people an idea
of the fullness of Christian doctrine taught by Christ and his
Church. The emphasis during this week of retreat is deliberately
laid on instruction rather than meditation (cf. II Tim. 4. 2), in
order that people may see Christianity as a whole, and see its
relation to the rest of life, and, in the knowledge of this added
dimension, that they may discover a greater sense of vocation
in their everyday lives. Consequently this book, which was
originally written as a résumé for those who had made one of
these retreats, can also be used by parish priests as a framework
for their instructions, and by lay people who wish to review the
Christian truths they learnt as children and acquire an adult
religious outlook.

H. MARDUEL

Foyer de Charité
Chateauneuf de Galaure
(*Drôme*)

Chapter 1

THE RECEPTION GIVEN
TO CHRIST

All wisdom has one source; it dwelt with the Lord God before ever time began—Ecclus. 1. 1.

The aim of this book is to give a synthesis of the Christian religion, not of its theory—this is the work of theologians—not by dealing with all the questions it raises—this would take several volumes—but by drawing the reader's attention to the links between dogma and daily life, taking those points of dogma which seem to us to have the greatest practical application. Our synthesis will be based on Love, because St John, by revealing to us that "God is Love" (1 John 4. 8, 16) gave us what must be the basis for all religious thought. The truth that God is love was not simply discovered by St John, but revealed to him by his master, Jesus Christ, of whom St Paul wrote: "The foundation which has been laid is the only one which anybody can lay; I mean Jesus Christ" (1 Cor. 3. 11). It is, therefore, to Christ that we must go to learn all the principles of our relationship with God, and especially the whole doctrine of Love.

It is Christ who comes to the world, it is he who takes the initiative, not we ourselves: "It was not you that chose me, it was I that chose you", he said to his disciples (John 15. 16). Similarly, he could say to each one of us: "It is not you who have called me, it is I who have come." The problem is, therefore, how to receive Christ. Not everybody succeeds in doing this, as St John tells us in the Prologue to his Gospel: "He, through whom the world was made, was in the world, and the world treated him as a stranger. He came to what was his own, and they who were his own gave him no welcome" (1. 10–11). We will start by examining some of the states of mind which

may prevent us from receiving Christ, then indicate those
which enable us to welcome him, and finally try to give an idea
of the problem of "the world". Only then shall we be able to
start on the main themes of this book.

St Mark's Gospel (9. 13–26) tells us an extremely revealing
anecdote, which it places immediately after the Transfiguration
of Christ on the mountain: "When he reached his disciples, he
found a great multitude gathered around them, and some of the
scribes disputing with them. The multitude, as soon as they saw
him, were overcome with awe, and ran up to welcome him.
He asked them, What is the dispute you are holding among
you? And one of the multitude answered, Master, I have
brought my son to thee; he is possessed by a dumb spirit, and
wherever it seizes on him, it tears him, and he foams at the
mouth, and gnashes his teeth, and his strength is drained from
him. And I bade thy disciples cast it out, but they were powerless. And he answered them, Ah, faithless generation, how long
must I be with you, how long must I bear with you? Bring him
to me. So they brought the boy to him; and the evil spirit, as
soon as it saw him, threw the boy into a convulsion, so that he
fell on the ground, writhing and foaming at the mouth. And
now Jesus asked the father, How long has this been happening
to him? From childhood, he said; and often it has thrown him
into the fire, and into water, to make an end of him. Come,
have pity on us, and help us if thou canst. But Jesus said to
him, If thou canst believe, to him who believes, everything is
possible. Whereupon the father of the boy cried aloud, in tears,
Lord, I do believe; succour my unbelief. And Jesus, seeing how
the multitude was gathering round them, rebuked the unclean
spirit; Thou dumb and deaf spirit, he said, it is I that command
thee; come out of him, and never enter into him again. With
that, crying aloud and throwing him into a violent convulsion,
it came out of him, and he lay there like a corpse, so that many
declared, He is dead. But Jesus took hold of his hand, and raised
him, and he stood up."
The interesting part of this account for us, in this present
context, is not the expulsion of the devil but the preceding
dialogue. It has one extraordinary feature: here is an unfortunate father whose son has been suffering for years from a danger-

ous affliction: "Often it has thrown him into the fire, and into water, to make an end of him", with fits which are probably unpredictable and give rise, in the father, to a mixture of pity and nervous irritation. To make matters worse, the disorder is unclean, for it is believed to be due to the presence of an evil spirit, and this only adds to the father's anguish and causes humiliation, anxiety for the future and fear that the evil spirit may take hold of other members of the family. Yet Jesus, usually so quick to relieve those who ask for help, seems to take no notice of all this misery; on the contrary he bursts into violent reproaches: "Ah, faithless generation, how long must I be with you, how long must I bear with you?" Why does he do this? The answer can be found in the father's opening remarks: "Master, I have brought my son to thee; he is possessed by a dumb spirit, and wherever it seizes on him, it tears him, and he foams at the mouth, and gnashes his teeth, and his strength is drained from him. And I bade thy disciples cast it out, but they were powerless." What do we find? A diagnosis: "He is possessed by a dumb spirit"; the symptoms: "Wherever it seizes on him, it tears him and he foams at the mouth, and gnashes his teeth, and the strength is drained from him"; finally: "And I bade thy disciples cast it out, and they were powerless." His attitude is sceptical and faithless and the result is more like the beginning of a medical consultation than an appeal to the Messiah, the Son of God, who is in fact treated like a common healer!

Then, and this is important to notice, Jesus plays the role that is expected of him and asks to see the child, as though he needed to make an examination. Having witnessed the victim's convulsions he questions the father as if he wanted further details about the case; but in doing this he gradually leads him to a better attitude of mind, to prayer and a desire for faith. Then, and only then, the miracle takes place; and the Gospel suggests that it did not happen in direct view of the crowd who had disputed with the apostles. Those who lacked faith would see that the miracle had taken place, but they would not see it happening.

Jesus always seems to play the part expected of him. To take some examples at random, when Jairus fell at Jesus' feet "imploring him to come to his house" (Luke 8. 41) to cure his

daughter, he goes, whereas, when the centurion points out
that there is no need for him to go himself (Mat. 8. 8), he heals
his servant at a distance. He only raises Lazarus from the dead
after having obtained from Martha an unequivocal profession
of faith; "Jesus said to her, I am the resurrection and life; he
who believes in me, though he is dead, will live on, and whoever
has life, and has faith in me, to all eternity cannot die. Dost
thou believe this? Yes, Lord she told him, I have learned to
believe that thou art the Christ; thou art the Son of the living
God; it is for thy coming the world has waited" (John 11.
25–7). This seems to be a kind of anticipatory application of
the famous maxim: "The measure you award to others is the
measure that will be awarded to you" (Luke 6. 38).

Approximately the same lesson can be learnt from the
conversation with Nicodemus (John 3. 1–21). Here we have
"one of the rulers of the Jews" who is well disposed towards
Jesus: "Master, we know that thou hast come from God to
teach us; no one, unless God were with him, could do the
miracles which thou doest." Even so, he has very great difficulty
in understanding what Jesus is teaching him, and the conversation ends in uncertainty: it is not stated that he found faith, nor
that he became a disciple; we only know from his subsequent
behaviour that he remained a supporter (cf. John 7. 50 ff., and
19. 39). He questions what Jesus tells him and his progress is
slow.

The meeting with the Samaritan woman offers a complete
contrast (John 4. 5–42). It starts badly; which is understand-
able in the circumstances, as Jesus is "tired after his journey"
and the woman naturally does not enjoy having to go down to
the well for water, and then carry it back up to the village in
the fierce, midday heat. It is not surprising, therefore, that her
first reply is unfriendly, especially as she can tell by his accent
that he is a Jew, and the Jews are enemies of her race and
nation, whom they despise. Furthermore, to human eyes, the
woman's character augurs even less well for the success of the
encounter, for she is openly a sinner: five men in succession and
the current one is not her husband. How does Jesus go about helping her? Firstly, he opens the conversation on the subject that
is already in her mind: water; and not by offering help but by
asking for it, so that she, by doing an act of kindness, becomes

receptive to good. Then Jesus quickly follows up the opening: "If thou knewest what it is God gives, and who this is that is saying to thee, Give me drink, it would have been for thee to ask him instead, and he would have given thee living water." At once the attitude of the Samaritan woman changes, she calls him "Sir". She understands only partly and slowly; it is difficult to imagine water "that flows continually to bring ever-lasting life". But at least she does her best, and when her mysterious companion reveals her faults, though she does quickly change the subject, she does not deny what he has said but recognizes that he is a prophet. Finally she is so overcome by her meeting with our Lord that, though not the type to concentrate on the spiritual at the expense of the material, she leaves her water-pot by the well and hurries up to the village and naïvely announces the event: "Come and have sight of a man who has told me all the story of my life; can this be the Christ?" The sinner has become not only an apostle, but a very effective one, for the villagers, on hearing what she says, go down to Jesus and get him to come up and speak to them for two days, after which many of them come to believe in him, and say to the woman: "It is not through thy report that we believe now; we have heard him for ourselves, and we recognize that he is indeed the Saviour of the world."

Jesus himself is sufficiently impressed by this incident to make an unusual gesture: he refuses the food they offer him saying: "My meat is to do the will of him who sent me, and to accomplish the task he gave me." This reminds us that we too must nourish ourselves with spiritual food and that man has a power not given to any other creature, that of being able to find his nourishment in God himself: for his mind, by entering ever more deeply into the understanding of the word of God; for his conduct, by conforming it to the will of God; and for his whole soul, by receiving the Eucharist.

Lastly, we can consider John the Baptist, who gives us a perfect example of how to welcome Christ into our lives (John 3. 25–36). John had already paid public tribute to Christ when he baptized him. But later John's disciples come to him and say: "Master, there was one with thee on the other side of Jordan, to whom thou didst then bear testimony. We find that he is baptizing now, and all are flocking to him." This amounted to a very grave temptation: that of competing with the very man whose way he had been sent to prepare. However, his disciples' error did at least serve to make John pronounce words which, for the purity of love and the depth of abnegation which they reveal, are among the most beautiful in the Gospels: "A man must be content to receive the gift which is given him from heaven, and nothing more. You yourselves are my witnesses that I told you, I am not the Christ; I have been sent to go before him. The bride is for the bridegroom; but the bridegroom's friend, who stands by and listens to him, rejoices too, rejoices at hearing the bridegroom's voice; and this joy is mine now in full measure. He must become more and more, I must become less and less." Not only is John determined, at whatever cost, to stay well within the limits of his mission, he also considers that he has found perfect joy in contemplating the happiness of his master. He likens Jesus, who has come on earth to found the Church and take her as his eternal companion—"I am with you all through the days that are coming, until the consummation of the world" (Mat. 28. 20)—to a bridegroom who takes his bride on their wedding day to remain with her for ever. He is only the best man who shares for a few hours in the joy of the bridegroom. When will we learn from John the Baptist that we have not to make a mission or a vocation for ourselves, but only to carry out the tasks that God has given us?

To sum up: the sins of the Samaritan woman do not prevent her from listening to Jesus or from becoming his herald, whereas the argumentative character of Nicodemus is enough to slow down his progress, and the father of the epileptic child only obtains the cure when he manages to pray for faith.

John the Baptist gives Christ a perfect welcome because he is full of abnegation and love. If we wish to receive Jesus as well as he did we must pray whole-heartedly, desire to have faith and cultivate a generous heart, and then we shall know the joy given to those who serve Christ.

Chapter 2

ALL-PERVADING LOVE

North wind, awake; wind of the south, awake and come; blow through this garden of mine, and set its fragrance all astir—
Song of Songs 4. 16.

In his discourse after the Last Supper, Jesus said to his disciples: "Live on, then, in my love" (John 15. 9), "not as in a temporary shelter, a tent put up just for one night,"—so Fr Huby happily puts it[1]—"but as in an all-pervading atmosphere of light and joy, which will envelop you and fill you completely. Dwell there, for although my love is faithful it does not force itself upon you; you are free to stay or to go." It is in such an atmosphere that all our Christian life should be lived and, also, that these pages should be read. We will now, therefore, define the qualities of soul which make up this atmosphere that we need in order to receive Christ and to listen to his teaching, and which create the climate best suited to the development of love.

The human soul that wants to love must become:

free, in order to be available and receptive to the calls made on it;

empty, so that the Beloved can fill it;

orientated towards God, consciously striving to come closer to him;

open and trusting, so that its love is not mean or calculated, which would make it unworthy of the name of love.

This freedom is born of interior silence, the emptiness comes from poverty of spirit, orientation needs desire, and open trustfulness comes from joy.

Silence

To love is to be attentive and receptive to the words of a person. Love is not content with merely observing the com-

[1] Huby, *Le Discours de Jésus après la Cène*, p. 79, Paris, 1942.

mandments, but actively desires to observe and listen to its
object. A Christian should be eager to hear the words of his
master, and this master does not care to speak loudly to us.
Elias in a moment of discouragement took refuge in a cave on
Mount Horeb, where Moses had received the Law: "Then
word came to him to go out and stand there in the Lord's
presence; the Lord God himself would pass by. A wind there
was, rude and boisterous, that shook the mountains and broke
the rocks in pieces before the Lord, but the Lord was not in the
wind. And after the wind, an earthquake, but the Lord was not
in the earthquake. And after the earthquake a fire, but the
Lord was not in the fire. And after the fire, the whisper of a
gentle breeze" (III [I] Kings 19. 11–12). It was in this gentle
breeze that God spoke to his prophet, and we also have to be
constantly on the alert for his word to be able to hear it.

Love needs privacy, it needs to live away from other people.
This is the reason for the family circle and for the honeymoon
couple. It pleases God to give all this to those he loves by taking
them into the desert, literally or figuratively, at the most
important moments in their lives; he did so for Jacob, for
Moses, for St Paul, and in modern times for Father Charles de
Foucauld. The chosen people also had to experience the
solitude of the desert, and they were led back there when they
strayed from the path. "It is but love's stratagem, thus to lead
her¹ out into the wilderness; once there, it shall be all words of
comfort" (Osee 2. 14).

Pure love needs a great purity of interior silence: it is only
in the calm of this "night" that one heart can speak to another.
We cannot really find God until we learn how to cultivate this
silence, until we refuse to be governed by the passions and
manage to calm the workings of the imagination; in short, until
we put into practice a certain asceticism, not at all easy in the
beginning, in order to eliminate everything which does not
lead us to him.

Poverty

We will consider just one aspect of it, that of spiritual
generosity: the desire to give something while knowing and

¹ "her" means here the people of Israel, referred to collectively in the
same passage as the mother of the individuals who make up the nation.

accepting that the giver will be made poorer by his act of giving. It means being always ready to act on all our Christian beliefs, even if this entails some sacrifice; more than this, we must desire these sacrifices knowing that, for God, to love us means to make demands on us. We have no need to be afraid of the suffering this brings, for does not the whole of Holy Scripture tell us "thy reward shall be great indeed" (Gen. 15. 1)? Look at Abraham. He was asked to do something almost unthinkable: for twenty-five years he had waited for the word of God to be accomplished. Then the miracle happened; he had his longed-for son when humanly speaking it was impossible. Isaac grew into a young man and his father had already begun to think proudly of the day when he would take his place at the head of the clan. But then came the terrible command: "Take thy only son, thy beloved son Isaac, with thee, to the land of Clear Vision, and there offer him to me in burnt-sacrifice on a mountain which I will shew thee" (Gen. 22. 2). Without making the least resistance, he journeyed for three days, built an altar, laid wood on it, and lifted the knife for the act which he knew would put an end to all his hopes. In the nick of time the angel stayed his hand and there came the divine reprieve: "I have taken an oath by my own name to reward thee for this act of thine, when thou wast ready to give up thy only son for my sake. More and more will I bless thee, more and more will I give increase to thy posterity, till they are countless as the stars in heaven, or the sand by the sea shore; thy children shall storm the gates of their enemies; all the races of the world shall find a blessing through thy posterity, for this readiness of thine to do my bidding" (ibid. 16–18). The reward is on the same scale as the renunciation; the sacrificed son is not lost after all, and with him is given a countless posterity and a blessing for the whole world.

Look at Mary: she also received her son contrary to all human possibility; for thirty years she surrounded him with affection, with such joy in her entire being. And for her, too, came the call for the total sacrifice: "Mary, take your son, your only son, him that you love, Jesus, and come and take part in his sacrifice on the mountain of Calvary"; and this time no angel came to stay the hand of the executioners. Christ had to pass through death and the tomb, but he, like Isaac, was not lost. His mother found him again on the glorious Easter morning. She, too, received the gift of a countless posterity, for every baptized Christian is truly her child. She gave much more than Abraham, and she received infinitely more, when we compare the blessing the old patriarch passed on to the world with her maternal influence on our eternal life. We can be sure that God's generosity to us, too, exceeds all our expectations, and when we have given up everything, we realize that it is all repaid to us, all and more besides. When we think of this, nothing else matters.

Now let us look at the story of Zacchaeus. He was a rich publican who was taken with the modest desire "to distinguish which was Jesus" (Luke 19. 3) as he was passing through Jericho. As he was a small man he could not see over the heads of the crowd, so he climbed up into a sycamore tree, and Jesus, looking up and seeing him, said: "Zacchaeus, make haste and come down. I am to lodge today at thy house" (ibid. 5). He only wanted to catch a glimpse of the Master, and now Jesus himself offers him hours of his company. This was enough for Zacchaeus; he understood at once: "Here and now, Lord, I give half of what I have to the poor; and if I have wronged anyone in any way, I make restitution of it fourfold" (ibid. 8). Like Zacchaeus, we should be willing to give beyond the demands of justice in answer to Christ's gift to us.

Desire

Love needs the presence of the beloved, it needs to be close to him, to be part of him, to feel him part of itself. It is never satisfied, it always wants to be closer, ever more intimate, and if this desire makes it suffer, it comes to love the suffering and feel lost without it, if it is not replaced by the joy of possession. The Christian would like to have these feelings towards his God, but he can only have them if he is one of those who feel that something is missing in his life; those who have everything they want do not need God. This is true of people who are "pampered, full-fed" like the Hebrews in Egypt (Deut. 32. 15); so complacent and content with what life has to offer them, they become incapable of looking for anything else. It is also true of those who, because they receive the sacraments and practise their religion to a certain extent, imagine themselves little short of perfection, and back away like the rich young man in the Gospels when the demanding nature of love is revealed to them. "If any man is thirsty, let him come to me, and drink" (John 7. 37), said Jesus, and the true believer answers him:

O God, my whole soul longs for thee,
as a deer for running water;
my whole soul thirsts for God, the strong, the living God;
shall I never again make my pilgrimage
into God's presence? (Psalm 41. 1–2).

But as for those who do not expect much, and do not want much, how can they be expected to find anything? They set little value on their God; in fact they disdain him. Is this an attitude likely to touch his heart and lead him to make himself known?

Joy

"Joy is caused by love."[1] Therefore it is a part of Christian spirituality, and we may conclude that charity is not real unless it leads ultimately to joy. There is a well-known saying: "A sad saint is a sorry saint." Nevertheless, many people are unable to live joyfully because they stop short at the trials and sacrifices asked of them by the Christian life, instead of looking beyond them, to God and all he gives them. Such people do not give themselves to God, they lend themselves—and only a part of themselves at that.

If we are fond of someone we will attempt to lose ourselves in the direct or indirect expression of our regard. And the same with the soul that really wants to give itself to God; faced with the demands of love, nothing else matters. If one can share with others in loving him, then a perfect joy springs up.

The joy of St Francis of Assisi, the joy of St Augustine, whose tears flowed when at last he found him he was looking for, the abounding joy of St Paul, the calm and strong joy of St John, and the inexpressible joy of Jesus whenever his thoughts turned to his Father—the true Christian shares in this joy, and without it there is no true religion.

[1] *Summa Theologica*, II^a II^{ae}, 28, 1.

Chapter 3

THE PROBLEM OF THE WORLD

The lover of this world has no love of the Father in him—1 John
2. 15.

Leo XIII in the Encyclical *Sapientiae Christianae* teaches us that
"to fix the gaze on God, and to aim earnestly at becoming like
Him, is the supreme law of the life of man".[1]

It is not difficult to see that "the world" is the opposite of
God, in as much as its characteristics are the opposite of those
of God.

The world is created, whereas God is the Creator;
it is limited, whereas God is immense (in the etymological
sense of the word—"without measure");
it lives in time, whereas God is eternal;
it is material in part, whereas God is pure spirit;
for the world it is Justice that is supreme, for God it is Love;
consequently the world is hard, whereas God is infinitely
good;
finally, whereas "God is light" (I John 1. 5), his opposite,
the world, lacks light and is darkness.

We are therefore faced with a fundamental choice, either to
take an interest in God and put him first in our lives, or else to
let the world occupy that place. Either we shall go towards the
light, or we shall seek the darkness; that is what will divide
men: "Rejection lies in this, that when the light came into the
world men preferred darkness to light; preferred it, because
their doings were evil. Anyone who acts shamefully hates the
light, will not come into the light, for fear that his doings will
be found out. Whereas the man whose life is true comes to the
light, so that his deeds may be seen for what they are, deeds
done in God" (John 3. 19–21).

[1] [Engl. tr. in, for example, *The Pope and the People*, p. 108. London
C.T.S., 1950.]

This drama of men who are unaware of their God begins when men are so fascinated by the world and its promises of comfort and pleasure that the unhappy creatures become incapable of seeing anything else. The modern world, wrote Stalin, is the product of a revolution which began in the sixteenth century. It was born of the fact that "men do not realize, do not understand or stop to reflect what *social* results these improvements will lead to, but only think of their everyday interests, of lightening their labour and of securing some direct and tangible advantage for themselves".[1]

This revolution has expressed itself chiefly in economic and technical terms, and so it has come about slowly, quietly and therefore implacably. Not having attracted attention it did not attract opposition. We have now reached a point where technical values have invaded the whole of life and are beginning to be taken for a new morality. Those who have made themselves its slaves are made uneasy by anything that goes beyond its scope, reaching the state of mind expressed by that abominable hero of Sartre's who cried: "I have delivered you. No more Heaven, no more Hell, nothing but Earth."[2]

The world of the twentieth century is, without any doubt, extremely well geared to the destruction of religious attitudes, not so much by persecution or argument as by subconscious suggestion. The thought of God disappears first from everyday life and then from the heart; it escapes in imperceptible stages.

Initially, men observe the exterior forms of religion, but practise them without love. This is in itself a sin: to be content with an ostensible conformity while rejecting the life that should inform it is completely contrary to the spirit of Christ. This error is practised collectively in many parishes where faith is largely a matter of routine. We should notice in passing that there is a certain way of talking in official circles which accepts and commends this error as normal, but it is dangerous to allow the religion of Christ to become nothing more than "the Churches", a mere "way of honouring God". This is to look at religion from a purely exterior point of view and therefore to place everything in an essentially false perspective.

[1] J. Stalin, *Dialectical and Historical Materialism*, p. 51. Moscow, 1951.
[2] Jean-Paul Sartre, *Lucifer and the Lord*, Scene X. [Engl. tr. by Kitty Black, London, 1952.]

If religion is emptied of its meaning men will gradually become aware of the empty frame, lose interest, and finally be disgusted with it and say: "I haven't the time", and they will only "pray when they are in a tight corner" and eventually abandon all forms of collective worship.

Finally, in the last stage, prayer is abandoned altogether in a life taken up completely by professional and family problems or simply by the passions. Phrases like: "I'm not a religious person but I'm better than many who say they are", are used to try to justify one's position, and gradually lack of faith and contempt of God are claimed as something to be proud of, and the passage to the enemy camp is complete. As St Augustine says, "turning to the works we turn from their author, turning our faces, after a sort, to the things made, and our backs to him who made them".[1]

This temptation, this tendency to lose the taste for the things of God is not new. On the contrary, it has been a permanent feature in the world since man's original sin, and Jesus warns us that it will continue in the Church: "In the days when the Son of Man comes, all will be as it was in the days of Noe; they ate, they drank, they married and were given in marriage, until the day when Noe went into the ark, and the flood came and destroyed them all. So it was, too, in the days of Lot; they ate, they drank, they bought and sold, they planted and built; but on the day when Lot went out of Sodom, a rain of fire and brimstone came from heaven and destroyed them all. And so it will be, in the day when the Son of Man is revealed" (Luke 17. 26–30).

This is a very characteristic text: we know that both before the flood and in the time of Lot abominations were being committed on earth (Gen. 6. 12, and 18. 20), but our Lord does not mention these, and the things he does speak of are not wrong in themselves: it is not wrong to eat or to drink, to get married, to sow crops, or to build. What is wrong is to do all these things in an atmosphere where God is forgotten: this is a greater evil than all the others, because it expresses a complete disdain for God, for him who deserves all our veneration. It is already the sin of "secularism".

---

[1] St Augustine, *Tractatus in Ioannem*, 8, 1.

If the light of God is no longer seen, if it is refused by the soul, things are nothing more than they are in themselves, that is to say, "Vanity of vanities, and all is vanity. . . . I have seen all things that are under the sun: and behold all is vanity and vexation of spirit" (Eccl. 1. 2 and 14).[1] The more men leave God out of their lives, even if this is not done deliberately, the less they are able to see any sense in life, or in the world. The current unawareness of God has deeply affected modern man, and he is tempted by an aversion to all that is real, an aversion sometimes, it would seem, even to himself.

The world which has abandoned God falls firstly into sin, then into dissatisfaction and finally into despair. Men feel caught up in a vicious circle from which they cannot escape, they are slaves unable to buy their freedom.

> No man can deliver himself from his human lot,
> paying a ransom-price to God;
> too great is the cost of man's soul;
> never will the means be his
> to prolong his days eternally and escape death (Psalm 48. 8–10).

"If creation is full of expectancy, that is because it is waiting for the sons of God to be made known. Created nature has been condemned to frustration; not for some deliberate fault of its own, but for the sake of him who so condemned it, with a hope to look forward to; namely, that nature in its turn will be set free from the tyranny of corruption, to share in the glorious freedom of God's sons" (Rom. 8. 19–21).

Intellectual Attractions

It would be pointless to speak of the attractions of the world in a general manner only; to say anything useful it is necessary to be more precise, so we will sketch at least the main features of the wiles whereby the world seeks to captivate and ensnare us in this twentieth century.

As far as its general mentality is concerned, our century has a preference for clear-cut, "committed" attitudes; the time of half-measures and compromises is past, and people want to be

---

[1] [Douay Version.—*Translator.*]

committed consciously and completely. When we meet with errors, therefore, these will no longer resemble the "heresies" of former times. The heretic is one who chooses from out of the full Christian doctrine some parts which he accepts and others which he refuses. Nowadays we are dealing chiefly with conceptions of the world which claim to be complete, and which differ radically from Christian doctrine. It is not by chance that the Encyclical *Humani Generis* bears the sub-title: "Concerning some false opinions which threaten to undermine the *foundations* of Catholic Doctrine."[1] It has been widely recognized that the Church's teaching is of an unassailable cohesion, and that, to combat it, its base must be undermined and a system set up as stable as is the Church's. Not least among the attractions of Communism is the fact that it forms a synthesis embracing the whole of life, and, in general, the more complete an error—any error—the closer it appears to be to the instincts of nature, the more attractive it will be. In these circumstances, a Catholic worthy of the name should be able to show his fellow men that he is thoroughly conversant with the doctrine he holds, and that he accepts it from A to Z, otherwise he will be judged to be half-hearted, inconsistent and weak.

We must not be deluded when systems which are fundamentally different from Christianity claim certain resemblances with it, sometimes using the Church's terminology to express completely different ideas, a trick which can create dangerous confusion. For example, the Christian wants to build the City of God on earth, he knows that that city should be agreeable to live in, and he will, therefore, be in favour of constantly improving the material welfare of mankind, especially the poorest of them, and of making use of the earth's material resources; but he knows that the perfect city only exists in the future and will not reach its final form until the world to come. The Communist replies that it is our duty to build a city which is of this world only, and that it is wrong for the least part of men's activity to be diverted from this goal. For him, even thinking of the other world is a crime because it distracts us from our preoccupation with this world. It is easy to see the consequences of this situation, and the outstretched hand must

[1] [Many editions in English are available, e.g. C.T.S. and *Catholic Documents*, London, The Pontifical Court Club.]

be refused, because after a period of apparent collaboration the differences between the two positions will make themselves felt, and if Communism wins it *must* persecute Christianity; this is an inevitable part of its own logic.

Where the salvation of the world is concerned, the Church does not invite its members to work out their own ideas but to adopt God's, to accept his teaching and to desire it, to be receptive to God, and not to allow themselves to be taken in by what Mgr Blanchet called "ideas that are idols".[1]

Attractions of the Senses

Clearly it is in this direction that the great mass of men are more compellingly attracted. This is not of course a new danger, but it is easy to see that it has increased considerably in our time. Scientific and technical progress has enabled us to be masters of the universe to a far greater degree than was possible for our ancestors, and has made available to a great mass of people pleasures more absorbing and more numerous than those previously reserved for a privileged minority, and far more people now enjoy a much greater degree of comfort. If one compares, for example, the life of a girl of twenty-five today who works in an office in any large town, with the life of her grandmother who at that age lived on her father's farm, the material differences in their lives are immediately obvious. What would our lives be like if suddenly the radio, the telephone, electricity, cars and trains were all removed at once? Yet all these discoveries are comparatively recent.

In addition, the stability of life seems to have disappeared; everything around us changes very rapidly, and we are constantly promised an ever-increasing comfort and ever greater amenities. So, when we are in difficulties, we are promised some new discovery which will solve all our problems and it is hard not to be taken in. Generally the solutions offered are not wrong in themselves, so it is not easy to draw the line between what is permissible in the circumstances and what is not, between the acceptable and the unacceptable. Gradually people give up making the necessary decisions, reason is replaced by feeling, and they tend to become adolescents, who

---

[1] *Semaine des Intellectuels catholiques,* 1949, p. 215. Paris,

grow old without ever reaching maturity. They become for all practical purposes pagans, happy with their pleasures, but selfish and indifferent.

In the midst of its material attractions the modern world has many serious defects. There is no need to elaborate on its hardness or the emptiness of an existence dominated by the pursuit of pleasure; nor will we dwell on the evils of some modern factories and offices where people have to work without knowing the purpose of what they are doing, or become slaves of a machine whose infernal rhythm they have to keep up with. We would like to concentrate more on the feeling, very widespread today, of being caught up in a chain of events for which we are in no way responsible and which, at first sight, influence our lives much more strongly than events which are under our control. It is true that good workers are always in demand, but when the cost of living goes up by 20 per cent and the buying power of money drops accordingly, there is nothing the worker can do about it. If the factory closes down, the good workers will lose their jobs as well as the bad ones. There again, there is nothing they can do about it. The closing down of the factory is probably caused by economic circumstances beyond the control of the management, or indeed of anybody at all. This is what weighs men down: the feeling of being enslaved and under some kind of malediction, which makes them turn even more desperately to pleasure to find solace and escape from their troubles.

The chain of events outlined above has certain notable results.

Firstly, the priest becomes isolated from those for whom he is responsible. Even in a parish that is outwardly "solidly practising" the parish priest is like a fish out of water among his parishioners. When he wants to raise their thoughts to spiritual matters they reply that the crops will be good, or that business is doing well, and the conversation continues at cross purposes and achieves nothing.

The other consequence is indicated by Pius XII who said: "It is true that the great progress that has been made in research and in the utilization of natural forces, and still more the emphasis that has been given to the spreading of purely earthly knowledge, have troubled the minds of many, so that they can barely perceive the supernatural."[1] The surrender to the things of the world has reached a point where many people are unable to think about the things of God, which no longer interest them and which they can no longer understand; a study or a hypothesis on the subject of the companion of Sirius would attract greater interest.

Finally, the fact that the world is forming itself into ever greater blocs tends to divide the mass of humanity: "Venerable brethren, you are well aware that almost the whole human race is today allowing itself to be divided into two opposing camps, for Christ or against Christ. The human race is involved today in a supreme crisis, which will issue in its salvation by Christ or in its dire destruction."[2]

We are, therefore, faced on the one hand with the spectacle of a world which increasingly conducts its affairs without reference to God, while on the other hand the Church continues to raise its voice to remind us of the triumph of Christ and of his continued growth in his Mystical Body. What is the Christian to do, and how is he to steer the right course in these complicated circumstances?

Some Human Solutions

The problem which we have set ourselves is one that troubles so many people that at least a start has been made at giving the solution: it is one of the main themes of contemporary literature. As this is not the place for lengthy erudition we will confine ourselves to the three types of solution offered by the characters in Anouilh's *Antigone*.

These are solutions of the simple, unelaborate type, not so different, after all, from those mentioned by Pius XII in his 1957 Christmas message. Firstly there are those who just don't care, as represented by the guards. Their indifference, indeed their incapacity to take an interest in anything outside themselves reaches a point where it is repugnant. In the face of the girl who is about to die, one of them is calmly talking about the

[1] Address to the students of the seminaries and Universities of Rome, 24 June 1939.
[2] Pius XII, Encyclical *Evangelii Praecones*. [Cf. *The Tablet*, 30 June 1951, p. 522, or *Catholic Documents*, V, p. 27.]

relative advantages of being a guard or a sergeant. But that type is Legion and can be seen in every bus, tube, and railway compartment.

Then come those who say an unqualified "Yes" to the world, as represented by Creon, Antigone's uncle: "I've both my feet on the ground, and both my hands in my pockets. Since I'm king, I've made up my mind to spend my time in trying quite simply to make the world a little less absurd than it is, if possible. You see, I haven't your father's ambition. What I propose to do is not even an adventure—it's an everyday job." In religious matters they are sceptics! "Have you ever heard the priests of Thebes recite the formula? Have you ever seen those poor, disillusioned timeservers with their hasty, skimpy gestures and gabbled words getting one corpse over so as to do another before lunch?" In the end they become so used to saying "Yes" that they become incapable of saying "No" even to avoid committing the basest of crimes.

In the face of all these compromises, Antigone reacts by a radical opposition: she is the type that says "No", choosing to die rather than alter her position: "I want everything at once. And I want it whole and entire. Otherwise, I refuse."[1] We cannot help admiring the fragile young girl who alone has the courage to prefer death to any compromise with human meanness. She attracts us, but her attitude is sterile because the world will kill her and her followers and when they have disappeared all will go on as before; nothing will have been changed and her efforts will be wasted.

Clearly none of these attitudes can be a Christian one, neither the proud "No" of Antigone nor the horrifying "Yes" of Creon, and still less the indifference of the guards. Then, what is the solution?

Let us turn to the Gospel. "You", says Jesus, "are the light of the world; a city cannot be hidden if it is built on a mountain top. A lamp is not lighted to be put away under a bushel measure; it is put on the lamp-stand, to give light to all the people of the house; and your light must shine so brightly before men that they can see your good works, and glorify your Father who is in heaven" (Mat. 5. 14–16). And again: "The kingdom of heaven is like leaven, that a woman has taken and

---

[1] Jean Anouilh, *Antigone*, pp. 71 and 75. Paris, 1946.

buried away in three measures of meal, enough to leaven the whole batch" (Mat. 13. 33).

The attitude of Jesus is quite different from all worldly attitudes. His followers "do not belong to the world" (John 17. 16) but they must stay in the world to act as light and leaven. The Saviour is sharing with us a divine prerogative: "God is light" (I John 1. 5). He himself is "the world's light" (John 9. 5), and here he is, saying that the same is true of his disciples. He means us to continue this mission. This privilege of carrying the torch is a particularly exacting one, it requires an effort which not all of us are prepared to make, because it is an intellectual effort and we are lazy; it consists in constantly distinguishing passing things from enduring ones and the admissible from the inadmissible. We are not asked to look at all human progress with a jaundiced eye. On the contrary, it is a question of using the discoveries of men in such a way that they give glory to God and liberate us for the spiritual. Neither should we spend our time indulging in nostalgia for times that have passed. To understand the times we live in, in order to be a light to them is not a permission which is granted to us, but an order that is given us. To go further, the leaven makes the bread rise only if it is mixed into it, and the Christian should always be on guard against deciding on any course of action simply in order to avoid temptation if this also entails a refusal to serve or an abdication of responsibilities. Those responsible for education have often erred on the side of cutting young people off too much from the outside world; and others engaged in good works have too often tended to confine their activities to the closed and comfortable circle of those who already share their ideas.

To achieve lasting results it is not enough to give money, either in small or large amounts, we must give ourselves and become involved; in matters of religion, we can only convert, only change our brethren by loving them, and it is only love that gives us any justification for trying to do so. If one tries to replace love by something else, the results are disastrous. For example, certain discussions on methods of Christian education or ways of running a parish can be pointless. Obviously in these as in other cases, there is a certain amount of technique involved but, however perfect the methods, no

B

results will be obtained without love as the first principle, and it is wrong to attempt to live quietly behind a barrier of foolproof systems that will eliminate the necessity to think and to learn from experience that love can be a disturbing element in life.

Finally we would like to point out two coincidences: a short time after Pascal had carried out the first experiments in modern physics and Descartes had perfected the mathematical instrument which would make possible the development of the sciences, Jesus appeared to an obscure nun and, showing her his heart, he said to her: "This is the heart that has so loved men." Then, as men did not listen to the message of Paray-le-Monial, and the corruption of the world continued, the Virgin Mary appeared to the children at Fatima; she showed them her heart and said: "The Lord wishes to establish devotion to my Immaculate Heart in the world. If what I say is done, many souls will be saved and there will be peace." The remedy that Christ offers for the evils of the world is to show us his heart and that of his Mother. "We have learned to recognize the love God has in our regard, to recognize it, and to make it our belief," said St John (I John 4. 16). The Christian solution to the problem and the desperate call of the world will always be to believe in love, to give ourselves up to it and so receive the will and the strength to serve others.

Chapter 4

GOD IS LOVE

In the depths of every human soul there is one tormenting question from which we cannot escape, even if we profess to be atheists. The future St Thomas Aquinas put it well when he asked the Benedictine monk who was entrusted with his education: "Master, what is God?"

This question has to be answered, for on it depends our inner life, and on that depends everything we do, and ultimately everything we are. A man is formed by the kind of god he worships. To take an example from within the sphere of Christianity, both Jansenists and Protestants reflect an unmistakable image of their interpretation of God.

It is a logical and psychological necessity for man to have a point of reference outside himself, to which he can direct all his human activities, and without one he deteriorates into worship of himself, and, as Thomas Merton says: "To worship ourselves is to worship nothing. And the worship of nothing is hell."[1]

This attitude does not always express itself in prayer or membership of any particular religious denomination. When St Paul complained of those for whom "their own hungry bellies are the god they worship" (Phil. 3. 19), he was not accusing them of celebrating Masses in honour of this part of the body, but of caring more about what they ate and drank than they did for the cross of Christ. There are other false gods: money, the flesh, personal honour, or even some other human creature for whom people will sacrifice everything, even the last shreds of their own dignity. In this sense it could be said that there is no such thing as atheism, but only false gods.

To be a Christian is, first of all, to admit that God has spoken to us and undertake to listen to his voice. He spoke to us, not

[1] Thomas Merton, *Seeds of Contemplation*, p. 23. London, 1949.

to teach us the structure of the atom or of the universe, or to explain our bodies to us or to give us a course in experimental psychology, but to make himself known to us, to give us "to know his Name". This means, in biblical language, to reveal oneself completely, to give oneself up entirely to the person to whom the name has been revealed.

This happened progressively. God's intention is to form an "alliance" with humanity, a very close union, so close that it can only be compared with the union of husband and wife. This conception is disconcerting to our modern minds, but it is a biblical conception, from the prophet Osee to the Gospel of St John and the Apocalypse, and so we see nothing to prevent us from using it, as we will do in comparing the period of the Old Testament to a betrothal, in which the future bride and groom come to know each other more intimately each day, without, however, giving themselves to each other completely. The New Testament is the wedding day, when God makes himself known and gives himself to man, expecting man to give himself in return. "I have made known to you *all* that my Father has told me; and so I have called you my friends" (John 15. 15).

"God the Father made a marriage feast for God the Son when he united him to human flesh in the womb of the Virgin; when he willed that he who was God in eternity should become man in time. . . . We can say, then, with greater clarity and assurance, that the Father made a marriage feast for his royal Son in as much as he united him to our holy Church by the mystery of the incarnation."[1]

The progress of this revelation is clearly indicated by passages like this: "I am the same Lord who revealed myself to Abraham, Isaac and Jacob; but although I revealed myself as God the Almighty [El Shaddai], my name Adonai [Yahweh] I did not make known to them" (Ex. 6. 2–3).

This name of Yahweh—"He that I am", remains a mystery; many biblical scholars think that it means a categoric refusal, or the impossibility of making himself known, something like "I am what I am". But however this may be, ever since the giving of the Law of Moses, humanity, betrothed to its God,

---

[1] St Gregory, *Homilia 38 in Evangelia* (formerly in the Roman Breviary for the Nineteenth Sunday after Pentecost).

has had sufficient knowledge of the nature of God to inflame its love.

(1) God is unique, or, rather, the only one of his kind, radically distinct from any other being: "Listen then, Israel; there is no Lord but the Lord thy God, and thou shalt love the Lord thy God with the love of thy whole heart, and thy whole soul, and thy whole strength" (Deut. 6. 4–5).

"What likeness, then, can you find to match me with? asks the Holy One" (Is. 40. 25). "I am before all; there is no other God but I" (Is. 44. 6), from whence the great importance of: "I, thy God, the Lord Almighty, am jealous in my love" (Ex. 20. 5). This statement repeated three times (cf. Ex. 34. 14) is characteristic, and gives shape to certain aspects of the Bible: the Holy One of Israel will not accept being placed on the same footing as anyone else whatever, for it would be against all truth and so is not to be admitted at any price. So, when his people worship foreign gods, he counts this sin as an adultery.

Surely, as a faithless wife leaves her husband,
so have you been faithless to me, O house of Israel (Jer. 3. 20).[1]

Let us never forget: God is he to whom we owe everything because he has given us everything. To prefer anyone else or anything else to him is to do him the same injustice, the same supreme injury as the adulterous woman does her husband when she turns her heart away from him and abandons him for a lover. Even if this insult is not made deliberately, do we not ceaselessly struggle against God's call for first claim on our love, by putting money, honours and our own selves in the place reserved for him? "Make it your *first* care to find the kingdom of God" (Mat. 6. 33).

(2) God possesses the earth and the entire universe because he is their creator.

The Lord owns earth, and all earth's fulness,
the round world, and all its inhabitants.
Who else has built it out from the sea,
poised it on the hidden streams? (Psalm 23. 1–2).

[1] This idea has been further developed in verses 1–13 of this chapter. [The translation quoted is that of the Revised Standard Version.—*Translator*.]

If he has created all this he is the absolute master of it, and he has every right over it. The comparison in the Bible of the potter who makes a vase of clay and then smashes it when it is not to his liking, is a limited one compared with the truth, for to make his vase the potter starts with raw materials; the Creator started with nothingness.

We have to go even further. Not only does the fact of creation give God every right over us, in the most absolute sense of the term, but we remain in a state of unimaginable dependence on him. Where we are concerned creation is not a thing finished and done with, it goes on, ceaselessly, and it could be said that we receive our being from God at every instant of our lives. Even more, every one of our thoughts and deeds, from the most open to the most secret and hidden, is subject to his almighty power, for if he were to wish that a certain thing should not happen, then it could not happen. At any moment, if he so wishes, he can plunge us back into the nothingness from which we have come. Therefore, to argue with God is vain, sterile and ridiculous, and if he chooses to lead us and the course of events by ways we find surprising, we must acknowledge his right to do so:

> How deep is the mine of God's wisdom, of his knowledge; how inscrutable are his judgements, how undiscoverable his ways! Who has ever understood the Lord's thoughts, or been his counsellor? Who ever was the first to give, and so earned his favours? All things find in him their origin, their impulse, the centre of their being; to him be glory throughout all ages, Amen (Rom. 11. 33–6).

Not mine, the Lord says, to think as you think,
deal as you deal;
by the full height of heaven above earth,
my dealings are higher than your dealings,
my thoughts than your thoughts (Is. 55. 8–9).

I acknowledge it, thou canst do all thou wilt,
and no thought is too difficult for thee.
Here indeed is one that clouds over the truth
with his ignorance!
I have spoken as fools speak,
of things far beyond my ken (Job 42. 2–3).

(3) Even if it is obvious that God is distinct from us, it does not follow that he is therefore a distant being. We may note in passing that from this point of view it is rather dangerous to compare him, for example, to the sun. It would be truer to say that he is intimately connected with us in the sense that the soul is connected with the body. He is within us, in every part of us, and "it is in him that we live, and move, and have our being" (Acts 17. 28).

The closeness of this contact has a most important consequence: there is no such thing as true indifference with regard to God. We can easily be utterly indifferent to an inhabitant of the Antipodes, because he has no connection with us and no influence on our lives. But it is impossible to remain indifferent to those who are close to us: either we become fond of them or else we detest them. The closer we are to someone, the greater the need to resolve the dilemma.[1]

Our proximity to God is beyond all imagination, since he is spirit, and spirit can penetrate right to the core of matter. Moreover, he is constantly at work in us, if only to give us our existence: "My Father has never ceased working," says Jesus (John 5. 17). His contact with us is continuous, so it would be dishonest to speak of neutrality where he is concerned: we are forced to make a radical decision between love and hate. One is absurd and leads us nowhere, the other is the way to happiness.

Psalm 138 sums up the feelings of a man meditating upon these things in an admirable way:

Lord, I lie open to thy scrutiny; thou knowest me,
knowest when I sit down and when I rise up again,
canst read my thoughts from far away.
Walk I or sleep I, thou canst tell;
no movement of mine but thou art watching it.

Before ever the words are framed on my lips,
all my thought is known to thee;
rearguard and vanguard, thou dost compass me about,

[1] This dilemma is sometimes not apparent in those who have had a strongly "secular" education, especially if this education has been characterized by great intellectual courtesy. There is no question of our attacking such people, they will have to be led gently out of their spiritual blindness. But this does not invalidate the principle we are expounding.

thy hand still laid upon me.
Such wisdom as thine is far beyond my reach,
no thought of mine can attain it.

Where can I go, then, to take refuge from thy spirit,
to hide from thy view?
If I should climb up to heaven, thou art there;
if I sink down to the world beneath, thou art present still.

If I could wing my way eastwards,
or find a dwelling beyond the western sea,
still would I find thee beckoning to me,
thy right hand upholding me.

Or perhaps I would think to bury myself in darkness;
night should surround me, friendlier than day;
but no, darkness is no hiding-place from thee,
with thee the night shines clear as day itself;
light and dark are one.

Author, thou, of my inmost being,
didst thou not form me in my mother's womb?
I praise thee for my wondrous fashioning,
for all the wonders of thy creation.
Of my soul thou hast full knowledge,
and this mortal frame had no mysteries for thee,
who didst contrive it in secret,
devise its pattern, there in the dark recesses of the earth.

All my acts thy eyes have seen,
all are set down already in thy record;
my days were numbered before ever they came to be.

A riddle, O my God, thy dealings with me,
so vast their scope!
As well count the sand, as try to fathom them;
and, were that skill mine, thy own being still confronts me.

Scrutinize me, O God, as thou wilt, and read my heart;
put me to the test, and examine my restless thoughts.
See if on any false paths my heart is set,
and thyself lead me in the ways of old.

(4) As early as the Old Testament, humanity began to
discover the goodness of God: "Give thanks to the Lord; the
Lord is gracious, his mercy endures for ever (Psalm 117. 1);
"Give thanks to the Lord for his goodness" (Ps. 135. 1). This
goodness and mercy extends to the most loving tenderness:

"I will console you then, like a mother caressing her son"
(Is. 66. 13); and it contains pity and patience:

How pitying and gracious the Lord is,
how patient, how rich in mercy!
He will not always be finding fault,
his frown does not last for ever;
he does not treat us as our sins deserve,
does not extract the penalty of our wrong-doing.
For his own worshippers,
the Lord has a father's pity;
does he not know the stuff of which we are made?
Can he forget that we are only dust? (Psalm 102. 8–10,
13–14).

But this love is as demanding as a husband's love for his wife,
and sometimes it inspires fear. God behaved as he did to the
stiff-necked people of Israel because their conception of
morality was still primitive, and they had to be handled with
a certain severity.

In spite of everything that had happened up to this point,
mankind was only at the very beginning of his knowledge of
God, he had only a feeble spark of light in the darkness. With
the coming of Jesus we are suddenly in full sunlight, where the
closeness of God to us will be revealed. The nuptial day has
come. As he says to the Samaritan woman: "Believe me,
woman, the time is coming when you will not go to this
mountain, nor yet to Jerusalem, to worship the Father. You
worship you cannot tell what, we worship knowing what it is
we worship; salvation, after all, is to come from the Jews; but
the time is coming, nay, has already come, when true worshippers will worship the Father in spirit and in truth; such
men as these the Father claims for his worshippers. God is a
spirit, and those who worship him must worship him in spirit
and in truth" (John 4. 21–4). The name Father, repeated three
times to make clear the majestic importance of what he was
saying, this word Father is the true Name of God. This is the
word which brings us most closely into union with him. For
indeed, beyond this word we know nothing, and in this word,
when it is fully understood, is contained the whole of Christian
belief.

Jesus felt so deeply about it, that he never referred to God by any other name, except when he was giving some specific explanation. And when he taught us to pray he did not tell us to say "My God", or "God, my Father", but quite simply "Our Father". The time has passed when devout men were wont to worship an unapproachable divinity. The "new man" (Col. 3. 10 and Eph. 4. 24) and the "new creation" (Gal. 6. 15) pay to their "Father which is in heaven" the homage of a perfect service in which the element of worship is, of course, still present, but completely absorbed now into the offering of their filial affection. For it is one and the same person who is God and who is also Father, wholly God and wholly Father, and not, as some Christians seem to believe, "the Almighty who, in some way, is vaguely paternal". This is an Old Testament idea and therefore two thousand years out of date. Surely this should make us ask ourselves how we stand in this matter, and whether God, to us, is not still purely and simply "He that exists". We should do well to learn to speak of God as "the Father", which is a precise and liturgical title fully in accordance with the Gospels.

God is a father because he has a son, Jesus, who possesses all that the Father possesses: "All I have is thine, and all thou hast is mine" (John 17. 10), to such a degree that "my Father and I are one" (John 10. 30). "Had you knowledge of me, you would have knowledge of my Father as well" (John 8. 19). The two live together in the closest and most complete intimacy; their oneness is perfect, and they have no secrets from each other: "The Father loves the Son, and discloses to him all that he himself does" (John 5. 20). That is not all; the Father passes all his prerogatives and all his powers on to his Son, in particular the highest of all, the one which sums up the divine privilege: the power over Life and Death.[1] "Just as the Father bids the dead rise up and gives them life, so the Son gives life to whomsoever he will. . . . Believe me, the time is coming, nay, has already come, when the dead will listen to the voice of the Son of God, and those who listen to it will live. As the Father has within him the gift of life, so he has granted to the Son that he too should have within him the gift of life, and has also granted him the power to execute judgement, since he is the Son of Man" (John 5. 21 and 25–7).

[1] Cf. Deut. 32. 39 and IV [II] Kings 5. 7).

Fatherhood consists not only in giving life but in the father's giving his *own* life, not in receiving *a* child but in receiving one's *own* child: in our case, the one destined for us from all eternity; in this case, the one that the Father eternally begets for himself in heaven. The completeness of this communication is beyond our understanding, and from it springs the double wonder of being made for each other and of being worthy of each other. And what greater sign of love is there than this gift of existence, of life, of the whole being, of this complete sharing of all thoughts and all powers? In the Godhead, the father-son relationship reaches a perfection and a beauty which cannot be equalled, precisely because the Father is able to make his entire self known to the Son, and because the Son is able to receive the whole of this gift from his Father. From this exchange flows a perfect happiness: the Father looks upon his Son with complete satisfaction as he sees in him a perfect reproduction of himself, and the Son looks upon the Father with admiration for the beauty and the generosity of him from whom he receives everything, of himself having nothing.

Therefore Jesus claims for himself all the fullness of being— "Believe me, before ever Abraham came to be, I am" (John 8. 58)—and also the knowledge of the Father: "But I have knowledge of him; if I should say I have not, I should be what you are, a liar" (John 8. 55), and it is this which allows him to say in all truthfulness: "My words are what I have learned in the house of my Father" (ibid. 38); "It is the will of him who sent me, not my own will, that I have come down from heaven to do" (John 6. 38); and again: "When you have lifted up the Son of Man, you will recognize that it is myself you look for, and that I do not do anything on my own authority, but speak as my Father has instructed me to speak. And he who sent me is with me; he has not left me all alone, since what I do is always what pleases him" (John 8. 28-9). This is indeed the central law of his existence: "Believe me when I tell you this, The Son cannot do anything at his own pleasure, he can only do what he sees his Father doing; what the Father does is what the Son does in his turn" (John 5. 19).

In short, we see that Jesus is the perfect answer to the Father's love, both by the witness he bears him in revealing him to the world, by his total obedience "which brought him to death, death on a cross" (Phil. 2. 8), and by his inner contemplation of him. Begetting is not a reciprocal act, and a son cannot give afresh to his father the life which his father gave him, not even if that son is God. Jesus seems to have wished in his human life to make up for this inability when he "yielded up his spirit" on the cross (John 19. 30). However that may be, it is certain that the love he bears his Father is the driving force of his whole life.

At this point we may make use of a comparison which springs to mind. The divine being shows itself to us as a kind of family, of whom the third member is the Holy Spirit. The Holy Spirit exists because Father and Son have a common activity, that of giving him life. They come together in this act which expresses their mutual love. More exactly, the Holy Spirit is nothing but the personification of their mutual love.[1] The Gospels hint at this double origin of the Third Person: "Well, when the truth-giving Spirit, who proceeds from the Father, has come to befriend you, he whom I will send to you from the Father's side, he will bear witness of what I was" (John 15. 26); "I say that he will derive from me what he makes plain to you, because all that belongs to the Father belongs to me" (John 16. 15).

He is placed on the same level as the Father and the Son, since baptism is given "in the name of the Father, and of the Son, and of the Holy Ghost" (Mat. 28. 19), and St Paul shows a remarkable liking for trinitarian expressions (cf. for example II Cor. 13. 13; Eph. 4. 4–6), and he shares in all the divine prerogatives with them, in particular that of giving life.

However, he differs from the first two Persons in that he does not give this life in the heart of the Trinity, but outside it; Jesus speaks to Nicodemus saying, "no man can enter into the kingdom of God unless birth comes to him from water, and from the Holy Spirit" (John 3. 5), and baptism appears to St Paul as "the cleansing power which gives us new birth through the Holy Spirit" (Titus 3. 5). After he has given us supernatural life, the Spirit "will be in us" (John 14. 17) to the extent that we "will be led" (Rom. 8. 14) by him, and he will

[1] *Summa Theologica*, I^a, 37, 1 ad 3.

become our constant companion and the unfailing guide of our existence. The apostles' thinking was impregnated with this truth of the presence of the Spirit in our souls. At the end of the Council of Jerusalem they wrote "to the Gentile brethren in Antioch, Syria and Cicilia" the famous phrase: "It is the Holy Spirit's pleasure and ours . . . " (Acts 15. 23, 28); and the day after Pentecost they were already proclaiming: "Of this, we are witnesses; we and the Holy Spirit God gives to all those who obey him" (Acts 5. 32). As for St Paul, was it not one of his favourite themes, when he said: "Do not quench the Spirit" (I Thess. 5. 19)[1], and: "Do not distress God's holy Spirit, whose seal you bear until the day of your redemption comes" (Eph. 4. 30)? Here he was using an expression from the book of Isaiah (63. 10) about the flight of the Hebrews from Egypt, and it is easy to see that he is speaking of someone well known to him.

The Christians of today no longer understand these things; at most, perhaps a few of the better ones remember the teaching of Leo XIII repeated by Pius XII: "It is enough to state that, since Christ is the Head of the Church, the Holy Spirit is her soul."[2] But in general they have not realized the power of the words Jesus used to his disciples: "But you are to recognize him; he will be continually at your side, nay, he will be in you" (John 14. 17). This is a great pity, because these are words that cannot die, any more than other words of the Master's can, and to pass over them is to rob his message of its full meaning. There is no need, we believe, for us to be given visible gifts of the Spirit like the early Christians in order to know him; it is sufficient to live with a community that is truly and unaffectedly devout, to feel that there is something in the atmosphere which cannot be attributed to the people themselves. And if "the power with which the apostles testified to the resurrection of our Lord Jesus Christ" (Acts 4. 33) did show itself in miracles, was it not, first and foremost, precisely an effect of authority, given to them by the collective presence of the Holy Spirit within the community? This same effect can still be seen whenever a priest has the good fortune to be able

---

[1] [Revised Standard Version.—*Translator.*]

[2] Pius XII, Encyclical *Mystici Corporis Christi.* [Engl. tr., *The Mystical Body of Jesus Christ,* C.T.S., 1943, p. 35, No. 55.]

to speak as the head of a fully Christian community, borne up by its collective life in the Spirit.

St John the Apostle, in his First Epistle, where he develops the teaching of our Lord's discourse after the Last Supper, tells us that "God is love" (I John 4. 8 and 16), that is to say, not only does he love, but he *is* love. Such an identification is possible only because although he is one and one only, he is not alone, as the divine being consists of three persons. One being alone would be reduced to loving itself, which would be a form of monstrous egoism. We must understand that Divine Love is of necessity three in one. It is for this reason that it will never be entirely accessible to our intelligence. For one thing, God is beyond our understanding. For another, as love is a question of the will, it is never completely intelligible to us. When some of the great mystics have reached the summit of love, they have had flashes of intuitive knowledge of the Trinity. The full light of this knowledge will be ours in heaven, for there nothing will come between us and our love for God. We shall now look at each of the three persons in the light thrown on them by St John:

The Father is Love given: he gives, he gives himself, he gives life—his life; in him all these expressions have the same meaning. He is *all* of love given, because it is his privilege to give himself wholly and entirely, to communicate his whole life.

The Son is the plenitude of Love, the plenitude of Life—received. To help us understand this unfamiliar expression, we may think of a child in its mother's womb: it receives its life and drinks it in with all its being, without leaving the womb; and so the Son, the Word of God, Jesus of Nazareth, receives life from the Father without being separated from his Father's bosom.

The Holy Spirit is mutual Love, that is to say, love plighted and exchanged, the plenitude of love exchanged (see above).

The Father is the source of Love, for just as it is impossible to follow a river beyond its source, so it is impossible to look further than the Father for the origin of love. There is nothing beyond, or, more precisely, it is not possible to go beyond him who is All.

The Son is the glory of Love, for it is in his child and through him that the Father radiates his eternal being. The Son shines forth from the Father, "God of God, light of light, true God of true God" (Credo of the Mass), and the Epistle to the Hebrews (1. 3) says: "A Son who is the radiance of his Father's splendour, and the full expression of his being", his living image, and his word expressing him who proffers it.

The Holy Spirit is the Joy of Love, for he is the consummation towards which all the love of the Trinity moves. It is *by* the Spirit that the Father and the Son love and cherish each other, and the consummation of all love is joy.[1] In our own lives, too, we may see that acts of unselfish love lead to joy and happiness.

Speaking more theologically we could say that there are two operations in God, both of them eternal as he is himself: intelligence, by which the Father expresses himself, speaks his Word, and begets his Son; and secondly, will, by which Father and Son love each other, and by breathing love produce the breath of love which is the Holy Spirit. But the first operation also is full of love, since it is an act of self-giving, and in it too St John's words hold good. It is for this reason that he writes that God is "light" and not "intelligence", for light makes things visible, therefore it transmits knowledge, whereas intelligence in itself is what accumulates knowledge and not what gives it. God, of course, only knows in order to give and make known.

What does he make known to us? He communicates his being and his nature which is life. In doing this he produces persons, and as he is able to communicate himself completely, he brings these persons to the highest degree of development possible, that is to say to a state of equality with himself by the complete possession of the divine nature. Such is the law of love, which always tends towards the giving of life, developing it and forming it into distinct personalities.

Without anticipating what we shall have to say further on in this study, we may indicate the main lines of it by referring to three texts of Holy Scripture: the first two have already been

---

[1] Cf. *Summa Theologica*, I*, 37, 2, and II* II**, 28, 1.

quoted, from the First Epistle of St John: "God is Love, God is light", and the third comes from the beginning of Genesis: "So God made man in his own image, made him in the image of God" (Gen. 1. 27). The purpose assigned to man from the beginning, therefore, is to build up as well as he can this divine image which is part of the Creator's plan. In other words our aim should be to become fully light and love, because God is Light and Love.

Chapter 5

THE CREATION AND MAN'S
DESTINY

"Look, beloved! All that is thine, and 'tis I who will give it thee"—Paul Claudel, *The Satin Slipper*, The First Day, Scene VII.[1]

When we speak of creation, there is one point that should be emphasized: creation is not something necessary. The Blessed Trinity is complete in itself and has no need of anything outside itself and certainly not of any created being. When the Father decreed the creation of other beings he took a decision that was completely free, required neither by any external law nor by any internal law of his divinity.[2]

However, although creation is not necessary for God, it is in accordance with his nature, for it is a characteristic of love always to want to love more and consequently to produce beings which it can love and which can repay its love. To be precise, creation does not add anything to God—it is impossible to add to him who is Everything in himself—but it adds a new note to his glory. If creation did not exist there would not be that current of love which can and which should rise up from creation to its Creator.

Being wholly love, God can create only through love, by love, and for love, to know and to be known, to praise and to be praised, to look on beauty and to reveal his own beauty, to give life and to receive from that life a response of life and of love.

To see how this aim is achieved in practice, we will look briefly at creation from one end of the scale to the other.

At the lowest end of the scale we have material creation, from the star to the atom, from the crystal of simple structure to the higher animals whose life is regulated by a delicate and

[1] London, 1931, p. 36.
[2] See *Summa Contra Gentiles*, Bk. I, Ch. LXXXI, and Bk. II, Ch. XXIII.

37

complicated mechanism. All the components of this part of creation have one thing in common: not being free they can in no way be unfaithful to the laws of their own nature, everything they do is strictly determined, so they offer to God the satisfaction of complete obedience. In addition they give to God and to us the joy of contemplating a marvellous beauty in which we can see a reflection of the glory and the beauty of God:

> See how the skies proclaim God's glory,
> how the vault of heaven betrays his craftsmanship!
> Each day echoes its secret to the next,
> each night passes on to the next its revelation of knowledge;
> no word, no accent of theirs
> that does not make itself heard,
> till their utterance fills every land,
> till their message reaches the ends of the world.
> In these, he has made a pavilion for the sun,
> which comes out as a bridegroom comes from his bed,
> and exults like some great runner who sees the track before
>   him.
> Here, at one end of the heaven, is its starting place,
> and its course reaches to the other;
> none can escape its burning heat (Psalm 18. 1–7).

And two thousand years later the eloquent voice of Blaise Pascal took up the song of the psalms with the same enthusiasm:

Let man then contemplate the whole of nature in her full and exalted majesty. Let him turn his eyes from the lowly objects which surround him. Let him gaze on that brilliant light set like an eternal lamp to illumine the Universe; let the earth seem to him a dot compared with the vast orbit described by the sun, and let him wonder at the fact that this vast orbit itself is no more than a very small dot compared with that described by the stars in their revolutions around the firmament. But if our vision stops here, let the imagination pass on; it will exhaust its powers of thinking long before nature ceases to supply it with material for thought. All this visible world is no more than an imperceptible speck in nature's ample bosom. No idea approaches it.

We may extend our conceptions beyond all imaginable space, yet produce only atoms in comparison with the reality of things. It is an infinite sphere, the centre of which is everywhere, the circumference nowhere. In short, it is the greatest perceptible mark of God's almighty power that our imagination should lose itself in that thought.

Returning to himself, let man consider what he is compared with all existence; let him think of himself as lost in this remote corner of nature; and from this little dungeon in which he finds himself lodged—I mean the Universe—let him learn to set a true value on the earth, its kingdoms, and cities, and upon himself. What is a man in the infinite?'

And if, in the light of modern science, we meditate along the same lines as Pascal, our meditation will gain in precision what it lacks in poetry, for we now know that the scale of the universe is beyond anything that we could have imagined.

In one second light travels 186,000 miles, i.e. seven and a half times the circumference of the earth; it still takes something more than eight minutes to reach us from the sun; it takes over three years to reach us from the nearest stars and one or two hundred thousand years to cross the Milky Way at its widest diameter.

In the Milky Way, "our galaxy", there are about a hundred thousand million stars. But we know of millions of other galaxies that are as large; the nearest, the Andromeda nebula, is one million four hundred thousand light years away. The further away these galaxies are, the faster they are retreating: it has been calculated that some of them are moving at twenty-five thousand miles a second. This makes a universe with a diameter of several thousand million light years.

There is an incredible variety in the composition of the stars: some are very hot and of tremendous brilliance (like several thousand suns), others are much cooler; some are formed of material of an incredible density (up to a hundred thousand times that of water) and very small, smaller than the moon for example, others, in contrast, are of very low density and so huge that the whole solar system would fit easily into one of them. Some are made of matter that is in states that are unknown on

---

[1] Blaise Pascal, *The Pensées*, First Part, Chapter 1, No. 84. [Engl. tr. by J. M. Cohen, p. 51. Harmondsworth, 1961.]

this earth. Today scientific instruments and knowledge can make us see further than our imagination was able to, and the effect is still more staggering.

If we pass from the world of infinite size to the world of infinite smallness, we come to the world of atoms. We know that to give the number of atoms contained in a few litres of gas at atmospheric pressure, we must write a figure with 23 noughts. The diameter of an atom of oxygen is about one ten-millionth of a millimetre and that of its nucleus is about ten thousand times less. In spite of their smallness, however, neither an atom nor its nucleus is a simple object; they are complex structures made up of elementary particles: electrons, protons, neutrons, and others that are still being discovered: mesons, neutrinos, positrons, antiprotons. These things are on a scale so minute that though we can form some idea of them, it is useless to attempt to picture them. In fact the infinitely small gives us the same feeling of disquiet as does the infinitely great. And, like the psalmist who invited the stars to sing of the glory of God, we can invite the atoms to join in too, with all their accompanying mysteries which are gradually coming within our range of knowledge.

But however beautiful we find the material world, and whatever joy we find in its contemplation, we must recognize that it has one fundamental defect: being incapable of intellectual knowledge it is also incapable of love. This is why it cannot give perfect joy to its Creator and why men must not love it for itself. Love, for its very existence, needs reciprocity, a resemblance between two beings that love each other, a mutual effort of each toward the other. I may consider that wine, gold or banknotes are good and that the starry sky is magnificent, but it is a degradation of love to give to wine, gold or banknotes that single-minded passion that draws the whole being towards the object it desires. If I try to love the stars with that sort of love, I can neither give myself nor receive anything in return.

The practical conclusion of all this is of the greatest importance: we use created things because we need them, but we must not let them become objects of our love, we should use them as means to strengthen the love that is in us. This distinction enables us to formulate a simple rule: we can use created things when we do so in such a way that they bring us closer to the one we are trying to love, but when they draw us away from him towards themselves, then we must reject them. This is the same principle as the famous "*tantum . . . quantum . . .*" of the Spiritual Exercises of St Ignatius.[1]

This distinction should not lead to any disdain of created things: the saint does not disdain them, because he is free to use them or not as he pleases. This is very noticeable in St Francis of Assisi who, writes Fr Gemelli, "crucifies himself, but without despising life".[2] When he was near the end of his life, when he had reached the depths of suffering and the heights of love, he liked to speak to the birds, and it was while he bore the marks of our Lord's Passion that he sang his famous *Canticle of the Sun*:

Most high omnipotent good Lord,
Thine are the praises, the glory, the honour, and all bene-
diction.
To thee alone, Most High, do they belong,
And no man is worthy to mention thee.
Praised be thou, my Lord, with all thy creatures,
Especially the honoured Brother Sun,
Who makes the day and illumines us through thee.
And he is beautiful and radiant with great splendour,
Bears the signification of thee, Most High One.
Praised be thou, my Lord, for Sister Moon and the Stars,
Thou hast formed them in heaven clear and precious and
beautiful.
Praised be thou, my Lord, for Brother Wind,
And for the air and cloudy and clear and every weather,
By which thou givest sustenance to thy creatures.
Praised be thou, my Lord, for Sister Water,
Which is very useful and humble and precious and chaste.
Praised be thou, my Lord, for Brother Fire,
By whom thou lightest the night,
And he is beautiful and jocund and robust and strong.
Praised be thou, my Lord, for our sister Mother Earth,

---

[1] "So it follows that man has to use them as far as they help and abstain from them where they hinder his purpose." *The Spiritual Exercises of St Ignatius Loyola*, Fundamental Principle. Transl. Thomas Corbishley, S.J., p. 22, No. 23. London, 1963.

[2] Agostino Gemelli, O.F.M., *Le Message de St François au monde moderne*, p. 24. Paris, 1935.

Who sustains and governs us,
And produces various fruits with coloured flowers and herbage.
Praise and bless my Lord and give him thanks
And serve him with great humility.[1]

Leaving on one side for a moment the middle degree in the scale of creatures, we pass to the top, to the angels. They share with God the privilege of being pure spirits, and since they can understand all things by their intelligence, they can give to the Father the joy of a love of unique strength, because there is no obstacle to prevent that complete union of their love with his which is inherent in their nature. The beauty of the angels is such that it can not be described in human terms, but clearly it infinitely surpasses any material beauty.

However, the angels do have certain limitations and deficiencies: by the very fact that they are pure spirits, but not infinite like God, they cannot transmit the life that they possess. Their love is sterile, strictly speaking; it produces nothing. In addition, without of course being cut off from the rest of creation, they are isolated to a certain extent by the very fact that they are pure spirits. When they express their love they can speak only each one for himself. For this reason the angels, like the material world, cannot provide that complete satisfaction which God has a right to find in his creation.

We will now come back to earth and consider man, that unique part of creation, possessing both body and soul and placed at the frontier of the two worlds of matter and of spirit. By his intelligence and his will, he is like the angels, capable of knowledge and of love. It is in his very nature to exercise these faculties and to direct them towards his Creator.[2] He is made to know him, to contemplate him and to rejoice in him.

Man also belongs to the material world and since his creation he has been called upon to "take command of the fishes in the sea, and all that flies through the air, and all the living things that move on the earth" (Gen. 1. 28). He has been consecrated master, after God, of the material creation,[3] and must use his

---

[1] Johannes Jörgensen, *Saint Francis of Assisi. A Biography*. Translated by T. O'Conor Sloane. London, 1912 (many reprints, e.g. 1956), p. 314. This work gives the original version of the *Canticle* with the above translation.
[2] Cf. Leo XIII, Encyclical *Sapientiae Christianae* (see note, p. 12 above).
[3] *Summa Theologica*, I*, 96, 1 and 2.

energies to order the world in such a way that God's plan is carried out. Those parts of creation such as the stars, over which he cannot gain direct mastery, he can possess by his intellect: "In space the Universe encompasses me and swallows me like a dot; in thought I encompass the Universe."[1] And through this knowledge he will sing the glory of God. Thus he will make himself the voice of dumb creation, he will love for all those who cannot love, and through him a song of praise to God's glory will rise up out of the world of matter. Man is made an image to reflect the glory of God, this is his destiny and when he tries to play any other role he is being untrue to himself. In relation to the rest of the universe, he has been given the role of priest who, by an act of perpetual adoration, offers up the creation to its Creator. Thus the material world, which has not of itself the freedom to give thanks to God, can do so through the liberty of man.

Finally, man has the power to co-operate with God in the creation of other men and the transmission of life. He can know the joys of giving and of giving himself, and can work with the Creator in enlarging the ranks of those able to participate in the exchange of love between heaven and earth. This then is the vocation of man seen from the point of view of creation, and it makes us see that man has been greatly loved and given a favoured place:

Thou hast placed him only a little below the angels,
crowning him with glory and honour,
and bidding him rule over the works of thy hands.
Thou hast put them all under his dominion (Psalm 8. 6–7).

But the voice of man is weak and feeble and cannot give to the Blessed Trinity that honour and praise of which it is worthy. Will God then be disappointed in man and will there be no one capable of rendering him the perfect homage that is due to him? Yes, for there will be Christ, true God and true man and, as such, a most marvellous synthesis of the whole order of being, possessing all man's capacities, but expanded to an infinite degree by reason of his divine nature. He will be able to represent humanity because he is the "Son of Man",

[1] Pascal, *op. cit.*, Chapter 3. [p. 101, No. 265.]

the "New Adam", and because the Father has "left everything in his hands" (John 13. 3):

> Thou art my son;
> I have begotten thee this day.
> Ask thy will of me, and thou shalt have the nations for thy patrimony;
> the very ends of the earth for thy domain.
> Thou shalt herd them like sheep with a crook of iron,
> break them in pieces like earthenware (Psalm 2. 7–9).

And as humanity's representative he is privileged in possessing an unequalled beauty:

> Thine is more than mortal beauty,
> thy lips overflow with gracious utterance;
> the blessings God has granted thee can never fail.
> Thy throne, O God, endures for ever and ever,
> the sceptre of thy royalty is a rod that rules true;
> thou hast been a friend to right, an enemy to wrong (Psalm 44. 3, 7 and 8).

Consecrated king of men, he also has command over the angels,[1] and can speak to the Father with the voice of all creation which is "summed up in him" (Eph. 1. 10).

So we begin to see the basic truth that Christ is the end, the goal of all God's activity; God does all things for Christ. And we can share the enthusiasm of the holy men of the Old and New Testaments, and of the whole Church which proclaims at the end of the Canon of the Mass: "Through him, and with him, and in him, to thee, God, almighty Father, in the unity of the Holy Spirit, is given all honour and glory, for ever and ever. Amen."

---

[1] Cf. Pius XI, Encyclical *Quas Primas*, 11 December 1925. [Engl. tr., *The Kingship of Christ*. London, C.T.S., p. 9.]

Chapter 6

THE MEANING OF LIFE:
DIVINE FATHERHOOD

The Spirit himself thus assures our spirit, that we are children of God—Rom. 8. 16.

As we said when speaking of the problem of the world, man, as a result of original sin, is no longer capable of understanding either the universe or his own life; today's Christians have little idea of why they have been put on this earth, and other people have no idea at all. It is easy to see what depths of moral despair this leads to. How is anyone to endure the pain and the difficulties of existence, if it no longer has any meaning? "How shall the soul justify itself, if neither God nor Christ exist?"[1]

The only answer is a revolt against life itself, and if something more than a purely negative attitude is wanted, we are forced to attach ourselves to some kind of system, which, even if it is false, at least gives us the illusion of understanding life and provides us with a purpose for all our efforts. " 'No dignity, no real existence is possible for a man who works twelve hours a day and still has no notion of what his work means.' Work must be made to mean something in cases like that, must achieve honourable status."[2]

We must solve this problem at all costs. What we have just said about creation and human destiny is not enough, for this was still written in the light of the Old Testament. So let us now look at the teaching of Christ, "the world's light" (John 9. 5), and of his Church.

Our childhood catechism answered the question: "Why did

---

[1] André Malraux, *Man's Estate*, Part 1, 4 a.m. [Engl. tr. by Alastair Macdonald, p. 62. Harmondsworth, 1961.]
[2] Ibid., p. 63.

God make you?" as follows: "God made me to know Him, love Him, and serve Him in this world, and to be happy with Him for ever in the next." This reply is correct, but it is insufficient, because its wording lacks vitality and, although everything is said, the essential part of it is not brought out and clearly expressed; it does not move us. We shall try to concentrate the truth into a shorter form which will mean more to us.

Why did God Create us?

The Father created us so that we might become his children. This vocation does not in any way clash with our destiny as free and intelligent beings, nor does it diminish that other magnificent vocation we have been speaking of, that of becoming the voice of all created things so that we are a living story of the glory of God. On the contrary, this destiny and vocation are strengthened and reinforced, so much so that any spiritual doctrine which attempted to ignore this fact would have to be accounted false. On no condition can we deny the great dignity of man, and everything we do must be guided by a love that is enlightened by knowledge, and a knowledge that is widened by love. There is no question of the Father's asking us to abandon our dignity and our freedom, on the contrary he increases them by giving us greater opportunities of knowing and loving. Therefore, everything we have to do as men we will still do as sons of God, but with greater demands made on us and, above all, with an entirely new approach, so that everything is done in a spirit of filial love.

The object of the rest of this book is to develop the consequences of this answer to our question, but one very remarkable consequence should be noted straightway: when a man and a woman join together to form a Christian home, the children born to them will be not just "human young" but also beings destined to become sons of the heavenly Father, future "heirs of God, sharing the inheritance of Christ" (Rom. 8. 17). We can see how greatly this enhances the dignity of the sacrament of marriage and how it gives a whole new dimension to the upbringing and education of children. The son of God is not to be brought up haphazardly, but in accordance with his Father's wishes.

Why does the Father Wish to Make us his Children?

To make us members of his divine family. The child joins his parents' family, he is part of it by definition. And so we are called upon to enter into the Godhead, which explains some of the sayings of Jesus, such as this one after the Last Supper: "You have only to live on in me, and I will live on in you" (John 15. 4).

Here we will limit ourselves to two important remarks: the first is that we are members of the divine family even while we are still on this earth: "Beloved," writes St John, "we are sons of God even now" (I John 3. 2).

The second is that as it is God's clearly expressed wish, Christian parents are in duty bound to give their children the benefits of baptism, and the newly-baptized child has the indefeasible right to know his heavenly Father in the same way as he knows his earthly one, and to ignore this point would be to rob the child of his right. This is one of the basic reasons for having Christian schools.

The family of God on earth should possess all its qualities of order, harmony and peace. The aim of the apostolate should be to develop these qualities as far as possible, and to increase the family by adding new members to it. What is evil is to try to break up God's family and diminish its good qualities; it is this that the Father condemns, and this is the way that leads towards a lack of love.

Why does God Wish us to be Members of his Family on Earth?

So that even now, here below, we may enjoy one of the benefits of this family: happiness. Man searches for happiness instinctively[1] and he is right, because that is what God made him for. So we should not attribute a divine value to suffering, and even less to unhappiness. Suffering is a means—a necessary means, moreover, and we should never try to minimize its necessity—but it is not an end in itself. The Church does not glorify suffering, she fights it. Here we should ask ourselves if we have not at some time seemed to recommend a complain-

---

[1] *Summa Theologica*, I*, 60, 2, resp.

ing, self-pitying frame of mind in which an air of gloom and
dissatisfaction were considered to be signs of distinction. When
this happens, the consequences are to be greatly feared, for
anything that is in any way healthy will soon begin to avoid
or abandon us.

We should remember that we are not made for just any
happiness, but for one particular happiness. Joy is the fruit of
love, and only love of God can completely satisfy us. If we look
for happiness anywhere else we are lost, for then we find only
"ersatz" beginnings of happiness and a certain cut-price joy,
all of which fades and leaves us with a terrible after-taste of
disillusionment, and nothing more. The beatitudes of the
Gospel, for all their air of paradox, are in fact an invitation to
us to abandon the second-rate kind of happiness so that we
may find true happiness.

Only in heaven can we find complete satisfaction of all our
desires, a satisfaction which leads to final beatitude, because
it is there that the Father's family will be reunited and we will
"see face to face" (I Cor. 13. 12). But here on earth we have
already been given a measure of joy as a foretaste of this greater
joy to come, and it is our duty to seek it out, for that is what
God wishes us to do. We will find it by giving, not only small
things or material objects, but also ourselves. Giving money,
for example, can be good and necessary, depending on the
circumstances, but it is not a substitute for the sacrifice God
asks of us—the giving of self. When Jesus spoke to the rich
young man, he told him to give up all his possessions, but he
added immediately: "Then come back and follow me"
(Mat. 19. 21). Perfection is to be found by walking with
Christ, for giving up wealth is only a preliminary condition
which is not asked of everyone. When a couple are engaged to
be married they give each other presents to show their love.
The happiness they foresee is not theirs yet for they do not yet
belong to each other entirely. But in the marriage ceremony
they give themselves to each other for life, and we all
know that it is not easy to keep on giving oneself anew every
day.

It is part of the most orthodox teaching of the Church that
the "state of glory" which we shall know in heaven is an
extension of the "state of grace" in which we are called to live

on earth.[1] In more familiar language we might say that the people who will be happy in the next world are the ones who have learnt how to be happy in this world, by giving themselves to God and their fellow men. And, equally well, those who have started being unhappy in this world, by refusing to give, are condemning themselves to eternal unhappiness. Hell is an unchanging egoism, solitary confinement with one's own eternal discontent.

The Prodigal Son

We can end these thoughts on the divine fatherhood by examining this parable which reveals a great deal to us about our Father in heaven.

"Then he said, There was a certain man who had two sons. And the younger of these said to his father, Father, give me that portion of the estate which falls to me. So he divided his property between them. Not many days afterwards, the younger son put together all that he had, and went on his travels to a far country, where he wasted his fortune in riotous living. Then, when all was spent, a great famine arose in that country, and he found himself in want; whereupon he went and attached himself to a citizen of that country, who put him on his farm, to feed swine. He would have been glad to fill his belly with husks, such as the swine used to eat; but none was ready to give them to him. Then he came to himself, and said, How many hired servants there are in my father's house, who have more bread than they can eat, and here am I perishing with hunger! I will arise and go to my father, and say to him, Father, I have sinned against heaven, and before thee; I am not worthy, now, to be called thy son; treat me as one of thy hired servants. And he arose, and went on his way to his father.

"But, while he was still a long way off, his father saw him, and took pity on him; running up, he threw his arms round his neck and kissed him. And when the son said, Father, I have sinned against heaven and before thee; I am not worthy, now,

[1] Cf. R. Garrigou-Lagrange, O.P., *The Three Ages of the Interior Life*, St Louis, 1947, Vol. I, pp. 29 et seq. Cf. also Pius XII, continuing the teaching of Leo XIII with regard to the habitation within us of the Divine Persons: Encyclical *Mystici Corporis Christi*. [*The Mystical Body of Jesus Christ*, C.T.S., 1943, pp. 48–9, No. 79.]

to be called thy son, the father gave orders to his servants,
Bring out the best robe, and clothe him in it; put a ring on his
hand, and shoes on his feet. Then bring out the calf that has
been fattened, and kill it; let us eat, and make merry; for my
son here was dead, and has come to life again, was lost, and is
found. And so they began their merry-making.

"The elder son, meanwhile, was away on the farm; and on
his way home, as he drew near the house, he heard music and
dancing; whereupon he called one of the servants and asked
what all this meant. He told him, Thy brother has come back,
and thy father has killed the fattened calf, glad to have him
restored safe and sound. At this he fell into a rage, and would
not go in. When his father came out and tried to win him over,
he answered his father thus, Think how many years I have
lived as thy servant, never transgressing thy commands, and
thou hast never made me a present of a kid, to make merry
with my friends; and now, when this son of thine has come
home, one that has swallowed up his patrimony in the company
of harlots, thou hast killed the fattened calf in his honour. He
said to him, My son, thou art always at my side, and everything that I have is already thine; but for this merry-making
and rejoicing there was good reason; thy brother here was
dead, and has come to life again; was lost, and is found"
(Luke 15. 11–32).

This story concerns three characters:
(1) The father: he clearly represents God and demonstrates
an *unfailing* paternal love: his affection is not diminished by the
bad behaviour of his children. He watches for the return of the
prodigal and throws his arms round his neck and kisses him
before the boy can apologize; he does not even let him finish
the sentence he had rehearsed to ensure a favourable welcome.
Then, when the elder son refuses to come into the house, he
goes out to meet him, he entreats him, he does not lose his
temper when this son reproaches him, but he explains his
behaviour simply, in words full of love. Why does the father
let the prodigal son go away in the first place? An earthly
father would surely not do the same thing in the same circumstances. The reason is that the Father in heaven wants us to
stay in his house out of love; he does not wish us to remain there

against our will. If someone does not love him enough to stay there, he prefers him to leave rather than to remain under false pretences. When the child has gone, he does not seek to punish him, for events will bring punishment enough. The punishment of a sinner comes from his sin, there is no need to inflict it on him from outside. This is sometimes true in this world, and always true in the next, for strictly speaking it is not the Father who damns the sinner, but the sinner who sends himself to hell by refusing the Father's gift of love.

(2) The prodigal son: he leaves home because he does not love his father enough to put up with the restrictions which are inevitably a part of family life. The orgy of spending he indulges in—we can leave it to his brother to accuse him of debauchery —is only the normal development and consequence of his sin, which is committed when he decides to go away and enjoy his possessions free from his dependence on his father. He pursues pleasure so feverishly that he ends up—he, a Jew of good birth— starving in a pigsty. Then, wanting forgiveness, he decides to return to his father's house.

We should make no mistake about this: he is forgiven as soon as he makes a move towards going back; he does not need to change his father's heart, but he has to change himself before he has access to the pardon which is always waiting for him. So it is in our own spiritual life as well: our problem is not to change God's attitude to us, but to change ourselves, so that we can benefit from his divine goodness. In instituting the sacrament of penance Jesus has not put an end to the ways to forgiveness mentioned in the Old Testament (cf. particularly Ez. 18 and 33); perfect contrition and a change of heart and life are sufficient for the remission of sins. It ought to be a perfectly simple matter for any Christian to use these ways to forgiveness and to go into the confessional to ask that his reconciliation with the Father should be completed by a reconciliation with the Church. How is it that Christians are so ignorant of this doctrine?[1]

(3) The elder brother: he returns to the paternal roof, which he has in any case never left, but he does not go in. He is there in the flesh, but he has no family feeling: he is bitter and jealous and incapable of understanding the father's forgiveness,

---

[1] This point is developed in the chapter on confession.

and he reproaches him for the most ridiculous things—for why go on about not being given a kid when he knows he has the entire inheritance at his disposal? The truth is that he was probably delighted to be rid of his brother and furious to see him return.

The last words of the father are: "My son, thou art always at my side, and everything I have is already thine." This is one of the keys to all spiritual life, and Jesus takes it up—and with great intensity—on the evening of the Last Supper (John 17. 10) to express the joy which fills him. Do we, too, know this joy?

One last observation: the parable finishes by leaving us in doubt as to whether the elder son decided to come into the house or not. Is this not symbolical of so many lukewarm people, those about whom one never knows whether they will ever consent, once and for all, to give their hearts to God?

Chapter 7

LUKEWARMNESS

No one who looks behind him, when he has once put his hand to the plough, is fitted for the kingdom of God—Luke 9. 62.

Man is free to love as he likes and so does not always love whole-heartedly. This lack of love is called sin and it requires a fairly attentive study. To say all there is to say on this subject would obviously take many volumes, but we will try to choose those aspects of sin which are most relevant to our time. We shall start by examining that painful and unhappy state of the soul that we call lukewarmness.

The term is not a human invention: it is used in the Apocalypse where one meets it in Chapter 3. 14–22, in the letter addressed to "the angel of the church at Laodicea"—probably the bishop: "Being what thou art, lukewarm, neither cold nor hot, thou wilt make me vomit thee out of my mouth", together with a description of the sickness: "I am rich, thou sayest, I have come into my own; nothing, now, is wanting to me. And all the while, if thou didst but know it, it is thou who art wretched, thou who art to be pitied. Thou art a beggar, blind and naked."

From this description we can see clearly one characteristic of lukewarmness: its insidious onset. The man who is in this state is generally unaware of the fact. He may sometimes suspect that all is not well but equally he may consider himself to be above average, even a saint. This is why it is necessary to describe it as accurately as possible and to list its symptoms so that it may be diagnosed.

If it is neither hot nor cold, it is obviously a state somewhere between that of the fervent man and that of him whose sins are many and serious. Theology defines the lukewarm person as one for whom "fully deliberate venial sins become habitual and ordinary."[1] We should notice that in this definition mortal sin is not absolutely excluded, but that the state of lukewarmness is characterized by a succession of small sins. It is clear that this attitude is far from that which the Christian is called to have. One made in the image of God has not the right to be mediocre, but if we keep up the sort of constant complicity with sin described above, our mediocrity is deliberate. This is why Father Lebret in his *Examination of Conscience* includes as faults:

Am I deliberately content with my own mediocrity?
Do I habitually fail to do my best?[2]

Straying so far from the authentic Christian calling has serious consequences: having become unworthy of God, the lukewarm man is unable to see the signs of God. When a star appeared in the east the Magi, who were devout men, recognized "the star of the King of the Jews", but to those who were indifferent it was only "a star". During his ministry, Jesus reproached the Pharisees and Sadducees vigorously for this inability: "When evening comes, you say, It is fair weather, the sky is red; or at sunrise, There will be a storm to-day, the sky is red and lowering. You know, then, how to read the face of heaven; can you not read the signs of appointed times? It is a wicked and unfaithful generation that asks for a sign; the only sign that will be given to it is the sign of the prophet Jonas" (Mat. 16. 2–4).

It is not difficult to guess the place that lukewarmness occupies in what might be called the devil's plan for bringing about the downfall of souls. If we take the case of a young man or a young girl who have been lovingly brought up in a Christian home and Christian schools and who, with all the vibrant eagerness of their youth, have given prompt obedience to Christ, is it going to be possible to start them on a downward path by tempting them to commit some grave sin? Of course

---

[1] Joseph de Guibert, s.j., *The Theology of the Spiritual Life*, p. 221, No. 269. London, 1956.
[2] L. J. Lebret & T. Sauvet, *An Examination of Conscience for Modern Catholics*. New York, 1961. In future when we quote Fr Lebret without further details, it is to be understood that we are referring to this book. For practical reasons, and because we do not always quote him literally, we have not given page references, which are in any case easy to find.

not. Some temptations would just not tempt them. Will the devil therefore give up? To think this would be to know little of him. He will begin a long-drawn-out campaign which consists of wearing down the soul little by little, starting off by suggesting sins that are so small they are barely noticeable. Then once the habit is established, he can gradually suggest more serious sins. "Indeed the safest road to Hell is the gradual one, the gentle slope, soft underfoot, without sudden turnings, without milestones, without signposts."[1]

As it is essential to be clear on this subject, it is worth noting those conditions with which lukewarmness should not be confused:

(a) Difficulty in praying: this is an important symptom about which one's spiritual director should be consulted, but it can be caused by other things than lukewarmness.

(b) Difficulty in acting on one's convictions: this may be caused by timidity, by an aversion to certain tasks or simply by a temperament lacking in will-power.

(c) Anguish about the demands of the spiritual life in times of trial: Jesus himself knew this anguish in the garden of Gethsemani (Mat. 26. 38), and many great saints have had it in their hours of difficulty.

(d) Fundamental weakness of soul: St Peter was weak since he denied Christ, but his reactions were never those of a lukewarm man; they were quite the reverse.

(e) The absence of conscious happiness: it is a dangerous modern mania to judge everything by one's emotions, and to imagine that things have gone wrong if one is not in a state of constant euphoria. We must not succumb to this aberration.

For the same motive of clarity, it is worth noting some of the false pretexts that are often given for venial sins:

(a) "It does not really matter." This can be true if it is a case of an isolated sin in an otherwise devout life, but if it is one of a long series of sins, then it does matter. Life is composed of a series of little things, and if most of these are spoilt by sin then the whole life is spoilt. Can one say that this is not serious?

(b) "Everybody does it." This principle is even more

---

[1] C. S. Lewis, *The Screwtape Letters*, p. 63. London, 1942.

dangerous because a conception that is in fact monstrous is given a disguise of respectability. Did Jesus ever say: "Do as everyone else does"? No; but he did say: "You are to be perfect, as your heavenly Father is perfect" (Mat. 5. 48), which is just the opposite. The Christian is the one who is often willing *not* to do what "everybody does".

(c) Sometimes, especially with older people, ugly sins will be given full rein, because they have become habits: curiosity, gossiping, tactlessness or vanity. Tendencies in these directions should be firmly controlled in youth, otherwise they may take a firm hold and do irreparable damage.

What is lukewarmness from a more psychological point of view? We feel that fundamentally it is the result of trying to reconcile two things that are irreconcilable: on the one hand a life that conforms to the attitudes of the world and on the other hand a life lived in the spirit of the Gospels, even—it may be—a life consecrated to God: or, if one prefers to put it another way, a Christianity from which the mystery of the cross is banished. It is characterized by two features:

(1) An absence of love, a want of charity. The lukewarm are permanently oscillating between good and evil, lacking the courage to take a radical decision and cut loose from their moorings. They are incapable of giving their hearts to their Father, and this means that they have little feeling for their brethren, coupled with a frightening self-centredness. It is this that revolts us, for this that it was written: "Thou wilt make me vomit thee out of my mouth."

(2) Complacency and self-satisfaction: "I am rich, thou sayest." There are many examples of this attitude in the Gospels: "I am not like the rest of men," says the Pharisee in the parable (Luke 18. 11). "I have kept all these [command-ments] ever since I grew up," says the rich young man who refused to follow Jesus (ibid. 21). And as these phrases have been branded with opprobrium since the beginnings of Christianity, others have been found since: "People like us, Father . . . "; or else: "I don't commit any sins, I come from a very good family." It would be impolite to elaborate.

How does the process of becoming lukewarm begin? By negligence. Often after a period of emotional fervour the first serious difficulties cause great discouragement: sometimes the slackness sets in after a period of convalescence or at moments of change in the routine of our lives. Other such moments occur in the middle of certain periods; the middle of the school year or the middle of life: it is one of the most common and dangerous temptations of "the dangerous age". At all stages in our lives, we need to be on our guard against the illusions of safety produced by a relative absence of temptations.

We can now speak of some of the most easily discernible signs of lukewarmness. People show these signs in greatly varying degrees, and some signs are much more serious than others. They could be studied under many different headings, but as we shall not, in fact, be discussing them again in any detail, this is a good opportunity to discover whether or not these are faults of which we are guilty. That explains why we are studying them at some length in this chapter.

(1) Prolonged neglect of prayer. This needs little explanation as it is a fairly visible sign. We should simply like to point out that for it to be really a sign of lukewarmness it must last some time, some months for example; it would be childish to worry because one had prayed little or badly for about a week. We should also add that to remain faithful in prayer, we must want to do more than cultivate our personal perfection, as this alone leads quickly to egoism and pride. We should pray with the wish to make a contribution to the love and glory of God.

(2) The progressive elimination of all forms of mortification. This word should be taken in its widest sense. The people that show this symptom appear to have taken as their motto: "Avoid the unpleasant at all costs", and if anything that would limit or inconvenience them comes into their lives, they turn away from it. Because of this they become increasingly negligent: anything is allowable, anything can be justified, any self-indulgence is permissible. They come to think of God as a kind of indulgent grandpapa and this can be seen in many different circumstances.

(a) Professional and personal duties: they pick and choose among their various duties, and finish by doing, or doing well, only those tasks that are interesting or satisfying. The rest is omitted or carelessly done. The social worker will carry out

a fascinating investigation with care, but take no trouble in
writing up her reports. The housewife will spend time, too
much time, on cooking and then neglect the housework. The
married man will be conscientious at work, and useless and
complaining at home. All this gives rise to habits that affect
the whole of one's life and cause a considerable "lack of
productivity".

(b) Satisfaction of the senses: firstly of those concerned with
the preservation of the individual. This is the realm of greed in
all its forms: the naïve greed that makes a religion of eating
well for any reason or for no reason at all—many people have
completely lost the idea that any privation is possible in this
domain; the animal greed of those who gorge themselves on
cakes, pastries, or sweets; the slaves of tobacco—the people of
the United Kingdom spend more on tobacco than on rent!—
and the tragic greed of alcoholism. Are people aware of the
havoc caused by drink? Families broken up, homes where life
is made impossible and children are seized with terror at the
sound of their father's key in the lock; financial ruin, the loss
of the most elementary dignity, appalling hereditary damage,
crowded mental homes, to mention just a few of the consequences. How can one get Catholics to react to this problem
otherwise than with indulgent smiles? How can one show them
how widespread is this evil which now reaches, sometimes with
certain refinements, upper-class circles and families that were
previously exempt, and which is rapidly spreading to women
who used to be less affected, and to regions once relatively
free from alcoholism? Drink can be responsible for untold evil.

(c) We now come to the sins of the senses concerned with
the preservation of the species. This brings us to the question of
immodesty of dress and of behaviour, on beaches, in public
places and on the dance floor, on the radio and on the screen.
These problems have too often been avoided, or referred to
only vaguely, and Pius XII himself has spoken of "the often
inadequate reactions of good people".[1] Teachers, and others
responsible for education, have not reacted firmly enough,
and some pious mothers go much too far in instructing their
daughters in the arts of attracting the male.

[1] Allocation at the Canonization of St Maria Goretti, 24 June 1950.
Acta Apostolicae Sedis, 42 (1950), p. 598.

"It is obvious to everyone that this is a most serious matter closely involving, in addition to Christian virtue, bodily health and the vigour and growth of human society. The ancient poet has well said: 'The beginning of lewdness is when citizens go about baring their bodies in public.' That being so, it will easily be realized that this question concerns not only the Church, but the public authorities also, whose desire it ought to be that physical strength and moral force should suffer neither weakening nor decline."[1]

If even after such grave warnings, anyone should still think that these things have only minor repercussions, he would do well to take into consideration two facts: the first is that large numbers of religious vocations among both men and women are lost for reasons of immodesty, especially, and this must be emphasized, immodesty in the home. This is today one of the causes, if not the principal cause, of diminishing numbers in seminaries and convents. The second fact is that impurity is a breeding ground for Communism and any concession in the domain of modesty tends to open the way to a total denial of religion.

We would like to add finally that this is a subject on which one has to be strict, especially where it is a question of giving a good or bad example: such as town-dwellers in the country or the families of those in prominent positions whose behaviour is always noticed. What may seem unimportant soon becomes the thin end of the wedge and more serious abuses creep in quickly.

(3) Excessive motives of self-satisfaction in the apostolate. This can be seen when people engaged in the apostolate seek to impose their own theories and their own systems, and consider that only they are capable of doing things properly. They seek their personal success and opportunities of showing off their clothes or their intelligence; they seek to command rather than to serve.

(4) The tendency to jealousy: they hate to see anyone else succeed, even in a field different from their own. This sign is particularly serious because jealousy, which becomes quickly embedded in our hearts, is completely opposed to brotherly

[1] Letter of the Congregation of the Council on Immodest Dress, 15 August 1954. *Acta Apostolicae Sedis*, 46 (1954), p. 45.

love and can easily degenerate into mortal sin. We should add that this sin is widespread and everybody knows the sort of havoc it causes. The Christian who finds himself nurturing feelings of jealousy must eradicate them vigorously for no concession can be allowed in this matter.

(5) The tendency to seek the company of those who have the lowest religious standards. It is well known among those engaged in education, in both boys' and girls' schools, that groups will appear, formed by individuals with certain things in common. Moral standards in particular give rise to the formation of such groups because we all feel the need for friends who share our attitudes in this direction. And if we notice that a youth or a girl changes friends, we should pay attention, because it is significant. We should remember the proverb: "Birds of a feather flock together", and we should look to see where our own preferences lie. It will give us a good idea of ourselves.

(6) An over-developed critical sense: this makes people disparage everything they see, and everything that is being talked about. When they give free rein to this hypercritical tendency, nothing finds favour in their eyes. This can cause great harm and has disastrous effects on the community and discourages everyone's efforts.

(7) The acceptance of formalism: this consists of adopting attitudes of piety or charity that have no interior reality. People with this mentality will go to church, but when they are there they will do little more than doze and chat. They may recite their prayers, but their heart is not with God. They think: "I must look as though . . . ", or: "I don't want to give the impression that . . . ". Such an attitude reveals a meanness of soul and a complete lack of respect for God. This is a tendency to which all ages have been prone and one about which the Bible is particularly cutting. These are Isaiah's views on the subject (Is. 58. 1–5):

Cry aloud, never ceasing,
raise thy voice like a trumpet-call,
and tell my people of their transgressions,
call the sons of Jacob to account.
Day after day they besiege me,
arraign my dealings with them,

a nation, you would think, ever dutiful,
one that never swerved from the divine will.
Proof they ask of my faithfulness,
would fain bring a plea against their God.
Why hadst thou no eyes for it, say they, when we fasted;
why didst thou pass by unheeding, when we humbled ourselves before thee?
Fasting, when you follow your own whim.
distrain upon all your debtors!
Naught comes of it but law-suit and quarrelling;
angry blows profane it.
A better fast you must keep than of old,
ere plea of yours makes itself heard above.
With such fasting, with a day's penance,
should I be content?
Is it enough that a man should bow down to earth,
make his bed on sackcloth and ashes?
Think you, by such a fasting-day,
to win the Lord's favour?

"Make no mistake about it; you cannot cheat God. A man
will reap what he sows," says St Paul (Gal. 6. 7). Not much
needs to be added to this except to point out the adverse effect
that superficiality in prayer has on the Church and on
Christians in general. It disgusts and shocks people, and rightly
so, because it is clearly a form of hypocrisy.

(8) Omitting faith from one's reasonings: this means
judging everything with reference to this life alone, sometimes
unwittingly in relation to money, but always by purely
worldly values. This is not even "behaving like everyone else",
it is acting as though Jesus had never spoken. It is a rather more
subtle sign, but not impossible to observe in ourselves. We can
for example take the advice of St Francis de Sales[1] and ask
ourselves where we stand "in our hope which is perhaps too
much set upon the world and upon creatures, and too little set
upon God and upon eternal things. In our sadness, if it be too
excessive for vain things; and in our joy, if it be too excessive
for unworthy things."

Generally the lukewarm person becomes embedded in the
state into which he has fallen, he suffers from a kind of spiritual

---

[1] St Francis de Sales, *Introduction to the Devout Life*, Part V, Chapter 7.
London, 1943, p. 258.

old age and hardening of the arteries. Such a state is extremely serious and this is how Fr Lallemant writes of its dangers: "The multiplication of venial sins is the destruction of souls [notice the strength of the expression] causing the diminution of those divine lights and inspirations, those interior graces and consolations, that fervour and courage, which are needed to resist the assaults of the enemy. Hence follow blindness, weakness, frequent falls, an acquired habit of insensibility of heart; because when once an affection for these faults is contracted, we sin without feeling we are sinning."[1] Happily, however, Providence can make good come even out of evil, and it often happens that some particular sin will have the effect of opening our eyes to the truth about ourselves, and provide a sufficient shock to make the soul shake off its torpor. St Andrew Hubert Fournet, a canonized saint, is said to have increased in virtue from the day when he was overcome with remorse for having refused alms to a poor man who knocked at his door.

We will end by giving some of the causes and the remedies for lukewarmness. Among the causes we can note:

(1) Fatigue, and notably nervous strain. This prevents the soul from maintaining proper control over its life and hinders it in turning freely towards the Father. The remedy, rest, is simple in theory but often difficult to apply in practice. It should be emphasized, however, that we must if necessary be prepared to cut down seriously on work or amusements to avoid this obstacle. For how many devout people has this not been the downfall! The lack of sleep is particularly dangerous because it tends to destroy the ability to pray, and the irritated body claims its revenge.

(2) Activism, or a lack of respect, in practice, for prayer. Prayer is at first replaced by real work but soon only by feverish and sterile activity.

(3) Monotony: this should be avoided as much as possible; by variety in one's spiritual efforts, by adapting prayer to the liturgical cycle, by enjoying one's spare time to the full and by doing a certain amount of intellectual exercise.

(4) The search for success: this makes men take all the wrong

[1] Fr Lallemant, *Spiritual Doctrine*, Principle III, Chapter II, article I, para. 3, p. 130. New York, 1885.

turnings that lead straight to egoism and arrogance. It can be avoided by conscientiousness in small things and a great affection for Christ which should be the motive for all our actions.

(5) Finally, lukewarmness can be a result of a false idea that God only looks at the big things in our lives. This is a mentality that must be corrected, and we can best do so with the aid of a good spiritual director.

The remedies of a general nature are indicated in the letter in the Apocalypse: "Come and buy from me what thou needest; gold, proved in the fire, to make thee rich, and white garments to clothe thee, and cover up the nakedness which dishonours thee; rub salve, too, upon thy eyes, to restore them sight. It is those I love I correct and chasten; kindle thy generosity, and repent" (Apoc. 3. 18–19). It is really a question of making a generous effort to practise the highest virtues, and these will not be found in books, but in the person of Jesus. The very fact of making this resolve, and the efforts it requires, make the soul rise up out of the dark and dismal fog which surrounds it. With the aid of God's grace a cure is possible and even normal, and it will lead us back again to that closeness with Christ that he desires: "See where I stand at the door, knocking; if anyone listens to my voice and opens the door, I will come in to visit him, and take my supper with him, and he shall sup with me" (ibid. 20).

Chapter 8

NOTES ON SIN

If thou, Lord wilt keep record of our iniquities Master, who has strength to bear it?—Psalm 129. 3.

In this chapter we shall be dealing with different aspects of sin, with the purpose of helping the reader to become aware of different sins, of their gravity and of their place in life, starting from the point at which we experience sorrow for them and seek forgiveness. We should say straightway that sin concerns everyone: Jesus sees nothing but sinners around him: "None is good, except God only" (Luke 18. 19), he says to the rich young man, while all men are evil: "Why then, if you, evil as you are, know well enough how to give your children what is good for them . . . " (Mat. 7. 11).

St Paul does not say any more than Jesus, although he speaks more strongly, quoting Psalm 13 for the purpose: "Jews and Gentiles, as we have before alleged, are alike convicted of sin. Thus, it is written, There is not an innocent man among them, no, not one. There is nobody who reflects, and searches for God; all alike are on the wrong course, all are wasted lives; not one of them acts honourably, no, not one" (Rom. 3. 9–12).

The fact that sin is universal makes it even more mysterious. To get to the heart of its mystery we shall proceed one step at a time.

(1) *The Supper Guests*[1]

"There was a man that gave a great supper, and sent out many invitations. And when the time came for his supper, he sent one of his own servants telling the invited guests to come, for all was now ready. And all of them, with one accord, began

[1] This section has drawn largely on Fr J. Lebreton, *The Life and Teaching of Jesus Christ Our Lord*, Vol. ii, Chap. 2, p. 55. London, 1934.

making excuses. I have bought a farm, the first said to him, and I must needs go and look over it; I pray thee, count me excused. And another said, I have bought five pair of oxen, and I am on my way to make trial of them; I pray thee, count me excused. And another said, I have married a wife, and so I am unable to come.

"The servant came back and told his master all this, whereupon the host fell into a rage, and said to his servant, Quick, go out into the streets and lanes of the city; bring in the poor, the cripples, the blind and the lame. And when the servant told him, Sir, all has been done according to thy command, but there is room left still, the master said to the servant, Go out into the highways and the hedgerows, and give them no choice but to come in, that so my house may be filled. I tell you, none of those who were first invited shall taste of my supper" (Luke 14. 16–24).

This parable gives a very grave warning: the master of the house, who represents God, invites a number of people to be his guests, but they all evade the invitation politely, without making up false excuses.

The reasons they give to justify their absence are far from being frivolous. And yet they are all condemned with no right of appeal. Why is this? It is because, by giving preference to their own affairs, however important these may be, over the call which summons them to the Kingdom of Heaven, they have disobeyed the great law of the Gospel: "Make it your first care to find the kingdom of God, and his approval" (Mat. 6. 33).

We should be on our guard, for it is very easy to commit sins in this way. Because we love the good things of this world, little by little they occupy all our affections, and inevitably the day will come when we shall find ourselves sinking into habits of egoism and injustice without noticing how odious such habits are. Fr Lebret notes the following as some of the ways in which we frequently go wrong:

> The love of money.
> The desire for riches.
> The desire for honours.
> Having ambition in excess of our abilities.

66 THE CHRISTIAN PURSUIT

(2) Sin as a Sickness of the Soul

It is quite possible to use the term "sickness" even for a mortal sin, because, as Pius XII teaches us: "Nor does all life depart from those who, though by sin they have lost charity and divine grace and are consequently no longer capable of a supernatural reward, nevertheless retain Christian faith and hope."[1] With this in mind, we should like to note three things:

(a) Sin is a real Illness and therefore a Reality

In spite of its apparent naïveté, this observation is not without point: it is a well-known fact that there is a whole school of modern thought which, as a reaction against past abuses and claiming as its basis the findings of scientific psychology, has arrived at a point where sin has so little meaning that in practice nothing is really our fault and there is an excuse for everything we do. Confronted with behaviour which does not conform to moral standards, they produce a "complex" to justify it.[2]

As it is not our purpose here to philosophize, there is no reason for us to attack the intellectual foundations of this mentality. But it is well within our mandate to point out that it is an attitude radically contrary to the whole of Judaeo-Christian thought as expounded in Holy Scripture and papal pronouncements.

We must go further still: our religion is based on a belief in redemption and in forgiveness. If the possibility of committing sin is ruled out, then the whole edifice collapses: dying on the cross is just a strange idea Jesus had, the Mass is useless,[3] and anyone who does penance is a misguided fool. Of course, we should not oversimplify and try to see sin everywhere, but neither should we go to the opposite extreme.

This sickness has its roots in our will; it is our will which

---

[1] Pius XII, Encyclical *Mystici Corporis Christi*. [*The Mystical Body of Jesus Christ*, C.T.S., 1943, p. 16, No. 22.]

[2] The condemnation of Dr A. Hesnard's book, *Moralité sans péché* (*Acta Apostolicae Sedis*, 48 (1956), p. 95) should help to underline, if this were necessary, the topical nature of what we have been saying.

[3] The main purpose of the Mass is not reparation for sins, but the re-enacting of the redeeming sacrifice of the cross, which would not have taken place but for our sins.

goes wrong, it leaves the loving dependence which links it with God to give itself up to the slavery of its passions, whether of the senses or of the mind. Here is how St Paul describes this alternative: "You know well enough that wherever you give a slave's consent, you prove yourselves the slaves of that master; slaves of sin, marked out for death, or slaves of obedience, marked out for justification. . . . At the time when you were the slaves of sin, right-doing had no claim upon you. And what harvest were you then reaping, from acts which now make you blush? Their reward is death. Now that you are free from the claims of sin, and have become God's slaves instead, you have a harvest in your sanctification, and your reward is eternal life" (Rom. 6. 16, 20–2).

Since it is man's free will which wallows in sin, sin is first of all an evil which comes from within. Outward behaviour may be regrettable without for that reason being very wrong, and we should take notice of Our Lord's warning: "It is from the heart that [a man's] wicked designs come, his sins of murder, adultery, fornication, theft, perjury and blasphemy. It is these make a man unclean; he is not made unclean by eating without washing his hands" (Mat. 15. 19–20).

We will come back to this particular truth when we talk about the healing of sin, and also when we talk about the way we confess our sins. There is one more thing we should like to mention while we are on the subject, and that is that we should not confuse the dictates of our feelings with those of our conscience. Very often our senses attempt to justify wrong behaviour by the pleasure we obtain from it—do not let us fall into this trap.

(b) Sin is a Social Disease

Because it always affects our way of life; sooner or later it touches those around us, so there is no use our taking refuge in phrases like "I'm not doing any harm to anyone else". It is a negative excuse, because it is not enough not to do harm, our business is to do good. From this point of view, even our thoughts, when they are evil or simply idle, rob those near to us of something that should be theirs, because they are preventing our hearts from loving, and if we are too much absorbed by them they will lead us into self-centredness. This is an extremely important consideration: if we go over the list of sins we are liable to commit, we shall see that the ones that are judged as being most serious are precisely the ones that harm others most.

(c) Sin is a Withdrawal into Oneself

Because it consists, either directly or indirectly, in preferring one's own will to the will of God. By giving in to this preference, the sinner is servant to his own desires; he becomes egocentric, or, if you like, he shuts himself up inside himself. He may do this in order to be able to indulge in various vices, which is the case of the ordinary sinner, the debauchee, the drunkard or the thief. He can also do it in order to contemplate his own virtues, like the Pharisee in the parable. But to remain enclosed within oneself is contrary to the whole movement of life, which consists in giving and receiving, in exchanging with others.

From the Christian point of view our life should consist in receiving from God and giving to our fellow men. From God, we receive not only the life of the body and the soul, but everything necessary for our sanctification: the presence of the Holy Spirit with his gifts, sanctifying grace, and the three theological virtues of Faith, Hope and Charity. Our duty to our neighbour is to give him our devoted service, our love and sometimes even our possessions. We cut ourselves off from God by *pride*, which we shall deal with in another chapter later on, and from our neighbour by *sloth and avarice*.

Sloth (we prefer this term to laziness, which nowadays seems to imply an amiable disinclination for over-exertion) is a refusal of the normal activity of our organism, a shying away from all effort. The slothful man would like to be able to do nothing, see nothing, feel nothing; he is half asleep, so that nothing disturbs his indulgence in the little world that begins and ends with himself.

There are different forms of sloth, or laziness, some of them quite subtle. Here are a few quoted from Fr Lebret:

Conservatism: no effort is made to adapt oneself to change.

Passive obedience: obedience is only perfect when it is the result of intelligent, thoughtful decision.

The absence of any effort at cultivating the mind: philistinism is a kind of sloth only too frequently met with among those we call "good Catholics".

Impulsiveness, or allowing one's behaviour to be governed by moods, and whims of the moment.

Wasting time, or spending too much of it on things of no importance.

Working carelessly, considering that what one does is always good enough for the money paid for it, or for the results one obtains from it.

Lacking firmness in decision, and leaving things unfinished.

Sloth is a serious evil, for it can make a whole life sterile, which is inadmissible in Christianity, since Jesus has asked us to "bear fruit".

Avarice also exists in many different forms, for it may apply to spiritual, intellectual or material possessions. It consists in always keeping things for oneself, in saving up God's gift when it is there to be used and put at the service of others. We will leave for the moment the question of material possessions, to ask ourselves what our attitude is to our possessions of intelligence and religion. For example, do we study with the sole purpose of accumulating knowledge, or to make ourselves more useful people? Do we know how to study so as to give others the fruits of what we have learnt?

Where our religious possessions are concerned, we may ask ourselves how we stand with regard to the apostolate. St Paul in prison could write that "there is no imprisoning the word of God" (II Tim. 2. 9). But if the pagans were unable to imprison it, Christians themselves have made it their business to do so ever since. How little of the apostle there is in most of us! St Catherine of Siena was already saying in her day that the world was "going bad for very silence". Her complaints would be only too appropriate today. So often we pride ourselves on keeping silent just when we should speak, and then we are astonished that Christianity spreads so slowly![1]

Let us remember the words of the Psalm:

[1] On this subject see Mgr Suenens' book, *The Gospel to Every Creature,* transl. by Louise Gavan Duffy, esp. pp. 47 ff. London, 1956 (many reprints).

To do thy will, O my God, is all my desire,
to carry out that law of thine which is written in my heart.
And I told the story of thy just dealings before a great
    throng;
be witness, Lord, that I do not seal my lips.
Thy just dealings are no secret hidden away in my heart;
I boast of thy faithful protection, proclaim that mercy,
that faithfulness of thine for all to hear it (Psalm 39. 9–10).

We should remember too that Mary did not keep Jesus to
herself but gave him to the world; just after the incarnation, by
bringing him to Elizabeth; later, by allowing him to go away
to carry out his ministry, and in the end, at the foot of the
cross, by sharing in his sacrifice.

(3) *Different Ways of Looking at Sin*

There are two ways of looking at it, both fully in accordance
with the spirit of Christ, both necessary and each—we should
not forget this—complementing the other.

(a) A certain act is wrong because it breaks a rule; it is, we
might say, an infringement of the code of our duties towards
God. Here we can perceive a law, a sinner and a judge, and the
point of view is that of a legal proceeding. It helps us to define
clearly the limits of what is allowed and what is forbidden, and
to teach these limits with precision. It is, therefore, most
valuable in helping to form the consciences of the very young,
who do not yet understand subtleties and need to have things
which they cannot analyse for themselves explained to them
perfectly clearly.

But if we stopped here, we should find ourselves facing very
serious objections, for God would appear as a judge whereas
he is our Father, and as a set of rules whereas he is Love. From
this way of thinking would come first a certain fear of the
judge and his judgement, and then the temptation to catalogue
our whole life, believing that all is well as long as we have not
committed any serious infringement of the code we learnt as
children. Last of all, this would take from us our love of life,
and leave us with our pride or our scruples—and sometimes
both. In short, this is playing a game which is not the Christian
game: "Love has no room for fear; and indeed, love drives out

fear when it is perfect love, since fear only serves for correction. The man who is still afraid has not yet reached the full measure of love" (I John 4. 18). And so we should not forget that we have to reckon with the second point of view, the psychological or subjective one.

(b) God does not just consider a good deed or a bad deed, he looks into the heart of the sinner. This view of sin leads us beyond the sin itself, to the deep-laid tendencies which gave birth to it. And here we make several discoveries: first of all that sin can consist of a state of mind; if for example I nurse a grudge against someone after a quarrel, I am in a state of wrong-doing, even if I have not started a new quarrel. Secondly, small sins may have their cause in more serious shortcomings; in a well-ordered life it may happen that occasions for grave sin are rare, but it would be a mistake to assume from this that one is little short of holiness. Lastly, even on the level of human relationships, nothing destroys friendship as quickly as repeated thoughtlessness and lack of consideration, and the same holds true on the level of our Christian life—a succession of sins against charity destroys our friendship with God little by little, they "quench the Spirit", as St Paul says (I Thes. 5. 19).

We should, therefore, complete our examination of conscience by looking into our hearts, while realizing that we should not judge our faults uniquely from this second point of view any more than from the first, for it does not give us an exact diagnosis of our sins, as there is the danger of unconsciously substituting an analysis of our feelings for a true examination of conscience.

One last observation: it is not for us to judge other people's worth: "Do not judge others, or you yourselves will be judged" (Mat. 7. 1). Judgement is the prerogative of God, and he delegates it only to the priest in the confessional.

(4) *Some Consequences of Sin in the Soul*

The first consequence is well known to everyone: it is the loss of charity and of sanctifying grace. Any good done by the sinner is deprived of its supernatural merit; it can only prepare his conversion.

Another lesser-known consequence is the awakening of

concupiscence: like spirituality and like love, sin takes on a life of its own. A man who allows himself sins of pride but who is shocked at the idea of committing sensual sins, wakes up one day to find that he is steeped in immorality. Another who thinks that by gratifying his desires they will be assuaged discovers that they become instead increasingly tyrannical.

A third consequence is that by losing our familiar contact with God we find it difficult to pray. We may note in this context that facility in prayer increases with purity of soul. When perfect purity is reached, then we arrive at contemplation: "Blessed are the clean of heart; they shall see God" (Mat. 5. 8).[1] The opposite is also true: certain hardened sinners seem to be almost physically incapable of saying the simplest prayer.[2]

Yet another consequence is that of estrangement from God. As the sinner ceases to be his close companion, a moment comes when he no longer knows God at all. Then comes the stage of temptations against the Faith, for as the soul does not miss God any more it is easy to believe that he does not exist. Here we should notice that there is no question of an intellectual process, and so it is useless to imagine that belief can be restored to the soul by mere reasoning, for, however convincing this may be, it will achieve nothing whatsoever. What has to be done is to make the sinner aware of his sins and to lead him back to repentance and prayer. Of course quite a different problem is that of the student or scientist whose faith is shaken because he does not see how to reconcile some assertion of profane learning with the doctrine of the Church.

In the end the sinner becomes a persecutor, and this can happen in three different ways:

Some turn against God and the Church, sometimes increasing their sins in an effort to rid themselves of their obsessive remorse—they seem to want to destroy the uneasiness of their conscience by going directly against it.

Others find it intolerable to think that just men lead a

---

[1] See also the *Catechism of the Council of Trent*, "De Oratione", No. 362.

[2] This trouble found by sinners in praying should not be confused with the difficulties of holy men and women in their meditations. In each case the distinction should be left to the spiritual director, who should be kept informed of the state of the individual soul, and of any inclination or reluctance which it feels.

different life from their own, and they would gladly say with the ungodly in the Book of Wisdom:

> Where is he, the just man?
> We must plot to be rid of him;
> he will not lend himself to our purposes.
> Ever he must be thwarting our plans;
> transgress we the law, he is all reproof,
> depart we from the traditions of our race, he denounces us.
> What, would he claim knowledge of divine secrets,
> give himself out as the Son of God?
> The touchstone, he, of our inmost thoughts;
> we cannot bear the very sight of him,
> his life so different from other men's,
> the path he takes, so far removed from theirs! (Wisdom 2.
> 12–15).

A third category professes the greatest disdain for the Church, which they accuse of being reactionary and out of date. We should beware of this kind of attitude, for can these people who are always clamouring against the Church prove that they on their side have done everything they can to understand the Church?

(5) *The World's Attitude and Christ's Attitude to Sin and the Sinner*

"One of the Pharisees invited him to a meal; so he went into the Pharisee's house and took his place at table. And there was then a sinful woman in the city, who, hearing that he was at table in the Pharisee's house, brought a pot of ointment with her, and took her place behind him at his feet, weeping; then she began washing his feet with her tears, and drying them with her hair, kissing his feet, and anointing them with the ointment.

"His host, the Pharisee, saw it, and thought to himself, If this man were a prophet, he would know who this woman is that is touching him, and what kind of woman, a sinner. But Jesus answered him thus, Simon, I have a word for thy hearing. Tell it me, Master, he said. There was a creditor who had two debtors; one owed him five hundred pieces of silver, the other fifty; they had no means of paying him, and he gave them both their discharge. And now tell me, which of them loves him the more? I suppose, Simon answered, that it is the one who had the greater debt discharged. And he said, Thou hast judged rightly.

"Then he turned towards the woman, and said to Simon, Dost thou see this woman? I came into thy house, and thou gavest me no water for my feet; she has washed my feet with her tears, and wiped them with her hair. Thou gavest me no kiss of greeting; she has never ceased to kiss my feet since I entered; thou didst not pour oil on my head; she has anointed my feet, and with ointment. And so, I tell thee, if great sins have been forgiven her, she has also greatly loved. He loves little, who has little forgiven him. Then he said to her, Thy sins are forgiven. And his fellow guests thereupon thought to themselves, Who is this, that he even forgives sins? But he told the woman, Thy faith has saved thee; go in peace" (Luke 7. 36–50).

This story is a perfect illustration of the contrast between Christ's attitude and that of the world. We do not have to go far in order to find examples of man's complicity with sin, or what occasions he has for falling into it and what clichés he finds to justify every kind of wrong-doing. But when the sinner appears before his fellow men—very often the very ones who contributed most to his downfall—he is treated with a harshness that is quite incredible. He is classed as belonging to a category from which he can never escape, he is labelled as a marked man; it is in this way that Simon thinks of the poor, unfortunate woman: "If this man were a prophet, he would know who this woman is who is touching him, and what kind of woman, a sinner." As for forgiveness, it is not even thought of. Jesus is regarded with scepticism and contempt; from the beginning to the end the Pharisee treats him disdainfully, and speaks of him coldly although he is his guest.

The behaviour of Jesus is the exact opposite of this. He has never been in the slightest way in league with evil, and so he can say to the Jews with his head held high: "Can any of you convict me of sin?" (John 8. 46). He has never ceased to teach a doctrine of the most uncompromising moral purity. But the guilty sinner has only to come to him in a spirit of repentance, and all he thinks of is forgiveness. Even in his manner of forgiving he is full of delicate attentions: he raises up the poor woman in front of all the other guests, her audacity has little importance for him, neither have her sins, for she is sorry for them and she shows great love, and this is enough for Jesus to forgive her. But every word he says in her defence is accompanied by a scathing rebuke for the Pharisee: "Thou gavest me no water for my feet; she has washed my feet with her tears, and wiped them with her hair. Thou gavest me no kiss of greeting; she has never ceased to kiss my feet since I entered; thou didst not pour oil on my head; she has anointed my feet, and with ointment. . . . He loves little, who has little forgiven him."

It is not possible to describe the charm and gentleness of divine forgiveness, it is inexpressible. But we may note that this forgiveness does not only proclaim us to be just men, it *makes* us so; it never humiliates a sinner, but, as in the case of the Prodigal Son, it at once gives him back his filial rights, in spite of the fact that he deserved to lose them by his sins.

> The quality of mercy is not strain'd,
> It droppeth as the gentle rain of heaven
> Upon the place beneath: it is twice bless'd;
> It blesseth him that gives and him that takes;
> 'Tis mightiest in the mightiest; it becomes
> The throned monarch better than his crown;
> His sceptre shows the force of temporal power,
> The attribute to awe and majesty,
> Wherein doth sit the dread and fear of Kings;
> But mercy is above this sceptred sway,
> It is enthroned in the hearts of Kings,
> It is an attribute to God himself,
> And earthly power does then show likest God's
> When mercy seasons justice. Therefore, Jew,
> Though justice be thy plea, consider this,
> That in the course of justice none of us
> Shall see salvation: we do pray for mercy,
> And that same prayer doth teach us all to render
> The deeds of mercy.[1]

And if one day we go into the confessional with our conscience weighed down with sins that we know are serious, we should not forget to ask God that the priest who hears our confession may have the grace to enable us to feel, in all he says to us, something of the kindness that is in the heart of Jesus.

[1] Shakespeare, *The Merchant of Venice*, Act IV, Scene I, vv. 184 ff.

Chapter 9

UNITY AND DIVISION

This message about what we have seen and heard we pass on to you, so that you too may share in our fellowship. What is it, this fellowship of ours? Fellowship with the Father, and with his Son Jesus Christ—1 John 1. 3.

We have seen that God creates in order to exchange love with his creation.[1] All parts of creation bear some resemblance to their Creator. This resemblance, as concerns men, is revealed in the Scriptures, and made clear by philosophy for the rest of creation. The result of this resemblance, of this exchange of love, is a unity, a communion between the Father and the beings that have their origin in him, and because this communion is the fruit of love, one can say that it is God's supreme aim. It is in this communion that God rejoices and that all creation should live.

At the same time, Satan has a contrary aim: to divide everything, to separate and to cause dissension.

(1) *The Unity of Heaven*

In early times men imagined heaven as an expanse of space situated beyond a vault from which hung the stars. This kind of image seems naïve today, and we can best describe heaven as the world of God, the universe of the Godhead. By this very fact it is the world of him who is one, the place of unity.

This unity is not just any kind of unity, but a full, absolute and total unity. It is Love that lives in heaven in the eternal and divine communion of the Three Persons and of the angels.

In heaven none lives alone, not even God.

In heaven life is lived "with" and "together".

In heaven the only way life can be lived is united.

[1] See Chapter 5, "The Creation and Man's Destiny".

In the visions of the Apocalypse not only the angels but also the elect always appear in "choirs", never alone.

In addition, nothing can affect the perfect and infinite union of the Three, because they are all-powerful, all-powerful in their love as in their life. From this union comes the tranquillity of perfect order. From this movement of love comes the boundless glory of God. This exchange of love within the Trinity is the unfathomable mystery of God and the culminating point of all things, to be adored eternally.

The unity of the Three is not a depersonalized uniformity—this is a speciality of the devil—the Father is not the same as the Holy Spirit or the Son; but together they form a community where everything is shared by love. In the heart of the Trinity there is no "yours and mine" only "you and I".

What is not love can never appear in God, never penetrate him or even know him, still less possess him. There lies its essential impotence, its torture, its rage, its inescapable defeat, the root of its eternal damnation.

God can be penetrated only by the Spirit of love, but "there is no depth in God's nature so deep that the Spirit cannot find it out. . . . No one else can know God's thoughts, but the Spirit of God" (I Cor. 2. 10–11). That depth which he alone can reach is the point where the mysterious exchange between the Father and the Son takes place or, to put it another way, where the life of the Son springs from that of his Father. But because "it was through him that all things came into being, and without him came nothing that has come to be" (John 1. 3), and because he has "chosen us out, in Christ, before the foundation of the world" (Eph. 1. 4), this point is also that from which all life comes and the source of all love; it is the central point of all the universes, the point from which everything comes and to which everything returns.

From this mysterious point, where he alone can penetrate, the Spirit comes forth to spread to the ends of the earth the life-giving forces of God. During the Octave of Pentecost the Church appoints for reading in the breviary Psalm 103, a hymn which contemplates the whole creation, as if to show us that the Spirit who "moved over the waters" (Gen. 1. 2) at the Creation continues to act in it and is the basis of life: "Then thou sendest forth thy spirit, and there is fresh creation, thou dost repeople the face of earth" (Ps. 103. 30).[1] The Spirit of Love, which originates in the Godhead, has the role of diffusing its force so that finally there is some trace of God in every being. The culminating point of this "centrifugal" action is the coming of the Holy Spirit to our Lady at the Incarnation of the Word, followed by his descent at Pentecost to become "the soul of the Church".[2]

Having achieved this outward movement, the Spirit of love then has the role of bringing all creation back to the Father. He accomplishes this by inspiring a twofold action wherein the Church raises men's hearts to God, and the angels, bowing down to Christ, join with his Mystical Body in adoration of the Father. In this way the whole of creation is reunited with its Creator and takes its part in the divine exchange of love.

The liberty of God consists in always being free to unite. The value of liberty in all its forms is derived from the fact that liberty is a prerequisite of love; and love is a willingness to unite. So at the end of this meditation we see God as him who is infinite Love at work, him who is almighty Power at the service of Love, him who is Freedom for Unity. These are formulas which will help us to be clear about our objectives. Do not all our efforts as Christians aim at freeing ourselves from egoism and all that prevents unity, and at using all our strength in the service of love so that our capacity for loving may become infinite?

(2) *The Attempt to Disunite*

The attempt to disunite did not originate from God or in God, but it did originate in heaven, in the world of spiritual creatures, among the angels. In God's plan the angels are united to their Creator both by their beauty as pure spirits, in which can be seen a reflection of God's own splendour, and by that exchange of love of which we have just been speaking.

But though the liberty of God never prevents him from keeping faith with his creatures, the same is not always true of the angels. Some of them refused unity. They said "No" to

[1] Cf. also Job 34. 14.
[2] Cf. Pius XII, Encyclical *Mystici Corporis Christi*. [*The Mystical Body of Jesus Christ*, C.T.S., 1943, p. 35, No. 55.]

the will of God and to his universal plan of love and in this
they disobeyed; they sinned. We shall now try to see what this
sin of the angels could have been.

It must of course have been a sin of the spirit since angels
have no bodies. This incidentally refutes a very widespread
error, that of considering the body as the source of sin; in fact,
the contrary is true, as sin originates in a conscious deviation
of the will of which the body is only the instrument.[1] In the
case of pure spirits, sin must consist in loving themselves more
than God or, to be exact, in preferring the beauty that is
inherent in their nature to that gift of God's grace which must
entail a loving recognition of their dependence upon him. To
put it in another way, the sin consists of trying to be like God
in possessing beatitude independently, instead of accepting it
as a gift.[2]

Up to this point we have only stated certainties, but it will
do no harm to explore the domain of probabilities, particularly
those which are honoured by tradition. We will start by pointing out that, to commit a sin, it is necessary to have an occasion
of sin, a test, and for a pure spirit the test must consist of being
faced with a conception, a divine plan which is accepted or
refused. Furthermore, if an angel is to be capable of rejecting
a divine conception, two conditions are indispensable: the
presence of a mystery—because an accomplished fact
is indisputable—and the impression that a refusal will
bring some advantage—otherwise there would be no temptation.

Precisely these two conditions are combined in the incarnation, which is the pivot of Christianity. The angels, like ourselves, find two great difficulties in accepting the incarnation.
The first is an intellectual difficulty, and the second is a
difficulty in believing that God's love for men could be so
extravagant that he would unite himself with sinful humanity
in this way, coming down himself to lift men up out of their sin.
In addition, the incarnation has consequences that the angels
could resent: in virtue of this mystery the man Jesus will be

[1] As a result of original sin, this statement is no longer strictly correct,
because the body is not always obedient to the will and often leads it into
sin. But the principle remains true, and it is this we wish to point out.
[2] *Summa Theologica*, I[a], 63, 3, resp.

King of Heaven.[1] Worse still, Mary will be Queen of Heaven and pure spirits will have to obey not only God made man, but a woman who, though without sin, is merely human and thus by her nature ranks below the angels. By these two beings and in them, part of the material creation will be placed above that of pure spirits!

If one accepts this hypothesis, many things become clear.[2] All the facts fit this explanation: the cause of the rebel angels' revolt is a mystery which will accomplish the greatest possible closeness between God and his creation, not only because the incarnation consists in a marvellous union between a human nature and a divine person—Jesus combining the two in one being—but also because this closeness is achieved by saving man from a state of affairs brought about by his own fault, and thus shows the strength of God's love continuing although it had been at first rejected. By striking directly at the unity existing between God and his creation, the bad angels damage God's whole divine dispensation and therefore, we may say, even the Godhead itself.

The sin of the angels will be reproduced on earth by men: the Jews will refuse to believe in the divinity of the Saviour; they will refuse to admit what appears to them as a lowering of God but is, in fact, a raising of the flesh. Thus the basis for salvation or the loss of it, for all creatures that are intelligent and free, will be the acceptance or the refusal of the divinity of Christ. It is faith in Jesus, in the Word made flesh in the womb of Mary, that alone brings salvation to every part of creation. It is for love that God humbles himself and it is his humility that scandalizes us: Jesus loses nearly all his disciples when he speaks to them of humbling himself in the form of bread (John 6. 67), and on the day of the supreme humiliation of the cross, only one disciple remains with him.

---

[1] "His kingship is founded upon the ineffable hypostatic union. From this it follows not only that Christ is to be adored by angels and men, but that to Him as man angels and men are subject, and must recognize His empire; by reason of the hypostatic union Christ has power over all creatures." Enc. *Quas Primas*. [C.T.S., p. 9.]

[2] As the angels live outside time, it is quite possible to suppose that God may have revealed the incarnation to them before the original sin was committed.

(3) *The Failure of the Attempt to Disunite in Heaven*

At the very instant that they sinned, the rebellious angels fell from heaven. Absence of love could not divide heaven because it was itself thrust out, excommunicated instantaneously.

The cry of Lucifer: "I will serve no more!"[1] was echoed by a voice powerful as an eternal judgement: "Michael?—Who is like God?" And this cry banished the rebels, flung them away to their Satanic world of adversity, to the depths of solitude and dereliction, to the gehenna of darkness, weeping and gnashing of teeth—to hell, the only alternative to love, where love is never given or received, and unity is eternally refused.

It is quite possible that when they learnt of God's plan the faithful angels themselves were troubled and mystified, but they never hesitated, and a thousand difficulties do not make a doubt. Later, one of them, announcing the mystery of the incarnation, will proclaim: "Nothing can be impossible with God" (Luke 1. 37). When they were tested they allowed no incomprehension or pride to separate them from God. On earth, at the moment when the crowd "walked no more with Jesus", St Peter rallied the Twelve and said: "Lord, to whom should we go? Thy words are the words of eternal life" (John 6. 69). Like the angels, the apostles had faith in the word of God, and it was this faith that gave them their victory over the world: "He alone triumphs over the world, who believes that Jesus is the Son of God" (I John 5. 5).

There was a war in heaven, a war of the spirit: "Fierce war broke out in heaven, where Michael and his angels fought against the dragon. The dragon and his angels fought on their part, but could not win the day, or stand their ground in heaven any longer; the great dragon, serpent of the primal age, was flung down to earth; he whom we call the devil, or Satan, the whole world's seducer, flung down to earth, and his angels with him. Then I heard a voice crying aloud in heaven, The time has come; now we are saved and made strong, our God reigns, and power belongs to Christ, his anointed; the accuser

[1] Traditionally inspired by the description of the Israelites' revolt in Jer. 2. 20.

of our brethren is overthrown. Day and night he stood accusing them in God's presence; but because of the Lamb's blood and because of the truth to which they bore witness, they triumphed over him, holding their lives cheap till death overtook them. Rejoice over it, heaven, and all you that dwell in heaven; but woe to you, earth and sea, now that the devil has come down upon you, full of malice, because he knows how brief is the time given him" (Apoc. 12. 7–12).

The devil and his angels have remained "the outcast" and "the fallen". When Jesus sees his disciples return from the mission he has entrusted to them, he says: "I watched, while Satan was cast down like a lightning flash from heaven" (Luke 10. 18). Not that the pronouncing of a few exorcisms by the disciples brought about the final downfall of the devil, but these incidents, minor in themselves, evoked for Jesus the vision that was always before him: the contrast between Satan whose spirit through his pride is cast down, and Mary whose body and spirit, through her humility, are exalted.

> What, fallen from heaven,
> thou Lucifer, that once didst herald the dawn? . . .
> I will scale the heavens
> (such was thy thought);
> I will set my throne higher than God's stars. . . .
> I will soar above the level of the clouds,
> the rival of the most High.
> Thine, instead, to be dragged down into the world beneath,
> into the heart of the abyss.
> And there thy corpse lies,
> with the moth for its shroud,
> worms for its cerecloth (Is. 14. 12–15 and 11).

One is reminded of what Jesus said to the Jews: "Why then, what is the meaning of those words which have been written, The very stone which the builders rejected has become the chief stone at the corner? If ever a man falls against that stone, he will break his bones; if it falls upon him, it will grind him to powder" (Luke 20. 17–18). The stone itself remains intact. It is useless to attack God in heaven. To attack Christ is equally vain; the loser is always the one that has dared to attack God.

And so the drama approaches. We have seen it coming: Satan is thrown down to earth where he arrives in a state of fury. Since he cannot fight against the world of God himself, he will turn his wrath against the works of God on earth and against man in particular. His time is limited: he has only the centuries of history in which to act, and what are they compared to eternity?

There is, therefore, and there will be as long as the human race exists, a combat in which man is both the soldier and the battlefield. God and the devil are waging war for the possession of man. The Christian, like those chosen before him to prepare the coming of the Saviour, is fighting in Christ's service against the Prince of Darkness. This war is the underlying explanation of all history; it is our sorrow and our glory. "It is not against flesh and blood that we enter the lists; we have to do with princedoms and powers, with those who have mastery of the world in these dark days, with malign influences in an order higher than ours. Take up all God's armour, then; so you will be able to stand your ground when the evil time comes, and be found still on your feet, when all the task is over" (Eph. 6. 12–13).

The Father's aim in this struggle is to make us his children and to give us by his grace all the qualities necessary for us to be able to share in his divine life, but Satan's objective is to separate man from his Creator, to sully and degrade him to a point, where whether in body or in spirit, he will be unable to carry the divine life within him. He wants to make man not only unworthy of this, but incapable of it. After this he would, if he could, wipe out the whole human race so that the divine life could no longer be spread among creation and God's plan would be nullified: "The thief only comes to steal, to slaughter, to destroy" (John 10. 10).

His offensives have been continuous. As soon as man appeared in the garden of Eden, the devil started his attack. Later his offensives were directed especially against the patriarchs and the prophets who tried to correct the Jews' misconceptions about the true nature of the incarnation. Then came his assault against Christ on Calvary, the heresies in every century, and in recent years, the materialist assault which aims at submerging men in an insidious solicitude for temporal things only, so that they lose the ability to think of God. It is easy to imagine the sneering joy with which Satan would hurl these men into total war to annihilate them; such are the objectives of evil.

(4) *The Loss of Unity on Earth*

In heaven, the devil's revolt met with total defeat. On earth where the conditions of the battle are different, so also is its course. The outcome will be the same, but in the meantime the devil will have some victories, both major and minor; the original sin was his first victory.

When man was created he received not only human life, but also a share in the divine life. It was as a son of God that he was to love his heavenly Father. Love finds its normal expression in sacrifice: when one loves, one exchanges one's possessions, one shares, and to share, one renounces one's own rights to these possessions. Today we express this love in the Mass where we share among one another the Christ, the gift that the Father has given us, and we offer up ourselves and our possessions.

Now let us see how the Bible describes Satan's attack on our first parents: "Of all the beasts which the Lord God has made, there was none that could match the serpent in cunning. It was he who said to the woman, What is this command God has given you, not to eat the fruit of any tree in the garden? To which the woman answered, We can eat the fruit of any tree in the garden except the tree in the middle of it; it is this God has forbidden us to eat or even to touch, on pain of death. And the serpent said to her, What is this talk of death? God knows well that as soon as you eat this fruit your eyes will be opened, and you yourselves will be like gods, knowing good and evil. And with that the woman, who saw that the fruit was good to eat, saw, too, how it was pleasant to look at and charmed the eye, took some fruit from the tree and ate it; and she gave some to her husband, and he ate with her. Then the eyes of both were opened, and they became aware of their nakedness; so they sewed fig-leaves together, and made themselves girdles" (Gen. 3. 1–7).

When we read that account in the perspective of this book, we must look primarily for the psychology of the fault. We find, at the root of it, a lack of love. When we love someone we are happy to do his will, and we respect his wishes even when it costs us something. But instead of putting her trust in God, Eve confides in the serpent, she discusses things with him and reveals to him the commandment God has given them and the penalty with which he has backed it up. The devil loses no time in working out his tactics. God has offered them a share in the divine life on condition they give him obedience. Satan offers a do-it-yourself technique. The sin of Eve and of Adam is, therefore, primarily an attempt at self-aggrandisement in the face of God, at equality with him, combined, of course, with a motive of personal profit and the desire for power. It is very obviously a sin of pride, which is to be expected as, in their state of original innocence, temptations of the flesh did not exist, because the flesh was perfectly obedient to the soul. However, there is one other point that is worth noticing.

There is one fruit, independence, that God cannot share with man and which will always remain forbidden to him for it is an incommunicable prerogative of the divine nature. God alone depends on no one else and enjoys complete autonomy. The liberty of man is not independence, which is incompatible with our nature; it is simply the power to choose our own master, or, to put it in another way, to choose the manner in which we will depend on God. In practice, whatever we do, our lives on earth are dependent on countless outside factors. In the way we dress and the way we eat, in our houses and in our habits, in our work and in our pleasures, we live according to the influences of our time and of our present circumstances. We may well live in a state of revolt against God, we shall none the less be subject to the laws of our nature: in spite of ourselves we shall be forced to act as men and not as dogs or as horses. This is a necessity, but it is scarcely a limitation— otherwise one would have to say, for example, that blood is limited when its circulation is confined to a network of veins and arteries. If we refuse our obedience, we get the impression that God is for ever constraining us and we spend our lives struggling and bruising ourselves like an insect that keeps hitting itself on the window-pane trying to escape. If, however, we obey out of love we feel the delight of filial affection and we can echo the words of the Psalmist: "Do but open my heart wide, and easy lies the path thou hast decreed" (Psalm 118. 32).

D

(5) *The Consequences of Original Sin*

"And now they heard the voice of the Lord God, as he walked in the garden in the cool of the evening; whereupon Adam and his wife hid themselves in the garden, among the trees. And the Lord God called to Adam; Where art thou? he asked. I heard thy voice, Adam said, in the garden, and I was afraid, because of my nakedness, so I hid myself. And the answer came, Why, who told thee of thy nakedness? Or hadst thou eaten of the tree, whose fruit I forbade thee to eat? The woman, said Adam, whom thou gavest me to be my companion, she it was who offered me fruit from the tree, and so I came to eat it. Then the Lord God said to the woman, What made thee do this? The serpent, she said, beguiled me, and so I came to eat.

"And the Lord God said to the serpent, For this work of thine, thou, alone among all the cattle and all the wild beasts, shalt bear a curse; thou shalt crawl on thy belly and eat dust all thy life long. And I will establish a feud between thee and the woman, between thy offspring and hers; she is to crush thy head, while thou dost lie in ambush at her heels. To the woman he said, Many are the pangs, many are the throes I will give thee to endure; with pangs thou shalt give birth to children, and thou shalt be subject to thy husband; he shall be thy lord. And to Adam he said, Thou hast listened to thy wife's counsel, and hast eaten the fruit I forbade thee to eat; and now, through thy act, the ground is under a curse. All the days of thy life thou shalt win food from it with toil; thorns and thistles it shall yield thee, this ground from which thou dost win thy food. Still thou shalt earn thy bread with the sweat of thy brow, until thou goest back into the ground from which thou wast taken; dust thou art, and unto dust shalt thou return.

"The name which Adam gave his wife was Eve, Life, because she was the mother of all living men.

"And now the Lord provided garments for Adam and his wife, made out of skins, to clothe them. He said, too, Here is Adam become like one of ourselves, with knowledge of good and evil; now he has only to lift his hand and gather fruit to eat from the tree of life as well, and he will live endlessly. So the Lord God drove him out from that garden of delight, to cultivate the ground from which he came; banished Adam, and posted his Cherubim before the garden of delight, with a sword of fire that turned this way and that, so that he could reach the tree of life no longer" (Gen. 3. 8–24).

The deliberate disobedience signifies the refusal of love, the rejection of God's plan for mankind; the unity between God and his creatures was shattered.

Separated from God who is life, man became subject to death.

Separated from God who is truth, he became ignorant, and acquired knowledge only with effort.

Separated from God who is happiness, he found unhappiness.

Separated from God who is strength, he found weakness; and work, instead of being a source of joy, became difficult. Instead of being "play" it became "toil".

Separated from God who is goodness, man became inclined towards evil: it is a strange aberration that makes men want to injure or destroy others instead of desiring their good.

Separated from God his Father, man lost the divine life and the gift of grace.

Separated from God who is holiness, he learnt the meaning of evil—by doing it.

Man remained a creature of God but he lost his rights as an adopted son and had "God's displeasure for his birthright" (Eph. 2. 3); separated from God, he became divided in himself, and subject to egoism, which is a false love of self. Because he rejected the fatherhood of God the transmission of his own life became subject to that inner conflict which is concupiscence. The noble desire for love in man became an ignoble urge to dominate, and in woman the wish to give affectionate obedience deteriorated into a slavish desire to be dominated. The temptation to evil would no longer be only from without but more often from within. On discovering this terrible fact man would blush on looking at himself, the soul be ashamed of its body, although the body had been made for the soul and for its service; each one of us can feel that he is a dangerous enemy for his own person. Adam has lost not only his God, he has lost his interior paradise and he has lost himself.

The original sin will not remain isolated but will produce a chain reaction. We shall see Cain kill Abel and break the unity between brothers. Ham will revolt against his father and the unity of the family will be destroyed. At the tower of Babel mankind itself will become divided and the work of evil will be complete. God's plan of unity will suffer an enormous setback; there will no longer be a family of man, only men divided against one another, a prey to the evils of war which will be constant and increasing; violence will reign over the earth:

The man that wounds me,
the stripling who deals me a blow,
I reward with death.
For Cain, sevenfold vengeance was to be taken;
for Lamech, it shall be seventy times as much (Gen. 4. 23–4).

These savage verses need no commentary!

However, unlike the sin of the angels the sin of man is not irreparable. When a pure spirit sins, it is of necessity the whole of its being that sins, so that the damage cannot be remedied. But the same is not true of material creatures; there always remains a part of them that is unaffected by evil and which can serve as the starting point for a conversion.[1] But humanity by itself was incapable of repairing the damage. Reparation could only be accomplished through the initiative of God and the incarnation of Christ, for redemption would have to achieve all that sin had undone: to bring about the triumph of faith over doubt, of good over evil, of sanctity over sin, of love over lack of love, of unity over division, of giving over possessing, of sacrifice over profit. The return to unity will come about through love, salvation will not be in isolation. Man will have to learn to be at the disposal of others in a spirit of filial obedience, to reverse, for the love of God, some of his natural tendencies. Thus, through the Saviour and all those who follow him carrying their cross, it will be possible to win back all that has been lost.

[1] See a more precise explanation in *Summa Theologica*, Iᵃ, 64, 2, resp.

Chapter 10

THE TESTIMONY OF CHRIST

*And what is the truth so attested? That God has given us eternal
life, and that this life is to be found in his Son*—I John 5. 11.

In this book there is no question of our writing, or even making
an outline of, a dogmatic theology of Christ, neither do we
plan a successive study of the mysteries of his life, such as the
one to be found in the *Exercises* of St Ignatius, or in Dom
Marmion's book.[1] But this chapter will have achieved its
purpose if it helps the reader to begin to know our Lord, a
discovery which, with our discovery of the Father, should
continue throughout our passage on this earth, to culminate in
eternal life, which consists in knowing them both (John 17. 3).

Christ is the only one capable of sending up to God a perfect
homage of praise and love from the heart of creation, and he
came on earth to be the Saviour of mankind. The angel said
as much to Joseph: "Do not be afraid to take thy wife Mary to
thyself, for it is by the power of the Holy Ghost that she has
conceived this child; and she will bear a son, whom thou shalt
call Jesus, for he is to save his people from their sins" (Mat.
1. 20–1).

Because of this double link with the Father and with mankind, and because of the complexity of the work of our salvation, he presents many different aspects that we may contemplate, aspects that complete one another without in any
way being in opposition. The synoptic Gospels do not even
attempt a synthesis of these "unfathomable riches" (Eph. 3. 8);
they are content to give us an account of events, and we have
to turn to St John and St Paul for a more elaborate interpretation.

"Jesus had one disciple, whom he loved" (John 13. 23), and

[1] Dom Columba Marmion, *Christ in His Mysteries*, London, 1923 (10
editions.)

for him the mission of the "Word . . . made flesh" (John 1. 14) was a double one: first of all it was a mission of enlightenment in the revelation of the Father (cf. John 1. 18); and secondly it was a mission of salvation, destined to embrace the whole human community, since its purpose was "that the world might find salvation" (John 3. 17), and this goes much further than simply saving souls; it means that Christ has given the world the means of salvation, available to everyone, even if everyone does not take advantage of it. This was accomplished when, according to the prophetic words of Caiphas, "he was to die for the sake of the nation; and not only for that nation's sake, but so as to bring together into one all God's children, scattered far and wide" (John 11. 51–2). Here we have a prospect which has a universal and cosmic point of departure.

The Apostle of the Gentiles, a man of a very different temperament, builds his doctrine round the idea that Christ "too is that head whose body is the Church" (Col. 1. 18). In order to become part of this body, we had to be freed from two forms of slavery; the slavery of sin—"Christ never knew sin, and God made him into sin for us, so that in him we might be turned into the holiness of God" (II Cor. 5. 21); and the slavery of the Law—"From this curse invoked by the law Christ has ransomed us, by himself becoming, for our sakes, an accursed thing. . . . Thus, in Christ Jesus, the blessing of Abraham was to be imparted to the Gentiles, so that we, through faith, might receive the promised gift of the Spirit" (Gal. 3. 13–14). Thus, "all the more lavish was God's grace, shewn to a whole multitude, that free gift he made us in the grace brought by one man, Jesus Christ" (Rom. 5. 15). And thus in accepting "an obedience which brought him to death, death on a cross" (Phil. 2. 8), he reconciles us with the Father, and with one another, "inflicting death, in his own person, upon the feud" (Eph. 2. 16). So, "with the cleansing power which gives us new birth" (Titus 3. 5)—meaning baptism—we have "had the seal set on our faith by the promised gift of the Holy Spirit; a pledge of the inheritance which is ours" (Eph. 1. 13–14). And so the Father's plan: "to give history its fulfilment by resuming everything in him, all that is in heaven, all that is on earth, summed up in him" (Eph. 1. 10), can be accomplished. The Pauline point of view, which is more concerned with explaining in detail the workings of our salvation, leads us just the same to the glory of the Father: "Everything is for you, . . . and you for Christ, and Christ for God" (I Cor. 3. 22–3).

Both St Paul and St John consider that the sending of Christ on earth to suffer death is the greatest proof of God's love for us, and their hearts are filled with profound gratitude: "Why did Christ, in his own appointed time, undergo death for us sinners, while we were still powerless to help ourselves? It is hard enough to find anyone who will die on behalf of a just man, although perhaps there may be those who will face death for one so deserving. But here, as if God meant to prove how well he loves us, it was while we were still sinners that Christ, in his own appointed time, died for us" (Rom. 5. 6–9). "What has revealed the love of God, where we are concerned, is that he has sent his only-begotten Son into the world, so that we might have life through him. That love resides, not in our shewing any love for God, but in his shewing love for us first, when he sent out his Son to be an atonement for our sins" (I John 4. 9–10). "God has proved his love to us by laying down his life for our sakes" (I John 3. 16). Even more than all this, Christ is not only sent to us, he is "given" to us: "If thou knewest what it is God gives" (John 4. 10), so that we are invited to exercise our rights of ownership in him: "To keep hold of the Son is to have life; he is lifeless, who has no hold of the Son of God" (I John 5. 12). He is not only "the Holy One of God" (Mark 1. 24), he is "our Christ" as well. Of course, we can only exercise this possession by means of love, for a free being cannot be possessed except by an exchange of love, but this had to be mentioned here to show the strength of love asked of us and the degree of closeness to God which is offered to us. This term "to keep hold of the Son" evokes the strongest affections in our human family lives, those of maternal, paternal and conjugal love.

It should be noticed that in Jesus the person and the mission are not separable; he does not only come to give light to the world; he himself is "the world's light" (John 9. 5); he does not only come to show us the way, to teach us the truth, to give us life; no, he is all these things himself: "I am the way; I am truth and life" (John 14. 6). That is why the attitude of a man who would say: "Very well, Christ has two natures. What has that to do with me?" is indefensible; one cannot understand his mission without knowing him, and, more than this, trying to get to know someone is the law of love, whereas saying: "This has nothing to do with me", shows a total lack of affection.

Reading the Gospels, we notice a striking fact: there is nowhere any description of the physical appearance of Jesus, nor for that matter of our Lady or of those close to them. Was the Master above or below average height? Was he slight or heavily built, dark or fair? We do not know, any more than we know what kind of voice he had. There is only one way of getting to know him, and that is the study of his actions and, better still, of his words which "are spirit, and life" (John 6. 64), and which inspired his disciples: "Lord, to whom should we go? Thy words are the words of eternal life; we have learned to believe, and are assured that thou art the Christ, the Son of God" (ibid., 69–70). Now his words are above all a testimony: "Believe me, we speak of what is known to us, and testify of what our eyes have seen, and still you will not accept our testimony" (John 3. 11), and Jesus' words are a testimony because, as he "abides in the bosom of the Father" (John 1. 18), he speaks first of all in order to reveal him to us. This is why we have chosen, as a way of coming closer to him, this aspect of his testimony which combines the different points of view of St John and St Paul. This testimony became a light for mankind, and those who heard it were called in their turn to be his witnesses "to the ends of the earth" (Acts 1. 8). And so, the message of salvation is spread by a chain of witnesses, and Christians are people who are willing to become one of the links in the chain.

We must have two intentions if we want to come to know Christ: the first is the intention of making everything he teaches us part of our life: "Only you must be honest with yourselves," invites St James; "you are to live by the word, not content merely to listen to it. One who listens to the word without living by it is like a man who sees, in a mirror, the face he was born with; he looks at himself, and away he goes, never giving another thought to the man he saw there. Whereas one who gazes into that perfect law, which is the law of freedom, and dwells on the sight of it, does not forget its message; he finds something to do, and does it, and his doing of it wins him a blessing" (James 1. 22–5).

Yes, but not without difficulties and suffering. Because the Christian message does not enter into a person's life in order to leave it as it is; it transforms it, and in order to transform it, it causes an upheaval, as Dostoyevsky's Grand Inquisitor said. No sooner was the incarnation accomplished, no sooner was Jesus present in Mary's womb, that she "rose up and went with all haste to a town of Juda, in the hill country" (Luke 1. 39), where she went to see Elizabeth; she left her home in Nazareth to travel on foot for two days along rough paths. The child she was carrying had already started to change her life, and the fact that he did so as soon as he arrived makes it seem as if he wanted to warn us that there would be a difference in us as well as soon as he was there. A difference so great, St Paul tells us, that "when a man is in Christ Jesus, there has been a new creation" (Gal. 6. 15); "No man can enter into the kingdom of God unless birth comes to him from water, and from the Holy Spirit" (John 3. 5).

From this we can see the trait common to all those people in the Gospels who refused to listen to Jesus: they were all "set in their ways": Herod at the time of his birth, and later the heads of the Jewish people. Satisfied with themselves and their position in life, they violently rejected the metamorphosis that Jesus asked of them. He is however unyielding on this point: "Nobody uses a piece taken from a new cloak to patch an old one; if that is done, he will have torn the new cloak, and the piece taken from the new will not match the old. Nor does anybody put new wine into old wineskins; if that is done, the new wine bursts the skins, and there is the wine spilt and the skins spoiled. If the wine is new, it must be put into fresh wine-skins, and so both are kept safe" (Luke 5. 36–8).

His listeners preferred to keep to the old wine (ibid.). They were just as paralysed in their habits and way of thinking as the sick man of Bethsaida was paralysed in body; but he wanted to get well, whereas they preferred literally to die of their illness rather than to make the effort of changing themselves.

The second intention that Jesus asks of us is that we should trust in him, with that trust which is not yet faith itself but which prepares the way for it, accompanies it and is the logical consequence of it. When the first disciples heard from St John the Baptist who Jesus was, as he walked by on the banks of the Jordan, they talked with him for two hours, and then the next day when he decided to go to Galilee, they went with him; they trusted him, and they were rewarded shortly after by the miracle of Cana, the first of the "signs" given by Jesus. The Gospel concludes the story of the miracle by saying that he "made known the glory that was his, so that his disciples learned to believe in him" (John 2. 11), so their trust led them to faith.

The same with the man blind from birth. This man had given up all hope; during his interrogation later he said clearly: "That a man should open the eyes of one born blind is something unheard of since the world began" (John 9. 32). In other words, he thought that even a miracle could not cure him. All the same, when Jesus said to him: "Away with thee, and wash in the pool of Siloe" (ibid., 7), after he had made clay with his spittle and spread it on the man's eyes—an act which in human eyes was absurd—the man did as he said. He trusted him in spite of his previous disbelief. He too came to have faith, for when Jesus found him later and asked him: "Dost thou believe in the Son of God?" he said: "I do believe, Lord, and fell down to worship him" (ibid. 35 & 38).

The whole of the Gospels could be interpreted as Jesus' method of teaching his disciples, a method which aimed at developing in them this same trust, the trust which is "strength of hope",[1] till it became so firm that it would survive the test of the cross, of death and of the tomb. So, when he asks anyone the same question as he asked the man born blind: "Dost thou believe in the Son of God?" he does not simply wish to know if the truths he taught are being accepted. Behind these words are grouped the three theological virtues—St Thomas already observed that, in faith, there is at least a beginning of love.[2]

We may go even further: "belief" in the Gospel context means the beginning of the total gift of self, of the surrender

---

[1] On this point consult *Summa Theologica*, II^a II^{ae}, 129, 6 & 7.
[2] Ibid., II^a II^{ae}, 5, 2, ad 2.

of the entire being.[1] And the first thing that the Saviour asks
of us is to accept his way of looking at mankind, at life and the
world. We find this disconcerting, because his way is not the
one our feelings encourage us to take.

For example, when we see somebody for the first time, the
first thing we notice is his face, or the clothes he is wearing; the
first thing Jesus sees is his soul. When he is considering events,
he judges them by their spiritual significance. When he was
told the story of the Galileans massacred by Pilate, he answered:
"Do you suppose, because this befell them, that these men were
worse sinners than all else in Galilee? I tell you it is not so;
you will all perish as they did, if you do not repent" (Luke
13. 2–3).

As we follow Christ, this way of thinking will have to become
our own, so will this way of looking at things, for such is the
law of love; it leads those who love each other to act in the
same way when they are faced with the same situation. This
of course forces us out of our small world of self; and faith
cannot live in us for long on its own, for it cannot grow without
charity.

Truths revealed by Jesus which we cannot verify by intellectual means cannot be looked on as a kind of insult to our
intelligence, for they do not come into the realm of theory;
they are facts. While false reasoning does insult the intelligence
the knowledge of a new fact enriches it; and if we find it
disconcerting, this should not be regretted but welcomed, for
it will start us off on a new and deeper enquiry. When we
learn that Jesus is God, that his Father is also our Father, we
are given the opportunity of a whole new field to work in which
would not have existed without this knowledge and which will
lead us to think out again our philosophy of life from the very
beginning.

A mystery is not a riddle, it is a truth which is only partly
comprehensible to the intelligence,[2] which is not the same

---

[1] Here we may quote the words of Pius XII: "In the same way, to
believe means, in the first place, to admit—and to penetrate as far as is
possible—the truths revealed by Jesus Christ, but, at the same time, it
means to draw from those truths the consequences they imply for our moral
life." Address to University Students, 15 June 1952, *Acta Apostolicae Sedis*,
44 (1952), Nos. 11–12, p. 584.

[2] *The Decrees of the Vatican Council*, p. 26. London, 1907.

thing; it is given to us for the light it transmits to us and the work it incites us to do, and not for its power to amaze us. And so when the Christian is given a new definition with regard to the faith he can only be delighted, for he sees in it an enrichment of his spirit and an invitation to widen his researches, because the newly revealed fact will no longer have to be queried, but will act as a basis for further study. The First Vatican Council decreed: "The doctrine of faith which God has revealed has not been proposed, like a philosophical invention, to be perfected by human ingenuity; but has been delivered as a divine deposit to the Spouse of Christ, to be faithfully kept and infallibly declared."[1]

Properly speaking, our religion offers us not ideas or ideals, but a God of flesh and blood to whom we can speak directly. Love seeks the face of the beloved; we cannot love an idea, we must love a person.

And so it is in Christ, through his words and his acts, that we should look for the Father. We have to have "sight of his glory" (John 1. 14) and if we "live on in" him and "live on in his love" (ibid. 15. 4 & 9), then we will become like St John and St Paul, impassioned followers of Christ who is the life of the soul: "For me, life means Christ" (Phil. 1. 21). We shall find happiness in contemplating his splendour and his radiant influence on the world: "He is the true likeness of the God we cannot see; his is that first birth which precedes every act of creation. Yes, in him all created things took their being, heavenly and earthly, visible and invisible; what are thrones and dominions, what are princedoms and powers? They were all created through him and in him; he takes precedency of all, and in him all subsist. He too is that head whose body is the Church; it begins with him, since his was the first birth out of death; thus in every way the primacy was to become his. It was God's good pleasure to let all completeness dwell in him, and through him to win back all things, whether on earth or in heaven, into union with himself, making peace with them through his blood, shed on the cross" (Col. 1. 15–20).

In order to remain closely attached to Christ and the Church we have to conquer a great modern temptation, which consists in seeing religion as something vague and indeterminate,

[1] *The Decrees of the Vatican Council*, p. 28.

something to admire from a distance because it consoles people and does them good. This is tempting because it makes little demand on our intellectual laziness; it is also tempting because it leads to attitudes like this: "I don't mind going to Mass, but not every Sunday; only when I feel I need it", which is nothing more or less than religious sensualism, and, as such, food for our egoism and self-indulgence. This attitude also involves a tendency to run away from precise and concrete things for fear of being committed; we manage to come to an arrangement with the God of our imagination. But somewhere in the Gospels, we remember, there is a certain Sermon on the Mount which hardly admits of compromise. Our complacency suffers other shocks as every Sunday the parish priest climbs into the pulpit and drums into our heads certain truths we would much rather forget! But this is the price of our finding God; Jesus is not content with lip service; he asks us to follow him, which is the most concrete commitment in the world.

If we listen to his testimony and listen to the voice of the Church reminding us of it as it explains it to us and brings it within our reach, we may be sure that we are in the way of truth. Fidelity breeds assurance and peace of mind which satisfy the needs of our minds and hearts. The first thing this testimony teaches us is not what God is in himself, but what he is in relation to us, how he thinks of us, how he sees us, how he behaves towards us. Through all this we come to perceive his nature. And this after all is the very heart of the problem: opposition to God is directed not against his existence, but against his attitude. The farmer whose crops have been ruined by a hailstorm and who blasphemes by saying: "If there was a God, such things wouldn't happen!" is not really expressing a doubt as to God's existence: he cannot understand that a good God could allow such a catastrophe.

"The flame dies if it is not passed on; we discover nothing for ourselves alone, and truth would wither in our hands if it did not become a mission."[1] Therefore, we in our turn must bear witness so as to show the world that God has an effect on things, and to show our fellow men that God cares about them.

---

[1] Jean Guitton, *Difficultés de croire*, p. 202. Paris, 1951.

To do this there is one mistake we must beware of: that of presenting them with a sentimentalized God; it attracts nobody. The world is waiting to be shown that Christianity is a strong and living faith. We are not asked to provide scientific proof of God's existence, but to show the world he exists by the way we live our lives. Any religious life which is not based on bearing witness to God's existence sinks into ritualism, and fills people with rightful disgust.

The Content of Jesus' Testimony

In one way it is the main purpose of this book to explain this content, but all the same it is worth giving a brief résumé of it here, and at the same time indicating certain practical consequences of Jesus' teaching, by linking them directly with its main themes. But if we want to get to the heart of the Gospels, we should bear in mind what Jesus himself said, namely, that he was speaking directly to the Jews: "I was sent only to the lost sheep of the house of Israel" (Mat. 15. 24).[1] He was not sowing in unprepared soil, for the Jews already knew certain things which are worth repeating because they are very much forgotten in these modern times:

(1) God is the Creator, and everything comes from him, so everything owes him homage and veneration. To deny this, says St Paul, is "to deny his truth its full scope" and this brings "God's anger" (Rom. 1. 18), which gives us an idea of the gravity of the fault, and we should not be surprised to see disasters strike the nations who are guilty of it. He whom they deny abandons them to their own devices. "And now", exclaims Pius XII, "men are trying to base the structure of the world on foundations which we have no hesitation in pointing out as mainly responsible for the menace which threatens humanity: an economy without God, law without God, and politics without God. The enemy has worked, and is working, to keep Christ out of the universities, out of schools, out of the family, out of the administration of justice, out of legislation, and out of the assembly of nations in which war and peace are decided."[2]

[1] [Revised Standard Version.—Translator.]
[2] Loc. cit.

In this respect, modern Christians should beware of two particular errors: the first consists in forgetting that nations themselves owe worship to God; official and public worship because "he has given to each the cycles it was to pass through and the fixed limits of its habitation" (Acts 17. 26); and the second is to allow ourselves to be drawn into a certain mystique of silence, when we should all be proclaiming God wherever we can.

(2) The Creator is wholly good, and evil does not come from him; it is a blasphemy to say the contrary. Evil comes from the devil and from the sins of mankind, "since the devil's envy brought death into the world" (Wisdom 2. 24). The Creator governs the world with an unceasing fatherly providence. The whole Bible is an affirmation of this providence.

(3) Retribution will come in the future, and the just man should not be shocked or even surprised to find himself suffering in this world; he should look death in the face and await it with confident serenity. "The souls of the just are in God's hands, and no torment, in death itself, has power to reach them" (Wisdom 3. 1).

This last conception only came to the Jews at a late date (possibly one or two centuries before Jesus) and it was not yet widely accepted among them; that is why the Saviour liked to underline it frequently by giving them striking parables, such as that of the man who wanted to rebuild his barns to store his superabundant harvest and who was to die the very night after he made this plan (Luke 12. 16–21), or that of Lazarus and the rich man (Luke 16. 19–31).

This teaching must be carefully studied, for today people forget it; we do not know how to die any more or how to envisage our death calmly; we do not know, and sometimes we do not want to know, of any possessions other than those of this world; that there are such possessions is the point which popular unbelief finds it hardest to accept, and so we should give particular emphasis to this aspect of our witness.

But the specific revelation of Jesus is:

(1) That God *is* Love, and not simply that he loves, or is lovable, that he *is* forgiveness, not simply that he forgives, and that his love is essentially merciful. We say of Mary too that she is Mother of God (in the *Ave Maria*) and Mother of Mercy

(in the *Salve Regina*). Now, love hopes to find in the beloved dispositions corresponding to its own movement of giving. God gives to him who gives, gives himself to him who gives himself, forgives him who forgives others. This last point is brought home strongly in the Gospel: "Your heavenly Father will forgive you your transgressions, if you forgive your fellowmen theirs; if you do not forgive them, your heavenly Father will not forgive your transgressions either" (Mat. 6. 14).

(2) That he is God, Son of God, and that "it was from the Father I came out, when I entered the world, and now I am . . . going on my way to the Father" (John 16. 28). And so in him everything comes from God, everything goes back to God; that is why he has divine prerogatives. Giver of life and of eternal life, Saviour of men, with the power of remitting sins—he is all these things because of his inner life which is hidden to us, and which is different from ordinary human life, for it is the very life of God. From this comes the very close union which we have spoken of,[1] and which results immediately in: "Whoever has seen me, has seen the Father. . . . I am in the Father, and the Father is in me" (John 14. 9–10). It will also follow that if we belong to Christ we shall share his passionate devotion to the Father.

(3) That we are called to share fully in his destiny: "If anyone is to be my servant, he must follow my way; so shall my servant too be where I am" (John 12. 26). He cares so much about this that it is his last prayer before the beginning of the Passion: "This, Father, is my desire, that all those whom thou hast entrusted to me may be with me where I am, so as to see my glory, thy gift made to me, in that love which thou didst bestow upon me before the foundation of the world" (John 17. 24). This is quite natural, for his Father is to become our Father as well: "I am going up to him who is my Father and your Father, who is my God and your God" (John 20. 17); and he himself having, as the Epistle to the Hebrews tells us, had to "become altogether like his brethren" (2. 17), his brethren should reciprocate by becoming altogether like him.

These are the truths to which it is now our turn to bear witness, and to do so we have to make them part of our lives, so fulfilling God's explicit and compelling demand for a "spirit

[1] See Chapter 4, "God is Love".

of sonship". Free from sin, free from servile fear, we will not replace the ancient slavery by a spirit of anarchy but by a spirit of love, which will make us feel that: "Just it is indeed and fitting, right, and for our lasting good"[1] to give our hearts to the Father of Jesus who has adopted us as his children: "Those who follow the leading of God's Spirit are all God's sons: the spirit you have now received is not, as of old, a spirit of slavery, to govern you by fear; it is the spirit of adoption, which makes us cry out, Abba, Father. The Spirit himself thus assures our spirit, that we are children of God; and if we are his children, then we are his heirs too; heirs of God, sharing the inheritance of Christ; only we must share his sufferings, if we are to share his glory" (Rom. 8. 14–17).

[1] Preface of the Mass.

Chapter 11

THE BLESSED VIRGIN

Peace shall flow through her like a river, the wealth of the nations shall pour into her like a torrent in flood—Is. 66. 12.

St Louis-Marie Grignion de Montfort called the short work in which he summed up his teaching, *The Secret of Mary*. He thus expressed a very true fact: devotion to the Blessed Virgin is little known, even by those who believe that they practise it fervently. In addition, it must be admitted that this devotion is sometimes presented in a way that appeals more to men's sentiments than to their reason, which may explain the invincible caution one sometimes finds today about our Lady.

We shall try to present Mary in the way that the Church does. Here it is significant that the first time a Council speaks of her it is to proclaim her Mother of God.[1] In the second part of the *Ave Maria*, which has been official for nearly four centuries now, we also say "Holy Mary, Mother of God". We shall begin therefore by considering this aspect of our Lady, for it is this maternity which has always marked her essential place in the redemption. St Paul says: " . . . till the appointed time came. Then God sent out his Son on a mission to us. He took birth from a woman, took birth as a subject of the law, so as to ransom those who were subject to the law, and make us sons by adoption" (Gal. 4. 4–5). Unless we remain in this perspective of Scripture and of the Church, we run the risk of losing ourselves in secondary details.

Why did Christ choose to be born of a woman, and of a particular woman living in a little village in Palestine? There was no necessity to do as he did. He could have appeared like Melchisedech, "without father or mother or genealogy"

---

[1] In 431 when the Council of Ephesus was convened to condemn the heresiarch Nestorius, it proclaimed that Mary had the right not only to the title of "Mother of Christ" but also "Mother of God".

(Heb. 7. 3),[1] and his incarnation would have been no less real. But though such an incarnation would have been real, it would have been less sincere, because by having Mary for his mother, and making this known to all, Jesus shared completely the common experience of men. Like us, he passed nine months in the womb of a woman, he was a baby, a boy and an adolescent, before becoming a man. He was of our flesh and blood, and, as St John says: "Every spirit which acknowledges Jesus Christ as having come to us in human flesh has God for its author" (I John 4. 2), so every spirit which acknowledges Mary as the origin of that flesh is likewise of God. History confirms that each time a heresy refuses or diminishes the honour due to Mary it ceases to preserve the truth about the mystery of the incarnation.

As Bishop Fulton Sheen shows us: "When God willed to become Man, He had to decide on the time of His coming, the country in which He would be born, the city in which He would be raised, the people, the race, the political and economic systems which would surround Him, the language He would speak, the psychological attitudes with which He would come in contact as the Lord of History and the Saviour of the World.

"All these details would depend entirely on one factor: the woman who would be His Mother. To choose a mother is to choose a social position, a language, a city, an environment, a crisis, and a destiny."[2]

If we pause for a moment to contemplate this mystery, we discover that the body of Mary is one of those privileged places where the human and the divine meet. Other such places were, under the Old Dispensation, the site of Jacob's dream (Gen. 28. 10–22), then the Tent of the Covenant (Ex. 33. 7 ff.), and later, the Holy of Holies in the Temple. For Christianity, the same is true of every church, since the Cenacle in Jerusalem, and of every host. In the heart of Jesus lies "all the fullness of the divinity".[3] But the place that is the origin of all the others in the New Testament is the womb of Mary, into which the Holy Spirit descended, according to the words of the angel

---

[1] [Revised Standard Version.—*Translator*.]
[2] Fulton J. Sheen, *The World's First Love*, Chapter 1. Dublin, 1953, p. 7; London, 1963, p. 13.
[3] Litany of the Sacred Heart.

(Luke 1. 25), to bring about the conception of Jesus, and where Christ himself, in whose person God and man are united, was content to rest for nine months. In Mary the mystery takes flesh, and it has been said of her that she is "at the same time the most spiritual and the most fleshly of creatures": the most spiritual, because everything in her is obedient to reason and to the guidance of the Spirit, and the most fleshly, because everything in her can find adequate expression even in her body; nothing remains fruitless in her mind; all there is penetrates her whole being. In her, the descent of the Word into the flesh prepares the ascent of all flesh towards God. When God became man, it was not so much in order that the divine might reach down to the human, but so that humanity in its entirety, both soul and body therefore, might be raised up to God. The incarnation is completed by the Ascension in the person of Jesus, by the Assumption in the person of Mary and by the resurrection of the flesh in each one of us.

If Mary is a mother, it is primarily because she was called to be just that, and the call was imperative, for she was told very clearly what was to happen: "Mary, do not be afraid; thou hast found favour in the sight of God. And behold, thou shalt conceive in thy womb, and shalt bear a son, and shalt call him Jesus. He shall be great, and men will know him for the Son of the most High; the Lord God will give him the throne of his father David, and he shall reign over the house of Jacob eternally; his kingdom shall never have an end" (Luke 1. 30–2). One is struck by the analogy with the call of Peter after the first miraculous draught of fishes: "Do not be afraid; henceforth thou shalt be a fisher of men" (Luke 5. 10). Neither Mary nor Peter had chosen the path that they were to follow. Mary had simply intended to remain a virgin, before and after marriage, and Peter had only wanted to be one of Jesus' disciples; the role that was proposed to each of them was beyond all human expectations, but such are the ways of God.

Yet although Mary's call was imperative, it was dependent upon her consent, for God would never violate any human personality, let alone that of the mother of his Son. Mary became the mother of Christ because she gave this consent to the angel and entered fully into God's plan. Moreover she was a mother more completely than any other woman because, as

Jesus had no earthly father, it was she who provided all the human elements in her Son. God does nothing by halves, but accomplishes everything more perfectly than we poor humans. "Behold the handmaid of the Lord; let it be unto me according to thy word" (Luke 1. 38). These are the words with which Mary accepts her vocation of motherhood, and the more one meditates on them the more one is struck by their precision and their greatness. "Let it be" is the Latin *"fiat"* and the same word as that used by God—in Genesis—at the creation. Jesus uses the same word in the Our Father: "Thy will be done", and in his agony in the garden.[1] To say that one is the servant or handmaid—literally the slave—of someone is the biblical way of expressing complete submission. We ourselves do not always give this answer when God calls us, and some of the great figures of the Old Testament were not always capable of doing so either. When God spoke from the burning bush to Moses and gave him the mission of freeing his people from the tyranny of the Egyptians (a task he had previously tried in vain to accomplish by himself), he refused: "Lord, have patience with me; wilt thou not choose some fitting emissary?" (Ex. 4. 13), and God had to insist and almost to threaten, before he accepted. He remained all his life a man to whom obedience did not come easily, and he seldom obeyed God's orders without arguing. Jeremiah also tries to evade his mission: "Alas, alas, Lord God, I am but a child that has never learned to speak" (Jer. 1. 6), and here again God had to insist. Jeremiah never lost this reluctance, and sometimes the persecution that his ministry entailed made him lose courage. The attitude of Isaiah, on the other hand, was quite the reverse—he offered his services without being asked: "And now I heard the Lord say, Who shall be my messenger? Who is to go on this mission of ours? And I said, I am here at thy command; make me thy messenger" (Is. 6. 8).

Mary does not hesitate in giving her acceptance, and this does not surprise us: we expect her reactions to be quick and whole-hearted. But we are puzzled at not finding in her the enthusiasm of Isaiah. In fact, however, Mary belongs to another spiritual family, to that of Samuel who said: "Speak on, Lord, thy servant is listening" (I Kings [Sam.] 3. 10), and

[1] It is throughout the same verb in the Greek, though in different tenses.

of Abraham who, on receiving the order to sacrifice Isaac, said nothing, but at once began to carry out God's instructions, and of the apostles who did not answer by words—or none that are recorded in the Gospels—but simply left everything and followed Jesus, as he asked them. This is the response of love at its highest: the acceptance pure and simple of the will of the beloved. The spontaneity of Mary's reply will be to her eternal glory because it is the proof of her wonderful readiness to do God's will: "One second! She took only one second to decide such a thing."[1]

This readiness was not a matter of temperament, it was the result of years of prayer and silent contemplation; and even more, the result of the Immaculate Conception, which is the origin of all that is mysterious in Mary. Here is what Pius IX says of this mystery:

> God ineffable . . . from the very beginning and before all ages appointed for his only-begotten Son the Mother from whom he would take flesh and be born in the blessed fullness of time. He chose her and fixed her place in the order of his plan. He loved her above all his creatures with such a surpassing love that in her in a most special way he found all his greatest delights. Therefore, drawing on all the treasures of his divinity, he filled her, above all the angelic spirits and above all the saints, with the abundance of all heavenly graces and poured upon her a wonderful wealth of gifts. This he did that she might ever be without spot, absolutely free from the slavery of sin, all beautiful, all perfect, with such total innocence and holiness, that, until one reached God, no greater can be imagined, no thought but the thought of God himself can measure its greatness.[2]

If the phrases: "He loved her above all his creatures", "He filled her, above all the angelic spirits and above all the saints, with the abundance of all heavenly graces" came from any ordinary source, one would naturally suppose that the author had been carried away by his piety to an extravagant degree, but this is not the language of simple piety, it is the word of the Church in the most solemn kind of document. Mary is, there-

---

[1] Paul Claudel, *The Tidings Brought to Mary*, Act IV, stage variant for Scene II. [Not in Eng. tr. by Louise Morgan Sill, London, 1916.]
[2] Pius IX, Dogmatic Bull *Ineffabilis Deus*, 8 December 1854.

fore, officially presented to us as a supreme example of sanctity, a sanctity based on absolute purity, from which everything that could prevent her from loving God with her whole heart is eliminated.

The effect of this freedom is an unequalled ability to love, and the intensity of her love fills the Father's heart with joy. It is his delight to shower his beloved child with gifts and add new qualities to those she already possesses, so that her capacity for love is ever-increasing: "Fair in every part, my true love, no fault in all thy fashioning! Venture forth from Lebanon, and come to me, my bride, my queen that shall be" (Song of Songs 4. 7–8). Jesus said one day about Mary: "Shall we not say, Blessed are those who hear the word of God, and keep it?" (Luke 11. 28), and in that short phrase he sums up the way to holiness for every soul, but especially for his mother, beginning with the moment of his incarnation. The Gospel tells us that she "kept in her heart the memory of all this" (Luke 2. 51), and we know without being told that her consent to her vocation was without reserve, and continually renewed, so that all her life she continued to say "Yes".

Jesus had barely been conceived in her when she "rose up and went with all haste to a town of Juda" (Luke 1. 39). What is the significance of this sudden departure? According to the customs of the times a young fiancée such as Mary was very closely tied to her own family and that of her future husband. But Mary's mission was to give her son to the world, and as this was not yet possible to effect completely, she brought him to the only two beings who were able to welcome him: Elizabeth and John the Baptist, who was due to be born in three months' time. We must remember that Jesus comes to us as he came to Mary, so that we may take him to our brothers, not keep him to ourselves.

The scene of the Visitation can teach us many things, but there are two that we should like to remark on particularly. Firstly, when Mary entered Zachary's house she "gave Elizabeth greeting" (ibid. 40). She probably said: "*Shalom aleïchem*", Hebrew words which mean: "Peace be with you", and at this greeting two miracles took place: Elizabeth was "filled with the Holy Ghost", and John the Baptist leaped for joy in his mother's womb (ibid. 41), signifying that he too was filled with the Holy Ghost, according to the prophecy of the angel Gabriel to his father (Luke 1. 15). So with two words, two miracles of grace were accomplished. During all his public life, Jesus did not grant any spiritual miracles as striking as these, which would appear to show that there are certain graces that he will give to souls only when he is taken to them by Mary; which explains the effectiveness of those who rely on her in their apostolate.

When Mary returned to Nazareth she was faced with a very unhappy situation. St Matthew's Gospel tells us that Joseph, seeing that she was with child, "was for sending her away in secret" (1. 19). It was a terrible situation for him too: Mary's virtue was evident, but even so she was clearly expecting a child. Mary herself could not feel ashamed—there was nothing to be ashamed about—or sad—the knowledge that she carried within her the Son of God could only fill her with joy. At the same time, the misunderstanding that this mystery created between herself and the man whom she loved dearly caused her much sorrow, because she could not tell him of the visit of the angel and the descent of the Holy Spirit. She could only pray and wait for help from above. We, like Mary, are not masters of the supernatural; there are times when we can do nothing, because we are sure that any attempt on our part would do more harm than good. In these moments we can remember Mary's times of waiting: before the angel came to Joseph, the stay in Egypt, the hours at the foot of the Cross, and all Holy Saturday.

We now come to a very important step in the unfolding of Mary's vocation, and one to which she continues to give her consent. It is the prophecy of the old man Simeon in the Temple at Jerusalem. The occasion is a joyful one: for the mother it marks the end of the legal period of uncleanness which follows childbirth for Jewish women. It is also the ceremony of offering the child to God, and then "buying it back" with the sacrifice of a lamb and a turtle-dove or if, like Mary, one was too poor to buy a lamb, two young pigeons would do instead. For Mary, this day was especially joyful: coming to the Temple meant bringing the child to the house of his Father, presenting him for his Father's delight, just as in a human family the mother takes the baby in her arms and shows it to its father. The rite of offering is accomplished uneventfully, so much so that there is no description of it at all, and then, to their amazement, the old man Simeon appears and begins his song of praise to God:

> Ruler of all, now dost thou let thy servant go in peace, according to thy word;
> for mine own eyes have seen that saving power of thine which thou hast prepared in the sight of all nations.
> This is the light which shall give revelation to the Gentiles, this is the glory of thy people Israel (Luke 2. 29–32).

Then suddenly the tone changes. He says to Mary: "Behold, this child is destined to bring about the fall of many and the rise of many in Israel; to be a sign which men will refuse to acknowledge; and so the thoughts of many hearts shall be made manifest; as for thine own soul, it shall have a sword to pierce it" (ibid. 34–5).

All this is hard for Mary to understand: the fall before the raising up, the sign which men will refuse to acknowledge, and finally the sword that will pierce her soul! And what can that sword mean but the death of her beloved child? It seems an astonishing response on the part of God to the joyful offering she has just made! We can therefore suppose that from the time she heard Simeon's prophecy, she lived with a poisoned thorn in her heart and that every event in the life of Jesus, even those tiny incidents which mothers notice with so much love, was sufficient to revive that fear which, though dormant, was never removed. One immediately wonders why it was that Christ inflicted such suffering on his mother. The reason is not hard to see: it was in order that she might share as closely as possible the state of his own soul. He himself could evoke clearly, at any time, the end of his ministry, his tortures and his death on the cross. Mary could not do this, but after the prophecy of Simeon she would share something of his own sufferings in this respect. So although her suffering was great, so too was her privilege, because it enabled her to be more closely united to her Son and her God.

Following the rhythm of the Gospels where they speak of our Lady, we will leave on one side for the present the long years at Nazareth and the months of our Lord's ministry, during which Mary effaces herself. We will turn to that tragic night when the news she receives of her Son becomes more and more terrible; first his arrest, then his trial, his appearances before Herod and Pilate, his scourging and finally the sentence of death. Then she is told that he has come out, carrying his cross, and for Mary too the Hour has come. "Now to stir abroad, and traverse the city, searching every alley-way and street for him I love so tenderly!" (Song of Songs 3. 2). "And why are thy garments stained in red? Why dost thou go clad like the men who tread out the wine-press? None other has trodden the wine-press but I only; out of all the nations, no champion came to stand at my side" (Is. 63. 2–3). "My son, why hast thou treated us so?" (Luke 2. 48).

So Mary went to Calvary. But what role did she play there? At the foot of the cross Mary was the new Eve beside the new Adam, the Woman *par excellence*, just as Jesus is the Son of Man, that is to say the Man *par excellence*. She was called to a new dignity: to represent here the soul, the spouse of Christ, and that means sharing his lot to the full. The hand of the tormentors did not touch her directly. Jesus would not have allowed this, but her union with him was such that his agony became hers also. Because of her love for him, and the humiliations, the insults, the agony and the mental anguish that her child suffered, she suffered too. She alone was able to do this, and she alone is now able to penetrate to the secret depths of the heart of Christ, just as he alone was authorized to penetrate within her body, for they are totally reserved for each other: "My bride, my true love, a close garden; hedged all about, a spring shut in and sealed" (Song of Songs 4. 12).

At the foot of the cross Mary represented the complete triumph of Christ. He said: "Sentence is now being passed on this world; now is the time when the prince of this world is to be cast out" (John 12. 31). And yet two thousand years have passed since then and Satan, alas, does not yet appear to have been cast out. But there is one place from which he has been completely banished, and that is the soul of Mary. If we look again at the quotation from Pius IX in which he says that God loved Mary "above all his creatures" and "filled her, above all the angelic spirits and above all the saints, with the abundance of all heavenly graces", we shall see the truth of Dom Marmion's penetrating reflection that "Christ above

all died for His Mother, to pay for her privileges".[1] Christ
found in Mary such a complete readiness for his redemption,
his work in her was so effective and gives him such a complete
and profound satisfaction, that if the impossible had happened
and no other soul had benefited from his sufferings, there
would still have been an element of perfection in his achievement.

Though Mary, St John and the holy women were at the
foot of the cross, there were some curious absences, for Peter,
the future head of the Church, was not there, nor were any of
the other apostles except John. What is the significance of this?
Those whom one would have expected to find with John and
Mary, and who were not there, all died as martyrs. But Mary
did not and neither did John. There are different vocations in
the Church, and if some die as martyrs, others live the sufferings
of Jesus in their hearts because of their union with him. These
latter do not need an exterior martyrdom; their martyrdom is
interior, and sometimes it is so intense that it is made visible in
their flesh, as in the cases of St Francis of Assisi or St Catherine
of Siena, and many others. Mary and John at the foot of the
cross were the first of a long line of contemplatives that will
continue throughout the lifetime of the Church. After years of
re-living what they suffered in their hearts beneath the cross
of Christ, any external martyrdom would have been
superfluous.

At the foot of the cross, it was Mary who presented Jesus to
the Father just as earlier she had presented him in the temple
at Jerusalem. She introduced him into his heavenly home just
as the first Eve introduced the first Adam into the Fall. It is
not that he was unable to do this by himself, but at that
decisive moment he wanted human collaboration, so that
through Mary humanity could say "Yes", so that she who
welcomed the Son of God into the world might send him back
as willingly when "the time had come for his passage from this
world to the Father" (John 13. 1). He accepted every human
suffering, but he is so truly a son that he wanted Mary to retain
for ever certain rights to him and thus be in a position to offer
up his Body "immolated to the Eternal Father by [her]

[1] Dom Columba Marmion, *Christ the Life of the Soul*. London, 1922, p. 375.

consent".[1] In this way she co-operated in this act of his priest-hood. She carried out for the first time the expression of love that the Church will prolong for ever in the Mass.

Through baptism we become the sons of God and so objects of love to his mother. She desires our salvation more ardently and more powerfully than anyone else. She is able to follow the course of each one of us, to know more than the priest about each Mass that he celebrates, about each judgement that he gives in the sacrament of penance, and each one of us, like Jesus himself, can know the inexpressible joy of being watched over by one whose maternal love sees all things in the light of God.

We should now be able to understand what devotion to the Blessed Virgin should mean. It should not be confined to a contemplation of the beauty of her Immaculate Conception, her virginity or her Assumption; all that is good and indispensable, but it is not sufficient. Still less can we be content with reciting ready-made prayers, even when we do this with pious and excellent regularity. True devotion consists in cultivating in our hearts the feelings of a child for its mother and gradually following her example in all our actions. This is no simple task; it is an immense one, and lasts a lifetime. When we have understood properly that we are children of our Heavenly Father, is it so difficult to accept as our Mother the one whom the only-begotten Son chose and formed to be his own Mother and whom he left to us on Calvary?

[1] Louis-Marie Grignion de Montfort, *A Treatise on the True Devotion to the Blessed Virgin*, Part I, Chapter 1, page 3. London, 1940. This is an idea that is taken up very frequently in French spirituality.

Chapter 12

VOCATION

In him it was our lot to be called, singled out beforehand to suit his purpose—Eph. i. 11.

The question of vocation can be treated in two different ways: either we make it our first concern to help people to discover the particular place that God has prepared for them within the Mystical Body of Christ; or, less practically, we emphasize the fact that the Father calls every Christian to him, and that a life of love cannot but be an answer to this call. It goes without saying that these different points of view are complementary.

The Practical Point of View

St Paul, writing to the Christians in Rome, says to them: "Each of us has one body, with many different parts, and not all these parts have the same function; just so we, though many in number, form one body in Christ, and each acts as the counterpart of another. The spiritual gifts we have differ, according to the special grace which has been assigned to each. If a man is a prophet, let him prophesy as far as the measure of his faith will let him. The administrator must be content with his administration, the teacher, with his work of teaching, the preacher, with his preaching. Each must perform his own task well; giving alms with generosity, exercising authority with anxious care, or doing works of mercy smilingly" (Rom. 12. 4–8); and he develops the same ideas, in more detail, in Chapter 12 of his First Epistle to the Corinthians. From these texts and others we could quote here, we can draw certain very clear conclusions:

(1) There are different forms of vocation, and not everyone is called to the highest ones. If we say, therefore, that we want

to do "whatever is best ", "whatever is hardest", we are working on a false and dangerous premise. Of course, we should "earnestly desire the higher gifts" (I Cor. 12. 31);[1] and of course we should wish to imitate Christ "in putting up with all injustice, all abuse, all poverty in reality no less than in the spirit,"[2] but what we have to do is to fulfil our own vocation, and not the vocation of some saint in a stained-glass window.

(2) "To each is given the manifestation of the Spirit for the common good" (I Cor. 12. 7).[1] So if we want to discover our vocation, we must look beyond our own selves. Every one of us has access to some field of action. For the Young Christian Worker and member of the lay apostolate this field will be his place of work; for the parish priest, his parish, and for the cabinet minister, the entire nation. In our field of action we are responsible for the people with whom we come into contact. Cain's answer to God was: "Is it for me to keep watch over my brother?" (Gen. 4. 9), but St Paul tells us we should feel responsible for those around us. Speaking of the eating of meat used in idolatrous worship, he exclaims: "Why then, if a mouthful of food is an occasion of sin to my brother, I will abstain from flesh meat perpetually, rather than be the occasion of my brother's sin" (I Cor. 8. 13); and Jesus proclaimed: "If anyone hurts the conscience of one of these little ones, that believe in me, he had better have been drowned in the depths of the sea, with a millstone hung about his neck" (Mat. 18. 6), and in a positive sense: "Blessed are the peace-makers; they shall be counted the children of God" (Mat. 5. 9).

My responsibility is to give my full measure, to go beyond what is strictly my duty: "When I preach the gospel," says St Paul, "I take no credit for that; I act under constraint; it would go hard with me indeed if I did not preach the gospel. I can claim a reward for what I do of my own choice; but when I act under constraint, I am only executing a commission. What title have I, then, to a reward? Why, that when I preach the gospel I should preach the gospel free of charge, not making full use of the rights which gospel preaching gives me" (I Cor. 9. 16–18).

---

[1] [Revised Standard Version.—*Translator.*]
[2] *Spiritual Exercises of St Ignatius Loyola*, in a New Translation by Thomas Corbishley, S.J. Second Week, "The King", p. 44, No. 98. London, 1963.

I must bear fruit: "My Father's name has been glorified, if you yield abundant fruit, and prove yourselves to be my disciples" (John 15. 8); "I am the true vine, and it is my Father who tends it. The branch that yields no fruit in me, he cuts away; the branch that does yield fruit, he trims clean, so that it may yield more fruit" (ibid. 1–2), and my duty remains even if my fruit is not accepted.

A lamp burns in the darkness, undeterred by the fact that beyond its circle of light lies further darkness. So it is sometimes that in our spiritual life we come across situations that we find disconcerting, such as that of the total failure of some priest who seemed to have everything that makes for success, or some social work which only manages to exist in the face of incessantly recurring difficulties, when it would seem to be more natural for it to function smoothly. God is glorified by persevering faith in the midst of trials and adversity. But we should not forget the parable of the barren fig-tree (Luke 13. 6–9): the manure that the vine-dresser wants to put round its roots will not save it from being cut down the next year if it does not produce any figs. And so for us, our Christian upbringing and the graces we receive are not a passport to glory, even less are they a screen we can hide behind to escape any kind of effort. On the contrary, they create responsibilities and they represent a duty.

A person who has thoroughly acquired this mentality of giving himself to God and serving his fellow men finds his vocation by asking himself what his aptitudes are, or, in more Christian language, what gifts he has received from God, natural as well as supernatural. Fr Lallemant has said that we must "be aware of the gift the Holy Spirit has given us and act in accordance with it". To sum up, finding our vocation always means learning to be ourselves as we are before God.

It is in fact a matter of common sense to realize that if God calls one of his subjects to carry out a particular task, he will most certainly give him the ability to do it, not without effort, but without its becoming an intolerable burden. Therefore, there can be no question of a religious vocation, for example, in a young man or woman whose health would not stand the discipline of the order which he or she considers entering, or who is not likely to be able to keep up an assiduous practice of piety.

It is also clear—and Canon Law itself mentions this with regard to certain very serious cases (Can. 542, 2°)—that no one should ever choose a way of life, however exalted it might be, if it goes against the pressing demands of charity.

Having said this much in order to clarify the issue, it should prove not without interest to run rapidly over the range of possible ways of serving. As we do so, we shall remember that we are always being called to imitate God's love, or, if you like, to become the instrument of his love. This love has two principal aspects: on the one hand it extends to everybody; Jesus was practising this kind of universal love when he spoke to the crowd, from the boat or on the mountain-side. On the other hand it surrounds certain people with special attention; in this manner he went to dine with Martha, Mary and Lazarus, he noticed the publican Zacchaeus up in his sycamore tree, he paid greater attention to his apostles, and one of them was the object of a preference sufficiently evident to enable him to refer to himself as "the disciple whom Jesus loved". The vocation of marriage is an imitation of this special love of Jesus. The sacrament directs the love of the man and the woman towards all the members of their family, and they should not rush about outside on the pretext of doing apostolic work, if it means that they are neglecting their home.

The celibate vocations reproduce the more general aspect of Jesus' love, and we can discern three categories of celibacy:

(1) The priest. The consideration which inspires the Church in asking its priests to renounce marriage is above all the wish to free their love so that it may be entirely at the service of God and the community. The priest belongs to everyone, and cannot allow his love to be monopolized by individual people, for this would limit his inner freedom. This is, therefore, a celibacy of dedication to others. We should remember that it is consecrated, on the day of ordination to the subdiaconate, by the most solemn vow of chastity known to the Church.

(2) The nun, the brother (male religious who is not a priest). Without of course excluding the considerations of dedication, this form of celibacy is inspired by the idea of making such a complete offering of the self to God that the body is marked by it too. In this way, as a married woman is an adulteress if she yields her body to anyone but her husband, so a nun is

unfaithful if she permits anyone at all to possess her body, which is offered up "as a living sacrifice, consecrated to God and worthy of his acceptance" (Rom. 12. 1).

In their various different ways religious of both sexes are, like the priest, called to love all those in their care with an equal love; the more contemplative their life, the more clearly marked is the universality of their vocation. Saint Thérèse of Lisieux, conscious of a vocation to pray for the whole world, realizes the Carmelite ideal, and the prayer of every consecrated soul is always aimed at reaching a world-wide dimension, like the holy sacrifice of the Mass, in which the priest presents the host "for all faithful Christians, both living and dead".

There is such a variety of different forms of religious life that it is quite impossible for us to go through them all. But we should like to make one or two remarks about consecrated men and women.

(a) The way they receive their call varies; for some it will be a desire for greater piety—the joy of holding a consecrated host in one's hands, the happiness of being entirely given up to one's Lord and Creator; for others the accent will be more on the desire for the apostolate—to do good, to save souls, to serve a noble cause. But he who is called knows and feels that he will be departing from the ways of love if he does not consecrate his entire self to the task. He should be helped to find his way without being either rushed or held back, and above all in a way that helps him to act of his own free will. The use of compulsion—whether open or hidden—in making people enter convents or monasteries is still a source of bitter tears for the Church.

(b) God puts a call to paternity in the heart of every man, just as he puts a call to maternity in the heart of every woman. These calls should not be suppressed by the priest[1] or the nun, but they should be spiritualized, because there is a real paternity which consists in imparting spiritual life to someone else by one's own devoted service and prayer. If this truth is not sufficiently taken into account, we shall end up by producing a shrivelling of the affections or else by giving rise to repressions

---

[1] On this subject see Pius XII's Exhortation to the Priests of the World, *Menti Nostrae*, 25 September 1950. [Engl. tr. *Catholic Documents*, IV, p. 4.]

E

and scruples; in short, the balance of the personality would be gravely endangered.

(3) *Celibacy in the world.* While we are on the subject, we might first of all ask ourselves whether this is really a vocation. In the past the answer used to be "No", at least in practice, and many a community of young women, founded on an idea not so very different in origin from that represented today by the Foyers de Charité[1] and similar institutions, eventually became a religious congregation—sometimes even enclosed— as did the Ursulines of St Angela Merici. At the present time we should certainly say that it is a true vocation, for wherever we look we see the need of Society for people devoted to its service in conditions which would hardly be compatible with marriage on the one hand, or on the other with ordinary religious life, which implies a special costume, special rules, life under a superior, etc. For examples of this devoted service we can mention the numerous tasks undertaken to help the clergy in their parishes; prison visiting, and the reclamation of prostitutes. It would seem that the Church herself, in organizing by the constitution *Provida Mater Ecclesia* a form of religious life whose members have no outward distinguishing signs and can so pass unnoticed among other people, has recognized this necessity and decided to provide for it. From a practical point of view, when one is unmarried and likely to remain so, one should organize one's life so as to serve God and one's fellow men as fully as possible, taking into account what we were saying at the beginning of this chapter. In this way we can save ourselves a lot of wasted time and useless waiting, and probably a lot of disappointment as well.

Sometimes people feel they are called in two ways: on the one hand their own innermost longings incline them to a life consecrated to God; on the other, there are circumstances which prevent them from embracing such a life; or else they receive a vocation which nothing permitted them to foresee. The Virgin Mary had a call to virginity in her heart, and she received from God a call to divine maternity. When we find ourselves in what appear to be similarly conflicting circumstances, we should await the turn of events. Childless couples experience a kind of double call since their desire for parenthood remains unsatis-

---

[1] See the Preface to this book.

fied; they must either come round to making their own family with adopted children, or else they should devote themselves together to some form of useful work, so that they are able to express their desire to live for others.

The Mystical Point of View

Every free being is of necessity called by God, because he was created out of love and love is God's call to us, it is a call to the fulfilment of life in joy and peace. The mystery is not in the call, but in the way we receive it, because the free will of man can refuse to hear the divine voice. There has to be a ceaseless effort to take hold of the gift of God, so that it does not remain like a grain of seed on a rock. The Father does not take back his gifts, but we can become untrue to them; the Christian should be a living "Yes" to God, just as the Word is a "faithful and unerring witness" (Apoc. 3. 14).

Human beings do not come from the hands of God mass-produced like cars off an assembly line; the call is personal and individual: "I know you by name," says Yahweh to Moses (Ex. 33. 12, 17),[1] and Jesus tells us that the good shepherd "calls by name the sheep which belong to him" (John 10. 3). "I am the good shepherd; my sheep are known to me and know me; just as I am known to my Father and know him. And for these sheep I am laying down my life" (ibid. 14–15). God asks us to return love for love, giving for giving, life for life, and his affection is immense for those who have persevered to the end and offered up everything to him who is Everything.

Vocation is not an outward form of life but an inner one; it is God who calls us and continues to lead us. This is true of all Christian life. In this context, sin consists in wishing to do God's work in one's own way instead of in God's way, and for one's own reasons instead of for God's reasons. By doing this, things which are supernatural are reduced to being merely natural, and human lives from being spiritual are made material, and love slowly rots and dies away. This is one of the forms of sin against the Holy Spirit, perhaps the most dangerous form. "You are the salt of the earth; if salt loses its taste, what is there left to give taste to it? There is no more to be done

---

[1] [Revised Standard Version.—*Translator.*]

with it, but throw it out of doors for men to tread it under foot" (Mat. 5. 13).

We should never forget that the Virgin Mary was incapable by ordinary human means of accomplishing the tasks which God gave her. This is also true for ourselves, even when our task is apparently a human one. We must not allow ourselves to be profaned and desecrated; we must put love into everything we do, and bring into the world the desire to make an offering of our lives.

Each choice made by God is eternal, but his call to us is its expression in time. It is Christ that God is calling in us, and as his love for him can never change, so his call to us can never cease. This is the unique and universal vocation shared by all humanity and all creation: "Blessed be that God, that Father of our Lord Jesus Christ, who has blessed us, in Christ, with every spiritual blessing, higher than heaven itself. He has chosen us out, in Christ, before the foundation of the world, to be saints, to be blameless in his sight, for love of him; marking us out beforehand (so his will decreed) to be his adopted children through Jesus Christ" (Eph. 1. 3–5).

Chapter 13

THE LAWS OF HUMAN LOVE

Now to stir abroad, and traverse the city, searching every alley-way and street for him I love so tenderly—Song of Songs 3. 2.

When we speak of human love, we mean in this context all the different forms of love known to the human heart: the love between husband and wife, parent and child, brother and sister, and the love of a Christian for his God. These different forms of love follow certain essential laws, which are the same for all of them. We will indicate here the three most important of these laws.

The Law of Abnegation or Ecstasy

The rather unexpected coupling of the two terms is suggested by St Francis de Sales: self-abnegation consists in denying oneself, forgetting oneself for others or for God; being in ecstasy is being outside oneself in a state where one forgets oneself; to love is to go out towards another being, and therefore loving also consists in coming out of oneself, denying oneself, being in ecstasy. Conversely, remaining within oneself means belonging to oneself and refusing to love. One belongs to oneself when one is at the same time the starting point and the finishing point of one's action: "I am going to buy myself a watch". It is I who am buying the watch (starting point), I am buying it for myself (finishing point). To come out of oneself one must eliminate the two pronouns "I" and "myself". It is quite simple to eliminate the second (myself), it is sufficient to perform one's action for somebody else: the father earns a living for his wife and children, the housewife works for her family, the soldier fights for his country, the Christian lives for his God.

It is more difficult to eliminate the "I"—there must be one

in the sentence! St Paul found the solution to this problem: "Those who follow the leading of God's Spirit are all God's sons" (Rom. 8. 14). For St Paul, the Christian is he who acts according to the promptings of the Spirit, he for whom the Spirit has become the starting point of his actions. Those who habitually live according to the promptings of the Holy Spirit can say with St Paul: "And yet I am alive; or rather, not I; it is Christ that lives in me" (Gal. 2. 20). They have adopted the advice of the *Imitation of Christ* (3, 27, 1): "My son, forsake thyself and thou shalt find me."

This is by no means easy and is not achieved without heart-searching and suffering and it is here that one must speak of "the uncompromising school of love" and remember that "not death itself is so strong as love" (Song of Songs 8. 6), and that the finding of this love entails an asceticism which includes, especially in youth, effort and mortification.

Whenever we limit our abnegation we limit our love. Jesus calls us to perfection and shows us the way when he says: "He [the Father] has not left me all alone, since what I do is always what pleases him" (John 8. 29); and: "It is the will of him who sent me, not my own will, that I have come down from heaven to do" (John 6. 38). The Christian is he who, like Jesus, is always doing the will of someone else, of the Father; his prayer is: "Thy will be done", and he takes it seriously; that is what it means—to lose oneself in order to give oneself—to be crucified with Christ.

We cannot preach a religion of love without preaching this abnegation and it cannot be taken lightly, for there are moments in our lives when the present and the future seem black and obscure, we do not know what decisions to make and we feel like echoing the words of Job:

Why is light given to a man whose way is hid,
whom God has hedged in? . . .
For the thing that I fear comes upon me,
and what I dread befalls me.
I am not at ease, nor am I quiet;
I have no rest; but trouble comes (Job 3. 13, 25–6).[1]

In such moments we are no longer our own masters; the time has come to trust in our Father with all our hearts, for he knows

[1] [Revised Standard Version.—*Translator.*]

the direction in which he is leading us. Sometimes our trust will need to be heroic, so that instead of despairing we may have the courage to send up out of the depths of our souls one of those prayers into which our whole being is poured like a challenge to the providence of God. We must not forget that we are still the spiritual descendants of Abraham who was capable of "hoping against hope" (Rom. 4. 18), and the brothers of Jesus who "accepted an obedience which brought him to death, death on a cross" (Phil. 2. 8).

We can, and we should, love ourselves in God[1] but we should not put our love for ourselves on the same level as our love for God because this latter should occupy the whole of our being: "Thou shalt love the Lord thy God with the love of thy whole heart, and thy whole soul, and thy whole strength" (Deut. 6. 5).

Abnegation is not an act that is accomplished once and for all; it is a state of the soul which should become more and more complete and affect all our actions. Love does not live in an armchair with its feet on the mantelpiece; a lazy monotony kills love and we must always be on guard against temptations in this direction. We must get the better of our natural inclination to settle down and make ourselves comfortable in life. This can only be achieved by means of continually renewed efforts. It is these efforts which produce the chastity of love: the seeking of another's joy and not one's own pleasure. Abnegation, properly practised and properly guided, does not mutilate the personality, it develops it. This is what André Gide, a somewhat irregular authority, has to say about abnegation:

> Abnegation is that ultimate word in which affirmation is perfected; everything you give up in yourself comes to life.
>
> Any attempt at self-affirmation is self-negation; any self-renunciation is self-affirmation.
>
> Perfect possession is proved only by donation; anything you cannot give has you in its possession.
>
> Without sacrifice, no resurrection.
>
> Nothing can flourish happily otherwise than through offering; anything you may try to protect in yourself, withers.

[1] *Summa Theologica*, II ª IIᵃᵉ, 25, 4; and 26, 4.

What is the sign that tells you the fruit is ripe?
The fact that it falls from the branch!
Everything ripens through giving and reaches perfection
through offering. . . .
I know that "unless the fruit die, it alone remains". O Lord,
grant that I may not wait for death in order to die!
It is when it renounces itself that virtue becomes perfect.
The extreme juiciness of the fruit has only one end—
germination.
True eloquence abandons eloquence.
A man is never more affirmative of himself than when he
forgets himself.
If one thinks of oneself, one hinders oneself.
Never do I admire beauty so much as when it no longer
knows it is beautiful.[1]

The Law of Incarnation or of Expression

On earth there is not, and there cannot be, such a thing as
purely spiritual love. Love is exercised by the whole of our
beings so that starting in our souls it descends into our bodies
and finds expression in our acts. The realization of this fact
makes us see how much Christianity is in accordance with the
desires of our nature: it is not only a religion of God, but the
religion of God incarnate, of the Word made flesh.

Plato's theme of the opposition between body and soul was
always completely foreign to biblical thought,[2] both body and
soul together are parts making up a single being, and they
generally move in the same direction. When St Paul opposes
the spirit and the flesh, he is talking about the "spiritual"
man, reborn in Christ and quickened by the Holy Spirit, on
the one hand, an unredeemed man, on the other hand. St John
shows us very strikingly that Jesus does not despise the realities
of the body: his first miracle is accomplished during a marriage
feast, to provide some one hundred and fifty gallons of wine!
When the Son of God came down from heaven it was not to
remain on earth but to bring to heaven with him all the
members of his Mystical Body. With the help of the Holy
Spirit, we are following in his steps towards the synthesis, the
marriage of God with humanity in a world at last transformed.

[1] André Gide, *Nouvelles Nourritures*, pp. 35–6. Paris, 1935 (34th edition).
[2] Cf. Claude Tresmontant, *Essai sur la pensée hébraïque*, Chapter II

As an example of the incarnation of love, we will consider a mother who gives a kiss to her little child. This kiss has several different effects:

It makes the child realize that his mother loves him; he is too small to understand this from the things she does for him but he can feel and enjoy his mother's kiss.

It makes the child, too, want to give a token of love, to return caress for caress.

It increases the mother's love.

The kiss is thus an outward and efficacious sign and the true sacrament of maternal love. Paternal love also has its sacraments: the giving of bread and the other necessities of life.[1] Jesus made flesh is the great sacrament, the great tangible sign of the Father's love.

The Church offers us seven sacraments that are seven signs of her love for us. Like the mother's kiss, they are efficacious in themselves, but an unresponsive attitude of the soul can prevent their effectiveness, just as the child can rebuff his mother's caress. The final result, therefore, depends both on the Church, which is responsible for giving the sacrament, and on ourselves, who are responsible for the way in which we receive it.

Each sacrament shows a particular aspect of God's love for us. Baptism, "the cleansing power which gives us new birth, and restores our nature through the Holy Spirit" (Titus 3. 5), represents the burial of the Christian with Christ in order to share in his resurrection into a new kind of existence (Rom. 6. 3–4). The rites performed in baptism are highly expressive: the entry into the church signifies our incorporation into the Mystical Body, the pouring of water on the head is a simplified form of immersion, the giving of a white robe symbolizes the purity of the soul, the lighted candle reminds us that we are to live in Christ who is light, the sacred oils are reminders and givers of strength. The place of the body in Christianity can be seen very clearly in the ceremony of consignation, that take place in the baptism of adults:

---

[1] Think, for example, of the scene in Claudel's *The Tidings brought to Mary* in which the father, although he is in a hurry to leave, agrees to stay to distribute the bread to his family for the last time before his departure. Act I, Scene III. London, 1916, pp. 55-8.

I set this sign on your forehead that you may take up the cross of the Lord.

I set this sign on your ears that you may hear God's commandments.

I set this sign on your eyes that you may see God's glory.

I set this sign on your nostrils that you may smell the sweet odour of Christ.

I set this sign on your mouth that you may speak the words of life.

I set this sign on your breast that you may believe in God.

I set this sign on your shoulders that you may take up the yoke of his service.

I set this sign all over you in the name of the Father, and of the Son, and of the Holy Ghost, that you may have everlasting life and live for ever and ever.   Amen.

Confirmation, which is the complement of baptism, is given by an anointing with chrism to remind us of the oil with which competitors in the arena were rubbed down, and in confirmation it signifies the strength necessary for one who will henceforth fight for the kingdom of God.

The same symbol is used in extreme unction where different parts of the body are marked by the oil to show that the strength of grace will make up for the weaknesses of the body and wipe out the sins committed.

The Eucharist, which is the food of the soul, is administered in the form of bread, which is the food of the body.

For the sacrament of penance to be valid, the sinner must give the priest some outward sign of his repentance, and the priest must pronounce the words of absolution.

In ordination, the key sacrament in the life of the Church, the transmission of the living force, the grace of the order, is made by the laying on of hands, which was a traditional gesture among the Jews.

We have left the sacrament of marriage until last, because it deserves special attention. It is the marriage contract itself that is raised by Jesus to the dignity of a sacrament (Can. 1012) so that the natural laws of conjugal love are strengthened but not modified, and the same acts, therefore, increase both human love and love for God. The bodily union of husband and wife is given the holiness of a sacrament; the joy that comes from the intimacy of their hearts is expressed and increased by the union of their bodies. By contrast, the physical union of two beings who have no real love for each other is shown up as being a terrible and empty travesty of love.

The Law of Extension

The trees in the forest produce new branches every year, and when they do so no longer, they are dead. Thus love can only live when it grows and extends outwards. It does this in two different directions: on the one hand, it draws us closer to the one we love with an ever-increasing intensity and strength, though sometimes with an added tranquillity, but we shall return to this subject in another chapter.[1] Secondly, it tends to draw along the one it loves with it towards a third person. For instance, in a family the father and the mother draw each other along towards the children, or, to give another example, the love that God gives to each man draws him out towards his brothers, and again, Christians draw each other towards the Father. If we refuse to let ourselves be carried on these currents that are set up by love, the love itself degenerates into a two-sided egoism that closes up the heart. In any circumstances closed circles are always fatal to charity. Because of this danger, a delicate balance must be maintained between the essential intimacy of the family circle and its hospitality to others. This balance cannot be achieved once and for all, it has to be continually readjusted. At certain times we entertain friends in our homes and at others it is the privacy of the family circle that needs to be re-established.

[1] See Chapter 18: "The Law of Spiritual Practices: Prayer".

Chapter 14

DIVINE LIFE

Yes, life dawned; and it is as eyewitnesses that we give you news of that life, that eternal life, which ever abode with the Father and has dawned, now, on us—1 John 1. 2.

One of the fundamental points of the message of Jesus is that his Father is also our Father (John 20. 17), he who gives us life. To be baptized means to receive this life, to be "born anew", to be "born of water and the Spirit" (John 3. 3, 5). "When a man is in Christ Jesus, there has been a new creation" (Gal. 6. 15); he has come "to share the divine nature" (II Peter 1. 4). Therefore, our religion is not some ideal that we create for ourselves, it is a gift from God: "If thou knewest what it is God gives" (John 4. 10), and like all life it is indivisible, either entirely accepted or entirely refused.

The distinction is important, for choosing one's own ideal means realizing one's own ambition and doing what one pleases, rather than doing what pleases God. It means wanting to be in exclusive charge of one's soul and in complete command over its development, rather than looking for fulfilment by living in God's love, in obedience to all his wishes. When we think of the Jews who crucified the Messiah, do we imagine they were inferior people, lacking in virtue? In fact the contrary is true. They were the true descendants of those who had carried devotion to duty to the point of letting themselves be tortured and massacred in great numbers to stop the Roman standards from getting into the Temple. But they had their ideal: the Law. Jesus came to teach us that we are sons of God who is Love. That did not fit in with their ideal, so he had to die. Judas himself was certainly not an evil man to begin with, or he would never have been chosen as an apostle; and if he changed later, so much so that he became a thief and betrayed his Master with the fatal kiss, it is very likely because the teaching of Jesus did not fit in with his own personal ideals.

The true purpose of the descent of the Son of God on earth is to give us divine life: "I have come so that they may have life, and have it more abundantly" (John 10. 10). And so there is only one authentic Christian spirituality, the one which follows Christ the giver of life, the one which accepts this life, to give it in turn to others. That is the thought that is going to dictate everything we do. Here we should like to mention one or two points of special importance.

Christian Strength, and Faith in Divine Life

There is at the present time much talk about "Divine Life". Young and old members of Catholic Action groups are fired with enthusiasm by the idea; the general public hears about it from the pulpit, and if preaching were enough we could almost believe that in this field victory has already been won and that all Christians think alike on this subject. Nothing could be farther from the truth. In fact, many of those who talk about it do not really believe in it, and sometimes do not quite understand what it is all about. Many a man who would like to be, or imagines or believes himself to be, in a state of grace has difficulty in acting in accordance with grace; he behaves as if it did not exist. If he has to overcome some difficulty, it never occurs to him to make use of spiritual forces, and he refers to very different realities in order to deal with and to resolve the problems of his life.

The result is quite clear: certain questions become insoluble, because God has arranged things in such a way that certain obstacles can only be overcome with his help. In actual fact our common sense is enough to tell us that where the body is concerned we should take physical action; if it is a question of our thinking, then we should use our intellectual processes, and when we are confronted with evil we should pray for grace. For a business man to try to stay scrupulously honest all through his life, for a healthy young man to try to keep from impurity, for a married couple to try to keep the laws of conjugal chastity in certain difficult conditions, in fact to try to solve all our social problems without the help of God, is to take a heavy risk. Mental hygiene may save a man from psychiatric trouble, but it is not a remedy for sin.

It must be admitted that there are moments in life when temptation is so strong and so subtly persuasive that any resistance seems impossible, we feel like a match in a whirlpool, and we are incapable of seeing where our duty lies or where wrong begins. In moments like these, if we want to stay faithful to Christ in spite of everything that may happen to us, we have to reckon with both human life and divine life, and call upon the powers of grace as well as those of nature.

We have already said that divine life is the gift we receive at our baptism. Its main characteristic is a certain presence of the Holy Spirit within our souls. It is as impossible to define this presence as it is to define any other contact between man and God. But it is definitely an active presence, since St Paul says: "Those who follow the leading of God's Spirit are all God's sons" (Rom. 8. 14; cf. Gal. 5. 18), and again: "The Spirit himself intercedes for us, with groans beyond all utterance" (Rom. 8. 26); and it is also an indispensable presence for even the most elementary Christian activity: "It is only through the Holy Spirit that anyone can say, Jesus is the Lord" (I Cor. 12. 3).

The Spirit brings with him a whole supernatural organism: sanctifying grace which makes us children of God and gives us a likeness to the divine nature, a likeness which is concealed here on earth but which will be revealed in heaven (I John 3. 2), the theological virtues of faith, hope and charity which enrich our faculties by enabling them to achieve direct contact with God, without which no Christian life is possible, and lastly, certain special aptitudes which are known as "gifts" and help us to act more easily in the way God wishes. As well as all these, he gives us the help we need to face special difficulties.

The type of man that Christ came to form on earth is one who lives in constant awareness of the Holy Spirit who lives in him as in his temple (I Cor. 6. 19). The Holy Spirit is so present in him that we might almost say that he becomes a new kind of being, composed of body, soul and Holy Spirit. This is certainly what St Paul was thinking of when he referred to "the spiritual man", and this is surely why he began his letters with the salutation: "Grace and peace be yours from God, who is our Father, and from the Lord Jesus Christ", without mentioning the Holy Spirit, precisely because grace and peace are sent to those in whom he resides. For the same reason, no doubt, St John wrote: "What is it, this fellowship of ours? Fellowship with the Father, and with his Son Jesus Christ" (I John 1. 3).

So therefore, if we are unaware of the Holy Spirit present and active within us, and if we do not bring into play the supernatural powers which he brings us, then we are behaving as incomplete beings, and we will always be weighed down and discouraged by the problems we meet from day to day. With this in mind we may read about the journeys of St Paul as they are described to us in the Acts of the Apostles. It is impossible not to be struck by the fact that in spite of his worries and his heavy responsibilities, in spite of the innumerable difficulties he has to face and the persecutions he has to endure, he never wavers, not even in the most critical circumstances. He does not even ask for light, but he always receives it, and strength as well, because the Holy Spirit is his close companion. Shortly before he died, he wrote to Timothy: "The spirit he has bestowed on us is not one that shrinks from danger; it is a spirit of action, of love, and of discipline" (II Tim. 1. 7). We may be certain that many of our troubles are only the consequence of our weakness, which comes from our refusing to put our trust in the power of God. If we restore whole-hearted faith to Christianity, we shall see that we have also restored its strength.

Divine Life, Love and Prayer

We have just seen that strength and life are two things, and two words, which are linked together. Strong people are those who are very much alive, weak people are those who refuse life. The saints have strength and serenity because they live life to the full. To this idea of divine life we must not add the two words and the two ideas of love and of prayer.

Divine life and love of God always go together; this should be obvious since "God is love" and his life in us can only mean that, prompted by the Holy Spirit, we return the Father's love for us. Therefore, we increase our divine life when we increase our love of God, and we lose our divine life when we lose our love of God, and we rediscover our divine life when we rediscover our love of God.[1] The soul that is filled with this love remains thoroughly well-balanced and shows all the signs of good health. We may note in passing that just as a child is by nature inclined to love its parents, so in the domain of grace the baptized person is by nature inclined to love God, his Father, and as long as he keeps his innocence of heart his supernatural development will be rapid and strong. This explains to us why a young child brought up in a truly Christian family has such a marvellous response to divine values. Parents should cultivate this response and they should respect the divine life of their children: they should never lie to them, never frighten them by making a fuss about things of no importance, and they should bring them up to be unselfish. Children should learn to look into the eyes of Jesus and speak to him from their hearts. In this way results can be achieved which surpass all expectation. Some problems do not even arise, and the guiding influence of the parents is greatly strengthened while still allowing them to remain gentle and kind.

Divine life and love of God express themselves and are developed by means of prayer. Without anticipating what we shall be saying later on, it is difficult not to say at this point how sad it is that so many Catholics have forgotten how to pray; they are incapable of meeting our Lord in this heart-to-heart way, incapable of intimate talk with him. It is even sadder that this should coincide with the efforts of our Protestant brethren who often try—and succeed—to recapture this feeling of personal contact with God, which is so clearly lacking in the modern world.

Some of the Consequences of Divine Life

Speaking of prayer and its influence on people, Carrel has no hesitation in saying: "It stamps its believers [better: faithful users] with a peculiar seal. The purity of the glance, the tranquillity of the bearing, the serene joy of the expression, the virility of the conduct, and when necessary, the simple acceptance of the soldier's or martyr's death, betray the presence of the treasure hidden in the depths of the organs and the spirit. . . .

[1] Cf. *Summa Theologica*, II[a] II,[ae] 25.

Peace radiates from them. And they carry peace wherever they go."[1]

What he says of prayer can be said of divine life in general. It leaves its mark on the whole personality and even on the body. Using everyday language, there is a Christian look, and there is a pagan look, and there is the look that a good priest has. A man's bodily health is expressed in his energy, his strength, his look of well-being. And his spiritual health is expressed in his gaiety, his serenity, his strength of character, his joy in living, and the peace, which Carrel noticed, radiating from him.

Sin, the sickness of the soul, also has its outward signs: a lack of strength, melancholy, discontent and bitterness; Christianity should lead to joy. People who go through life wearily dragging their feet are not people who live by love. Physical tiredness may very often disturb certain aspects of our spiritual life, but it does not affect that life itself, and does not show the same symptoms.

One thing we should always remember: in our life here on earth, sickness of the soul can always be cured. Nowadays, the more people try to reduce the domain of sin, at least in practice, the more they have the idea that sin is irreparable and unforgivable. We meet so many people who think that all is lost and sink into despair if ever they have committed a really serious sin. One wonders where their faith in the Gospel is and what confession means to them! In fact, not only can sin be cured, but it can be cured more easily than the ills of the flesh, because the remedy, which is first of all the sacrament of penance, has greater certainty.

A man whose soul is sick expects much understanding and gentleness from the priest who is his doctor. He needs it even more if he is in a state of serious sin; the soul which returns from far off is like the body on the threshold of death: rough handling will kill it.

But he should also expect plain speaking; we go into the confessional to receive forgiveness and not to receive compliments, even less to find an accomplice who will help us gloss over our sins. Asking a priest for assurance that all is well when

[1] Dr Alexis Carrel, *Prayer*. [Transl. by Dulcie de Ste Croix Wright, pp. 40–1. London, 1947.]

we know we are in the wrong, and by doing so becoming committed to further wrong-doing; this is doing the devil's work for him, for it means using a sacrament which is there to destroy our sins, and to help us not to fall again, to make sinning easier.

Lastly the confessor must be patient, for there are many faults which cannot be conquered quickly, and it is no use demanding immediate results, for that would be treating a man like a piece of machinery and might break him altogether. But usually it is the sinner who is impatient. So many of us would like to be given an infallible recipe for getting rid of temptation, rather than the sins themselves, and seem to dream of a kind of spiritual medicine-chest, with shelves neatly lined with the prayers or the novena which, on demand and at small cost and no trouble to the sinner, will cure him of all his spiritual ailments. What do we think the Church is, and who do we think we are?

The Nobility of the Christian: the Fruits of the Spirit and the Fruits of the Flesh

Because he has become a son of God by his baptism, the Christian feels the love of the child for its father growing within him. From this moment onwards he is marked by a special character which he will always keep, in this world and in the next. We have a right to heaven because we carry the divine life within us, and if we lose this right by our sins, even if we go to hell, we remain a fallen son of God and not just a human creature. The consequence of this truth is expressed in the words of St Leo the Great: "Christian, be aware of your dignity."[1] We have now to explore the implications of this dignity.

To become a child of God is to be raised to heights which surpass anything that human ambition could hope for; it means having a kind of nobility which has no equal among worldly values. We must then act in accordance with it, and above all remember this dignity in our daily life. We are not expected to diminish our value as human beings on the pretext that it will increase our value as Christians. The human being

[1] St Leo the Great, *Sermon I on the Nativity.*

is good in himself; if he were not, we should be accusing God of creating evil; the Holy Spirit, by coming to live within us, takes charge of all the good in us, and far from destroying us, he brings us fulfilment. Within the Mystical Body of Christ, all our gifts should bear fruit and develop in the best possible way. The only thing is that they must be used in the service of love. Any man who buries his talents instead of putting them to use will be rejected as a bad servant (Mat. 25. 14–30).

With this in mind we should no doubt ask ourselves whether we as Christians have not made mistakes in this domain. In some places there has grown up a race of mean, stunted, devitalized Christians: "Because they have neither the strength nor the grace to take their place in nature, they imagine that they are grace itself. Because they lack earthly courage they imagine that they are halfway to eternity. Because they have not the courage to be part of the world, they imagine they must be part of God. Because they will not take sides on any human issue, they imagine they are on God's side, because they are not really men they imagine they are near to God, and because they love no-one they imagine that they love God. . . . But Jesus Christ himself has been a man." This passage from Péguy's *Note Conjointe*, which takes up the idea of St John: "If a man boasts of loving God, while he hates his own brother, he is a liar. He has seen his brother, and has no love for him; what love can he have for the God he has never seen?" (I John 4. 20), has not lost its topical significance. If that is so, it is serious, not only because it is abominable to see religion serving as a pretext for small-mindedness and meanness, and because it is terrible to see human personalities spoilt and stunted, but also because it is a disaster from the point of view of society. The world needs fine men and women, parents and citizens, conscious of their duty and concerned with taking their part in the life of their country. If these fine people do not come from our schools and colleges, from our Catholic Action groups, or, in a word, from the Church, people will look for them elsewhere; they will set up the heroes of antiquity or Nietzsche's superman as an ideal in their place.

The Christian should be "set free" by the truth (John 8. 32). All through his life he must aspire to that liberation which will free him from the slavery of sin and of the Law. Naturally, he will observe the Law,[1] like his Master, who could ask the Jew with his head held high: "Can any of you convict me of sin?" (John 8. 46), but he will do so in a transcendent way, borne up by love. Then he will be able to reap the harvest of the Spirit: "a harvest of love, joy, peace, patience, kindness, generosity, forbearance, gentleness, faith, courtesy, temperateness, purity. No law can touch lives such as these" (Gal. 5. 22–3). And when men realize that the effect of Christianity is one of liberation instead of one of restriction, they will be better able to understand its message; and when this harvest of the Spirit can be seen in the lives of Christians, it will be a revelation and an inspiration to the world.

At the other extreme, by refusing to be led by the Spirit, we fall among the things that "proceed from corrupt nature; they are such things as adultery, impurity, incontinence, luxury, idolatry, witchcraft, feuds, quarrels, jealousies, outbursts of anger, rivalries, dissensions, factions, spite, murder, drunkenness, and debauchery" (ibid. 19–21). Then, "when sin has reached its full growth, it breeds death" (James 1. 15); and not only death of the soul. We must remember that attempts on human life are not uncommon. There are abortions by the million in Europe alone, there are old people who die of neglect, there are ill-treated children. As soon as Christ and his Church disappear from countries that have once been Christian, the moral order slowly disintegrates, until even the most elementary rules of decent behaviour are no longer respected.

We have already spoken of the well-balanced state of the man whose heart is filled with the love of God. We should add that there are two ways of sinning against this equilibrium: either by wishing to live a good life while putting charity into second place—this produces a race of sectarians; or else by wanting to live in charity without understanding that it should perfect the other virtues and not replace them. This produces sentimentality, which is a short-lived and fruitless caricature of love. The man who is truly obedient to the Holy Spirit "is never insolent" (I Cor. 13. 5), but is able by instinct to avoid these two extremes, and so always steers its course aright.

---

[1] Naturally, the Christian no longer has to observe the Jewish Law. But it is, alas, only too easy for him to return to the old ways by basing the whole of his life on legalism, forgetting that charity comes first.

Chapter 15

THE LAWS OF DIVINE LIFE:
RENUNCIATION

True, also, I am fastened to the cross, but my cross is no longer fast to anything—Paul Claudel, *The Satin Slipper*, The First Day, Scene I.[1]

Divine life is subject to certain laws which are similar to those of human love, although less subject to exceptions. Each one of these laws, in the sense we are giving them here, consists of a set of rules which cannot fail to produce their effect if they are really applied.

There is no question of our pandering to that morbid desire for infallible recipes, which we have just been attacking; the rules we are going to deal with in this chapter are quite a different matter, for they show us how and where to apply our efforts; they do not replace them, neither do they make them automatic. We should like to study three of these laws of divine life.

(1) The law of preparation or of renunciation, which is the subject of this chapter;

(2) the law of spiritual exercise; and

(3) the law of nourishment, both of which we will discuss in later chapters.

The principle of the law of preparation is easy to understand, for a delicate plant, if it is to grow, must be given the right climate and the right soil, which must be fertile and also cleared of all weeds which might choke it or impair its growth by using up all the goodness in the soil. In the same way the divine life within us needs the "climate of love" we have spoken of in an earlier chapter, and it also needs well-prepared ground. By conforming to the law of preparation, we clear our souls of

[1] London, 1931, p. 2.

spiritual weeds. At first glance this seems to be a negative occupation, and so it is, but it must never be neglected, because weeds never stop coming up again. These weeds are the deadly sins, the seven deadly sins, or forms of perverted love, which tend to fill our hearts and souls:

Pride, the love of oneself.
Anger, exasperated love of oneself.
Envy, the love of other people's possessions.
Covetousness, the love of one's own possessions.
Sloth, the love of doing nothing.
Gluttony and Lust, the love of sensual pleasure.

To fight these tendencies, it is not enough to avoid committing the sins; we have to learn to do without certain permissible pleasures, in other words, to practise mortification. Its practice is essential to give the soul complete liberty, and to free it from everything which might hinder it in its search for union with God. By deliberately allowing ourselves to indulge in every pleasure which is not a sin, we are making ourselves the slaves of our passions, and making it extraordinarily difficult for ourselves not to go beyond the limits of what is permissible. By choosing penance we are imitating Jesus, who "to win his prize of blessedness, endured the cross" (Heb. 12. 2), and we are making it easier for ourselves to keep on the right road.

Rather than go into details of how to combat each of the deadly sins, it will be more helpful to study where we must use renunciation and how we can practise it. There are three spheres.[1]

(1) *Our Social Life*

In this sphere, what we have to do, quite simply, is to give up anything which could do harm to ourselves or other people. What harms *us* is first of all what leads us into sin: unhealthy friendships, letting ourselves be drawn into bad company or influenced by the moral code of our non-Christian friends. This is a very difficult problem, for it may involve us in making heavy sacrifices; for example, Jesus, and the apostles after him, were rejected by the Jewish people, which was after all their

[1] According to Fr Lebreton, *The Spiritual Teaching of the New Testament*, London, 1960.

own. The first Christians had to keep true to their faith in the most difficult circumstances, for at every moment they were risking their lives for Christ. Nowadays, we ourselves, living in a society which in many ways has become pagan again, often have to show very great courage. For example, in the situations which result from the practice of divorce, or in the case of the poorly-paid working-girl forced to choose between giving in to her boss's advances or losing her job, or again of people working for an employer whom they know to be dishonest. Sometimes, by ordering people to break off certain relationships, the priest gains a reputation for undue severity. When this is so, it is because we have no idea of the true value of our souls, and we fail to see that it far outweighs any advantages which might accrue to our bodies.

To avoid positive sins is still not enough, for we must have the greatest liberty in which to accomplish the good we intend to do. This sometimes leads to painful misunderstandings and separations, for instance between a young man and his parents who oppose his work in the apostolate or his entry into a seminary. This is the moment to remember the words of Jesus: "He is not worthy of me, that loves father or mother more; he is not worthy of me, that loves son or daughter more" (Mat. 10. 37).

We must stop doing anything which could harm our souls, and we have even greater reason to avoid without exception everything which might harm other people: "If anyone hurts the conscience of one of these little ones, that believe in me, he had better have been cast into the sea, with a millstone about his neck" (Mark 9. 41). Here we should be on our guard, for an action which is not bad in itself may well be forbidden to us because of the scandal it would cause to others. St Paul, speaking of meat used in idolatrous worship, concluded that it might be eaten without committing a sin. Then he adds: "It is for you to see that the liberty you allow yourselves does not prove a snare to doubtful consciences. . . . When you thus sin against your brethren, by injuring their doubtful consciences, you sin against Christ" (I Cor. 8. 9, 12). We cannot remain indifferent to the effects of our behaviour on those around us, and we must never forget that sometimes it takes very little to tempt someone into wrongdoing; we can do it by a thoughtless word, an expression, or even by our general attitude. Whatever happens, we should realize the great responsibility we have in the way we behave to others. This is not a subject which Jesus treats lightly.

As a reward for this renunciation of certain aspects of our social life we have a special compensation—that of being part of a community that respects and loves life. By their endless sacrifices, our ancestors in the faith have produced one very wonderful thing: the truly Christian family; and yet another wonderful thing is the number of communities who live together in Christian unity as Christ has asked us to. Our own efforts should be directed towards perfecting these communities and institutions, where we can—and should be able to—see "how good and how pleasant it is for brethren to dwell together in unity" (Ps. 132. 1).[1] The way for us to do this is to find and to show our agreement on both large and small matters, and to be completely open in all our dealings with one another.

(2) *The Good Things in Life*

Where these are concerned, we can see two problems, one of mortification and one of Christian poverty.

We have already discovered the necessity of accepting a certain degree of penance, and we can see it here when we consider the different spheres of our work and pleasure. There is little to be said about work; for penance, here, lies mostly in overcoming boredom, discomfort and fatigue, so that we may do whatever we have to do as well as we possibly can, taking to heart the words of St Paul to slaves: "You who are slaves, give your human masters the obedience you owe to Christ, in anxious fear, single-mindedly; not with that show of service which tries to win human favour, but in the character of Christ's slaves, who do what is God's will with all their heart. Yours must be a slavery of love, not to men, but to the Lord; you know well that each of us, slave or free, will be repaid by the Lord for every task well done" (Eph. 6. 58).

As for sensuous pleasures, the Church nowadays asks very few official privations from us—no meat on Fridays, four days of fast in the whole year—but they do seem to indicate that

---

[1] [Douay Version.—*Translator.*]

there is room for further effort in this domain. Many people forget to observe this obligation, or pretend that the effort is too much for them; others inflict on themselves excessive personal restrictions which harm their health and end by providing them with excuses for total inertia. Here a happy medium should be found, but all the same, how many of us might undertake to reduce just a small amount of our smoking, drinking or eating, without feeling that our health was in any way endangered!

Lastly, an attitude of penance should be applied to things of a sexual nature. For example, by keeping our hearts for real love, by attempting to keep our thoughts pure, by a certain modesty and dignity in the way we dress, by a way of behaviour that is at all times worthy of children of God. Also by avoiding dubious entertainment, reading and conversation, and by a certain moderation in our use of the rights of marriage.

The problem of poverty has always been a difficult one. Here we have the example of Jesus to look at: he came into the world born in a stable, cradled in the straw, and the day of his presentation in the Temple his mother could only afford to make the offering of the poor: "a pair of turtle-doves, or two young pigeons" (Luke 2. 24). He was "the carpenter's son" (Mat. 13. 55), a carpenter himself (Mark 6. 3), and during the period of his ministry he had "nowhere to lay his head" (Luke 9. 58). Then, his teaching repeats the same theme repeatedly, categorically, so that there can be no doubt in our minds as to what he means, and so that we should be disturbed in our innermost hearts by his words: "Blessed are the poor in spirit" (Mat. 5. 3); "Blessed are you who are poor" (Luke 6. 20); "But woe upon you who are rich; you have your comfort already" (ibid. 24); "You must serve God or money; you cannot serve both" (Mat. 6. 24); "Believe me, a rich man will not enter God's kingdom easily. And once again I tell you, it is easier for a camel to pass through a needle's eye, than for a man to enter the kingdom of heaven when he is rich" (Mat. 19. 23–4). And again: "None of you can be my disciple if he does not take leave of all he possesses" (Luke 14. 33). This last warning is not addressed to the little group who are close to him, but to a big crowd, which clearly shows that he does not include poverty as an optional extra, but as an intrinsic part of Christian life.

St Paul was only confirming the words of Jesus when he wrote to Timothy: "The love of money is a root from which every kind of evil springs, and there are those who have wandered away from the faith by making it their ambition, involving themselves in a world of sorrows" (I Tim. 6. 10).

For a very long time it has been an established fact in Christian tradition that the man who chooses poverty relieves himself of a burden. We become so preoccupied with the worries and responsibilities of money that they form a thick undergrowth in our hearts which chokes the word of God within us. We know from experience that a man who has a taste for money ends by losing his taste for the things of God. He puts his trust in bank-notes rather than in God, and often everything he does is dictated by his one purpose in life, which is to make money. He has replaced Christian hope by a merely human hope. We should always remember that the true Christian is not a man who makes a virtue of riches, but a man who is happy with what God gives him.

All the same, everyone knows very well that in spite of the example and teaching of Jesus, in spite of the exhortations of the Church, the virtue of poverty is very little practised among the mass of Christians, and very often we even deny its necessity. The reason is very simple: on the one hand poverty is one of the things which change our lives most profoundly; it goes right through to the smallest details of our existence and leaves its mark on them. On the other hand, we cannot live without money—somebody has to pay the grocer's bills—and therefore complete renunciation can only be in our hearts. It is not easy to decide on what is the precise limit between reasonable and superfluous expenditure, between what is a luxury and what is not, and the devil makes use of this difficulty to discourage us and lead us to give up the struggle altogether. So what we have to do is to discover a kind of poverty adapted to our own particular lives, and then to put it resolutely into practice, and the solution can only be found in some kind of compromise. Even in the religious orders, the poverty of the Carthusian is different from the poverty of the Trappist, and among the congregations which take simple vows there are even greater differences. And the layman does not, unless he has a special vocation, need to imitate the way of life of any one of these religious orders. Various attempts at doing so have frequently turned into ridiculous excess or caricature, which bears no relation to true charity. Therefore, it is up to each one of us, inspired by Christ, to find the solution which will allow him to live the beatitude of the "poor in spirit" in the circumstances in which God's will has placed him. But how are we to achieve this?

We should not confuse Christian poverty with utter destitution. Destitution means *not* having enough to live on, and Christian poverty means having *just enough* to live on. Thus, destitution can never be advised or encouraged, for where the necessities of life are lacking the practice of virtue is impossible; it is enough to have seen really bad slum conditions to realize that if human dignity is preserved there, it is by some kind of daily miracle. Therefore, this kind of life is something which should be got rid of, and should certainly not be taken up for the purpose of personal perfection.

Having said this much, we should like, with the help of Fr Lebret, to mention some of the offences most frequently committed against the virtue of poverty:

> To see people who are obviously very hard up and to feel it is none of our business.
> To assume that all those who are poorer, less well-educated or less successful than ourselves are necessarily inferior to us.
> To take advantage of someone else's need and misfortune in order to exploit him.
> To delay in paying what one owes.
> To forget to give back, or keep indefinitely, things which have been lent to us.
> To consider as our right any advantages we may have inherited or acquired.
> To keep for ourselves things we do not really need.

These two last points lead us right to the centre of the resistance that is put up, as soon as we discuss the problem of poverty in front of an audience of people who are reasonably affluent. Many of them have a tendency to think that, because they have acquired a certain wealth, they themselves and their children have some kind of divine right to the ease and comfort which it buys for them. And they are most indignant at the suggestion that times might change. This is not very Christian of them, for it shows a refusal to accept trials and difficulties, nor is it very logical, since we only have to look at the history of human society to see that it is constantly changing and re-forming itself, and that conditions in the standard of living of any particular family are liable to change from one generation to another, without there being anything that we can do about it. In the same way, the idea of not treasuring up one's super-fluous possessions appears to many of them as an offence against the tenets of ordinary decency. And yet Leo XIII told us, more than seventy years ago, that "when what necessity demands has been supplied, and one's standing fairly taken thought for, it becomes a duty to give to the indigent out of what remains over".[1] By saying this he was only developing the doctrine of St Thomas Aquinas, according to which worldly goods belong to all men in general before they belong to some men in particular. Therefore we are committing a sin against justice when we keep for our own use any more than necessity or propriety demands. And if we do so, we are depriving those who do not even possess the basic needs of existence. St Basil said: "The pair of shoes you own but never wear, belongs to the man who has no shoes at all." In that case, we can see there is no question of our giving away something of our own in a gesture of laudable generosity, but of giving him what is his by right.

  If we want to practise true poverty, and yet not leave the state of life in which God has placed us, we should listen to the words of St Paul, that master of sound practical advice: "Warn those who are rich in this world", he writes to Timothy (I Tim. 6. 17–19), "not to think highly of themselves, not to repose their hopes in the riches that may fail us, but in the living God, who bestows on us so richly all that we enjoy. Let them do good, enrich their lives with charitable deeds, always ready to give, and to share the common burden, laying down a sure foundation for themselves in time to come, so as to have life which is true life within their grasp"; and to the Corinthians he said: "You do not need to be reminded how gracious our

<hr />

[1] Leo XIII, Encyclical *Rerum Novarum*. [Engl. tr. *The Condition of the Working Classes*. London, C.T.S., p. 17, No. 19.]

Lord Jesus Christ was; how he impoverished himself for your sakes, when he was so rich, that you might become rich through his poverty" (II Cor. 8. 9).

Here the apostle shows us the way to achieve active poverty; this is, to make ourselves poor by giving. The way to achieve this is by fighting against our instinct of security, which is allied to our instinct of ownership. For example, we may learn to lend things, not just things of little value but valuable things, such as our silverware, or our country cottage. And in doing so we should be prepared to accept a certain risk to our belongings, such as their damage or their loss. Again, we may put certain sources of income to a common use, and lastly and above all we should give more and more generously to charity.

Another way, somewhat different, lies in trying to reduce our own needs: "If we have food and clothing to last us out, let us be content with that" (I Tim. 6. 8). Very often we may ask ourselves whether things we consider to be indispensable could not in fact be very well done without, not only without our suffering in the very slightest, but also without our upsetting the social conventions. Even a modest effort along these lines, if it is faithfully maintained, will give results that will astonish us. And if everybody would do this it would free large resources which could go towards increasing the salaries of those who are underpaid, financing works of charity, and in short enabling us to play our role as Christians in the fullest possible sense.

Last of all we should remember that poverty does not mean in the least that we should despise the good things which God has put at the disposal of man; such an attitude would be suspect, seeming to conceal feelings of spite or pride. The man who lives in Christian poverty does not despise the good things of life; he may possess them, but he is not possessed by them. His heart is free and he is untroubled, even at the idea of losing everything he owns.

(3) Ourselves

The third thing to be renounced is ourselves, and we must attempt to define what we mean. Here we should like to say that in our opinion one does not very often find a reliable explanation of this.[1] Sometimes, on this subject, hyperbolic expressions are used in which the writer seems to take a pleasure in dwelling on the crushing torment which this renunciation brings upon our souls; but it is difficult to see how this can be reconciled with a proper respect for our personalities. At the other extreme, all we are told is that we must correct our bad habits, which certainly does not express the fullness of Christ's thinking.

We feel that an example taken from daily life will say more than any theories: You may know a girl of nineteen; you do not see her for some time, and when you see her five years later she is married and already the mother of a child. She is still the same person, but all the same she has changed a great deal. Each important moment in her life, her engagement, her marriage and her motherhood, has made its mark on her. Her interests and values have been completely transformed by the love of her family. This is what happens when the love of God is allowed to take possession of a soul: slowly, but with infinite tenderness and strength, he transforms it, although the changes are at such great depth and so subtle that it is impossible to describe them in detail.

To renounce ourselves means in fact to let ourselves be transformed by the love of God which fills our whole soul, but even more, it means doing something to encourage this change. It is hard for us, because we like ourselves as we are. It becomes easy if we do it out of love, and realize that our renunciation is merely the convex surface to the concave surface of love. It is a long, slow business which requires patience and care. Above all we must make Christ's will our own, loving what he loves, being interested in what interests him, and seeing all things in relation to him, and, as it were, through him. In this way, little by little, we may achieve our purpose; Christ takes hold of our souls, and it is he who achieves their transformation.

[1] Fr Lebreton, *The Spiritual Teaching of the New Testament*, pp. 190–197, London, 1960, gives the best that we know.

Chapter 16

THE SPIRIT OF CHRIST
AND ITS ENEMIES

*He who is not with me, is against me; he who does not gather
his store with me, scatters it abroad*—Luke 11. 23.

We have seen that Christ did not come down on earth only to
save men; he also came so "that the world might find salvation
through him" (John 3. 17), not by setting up a political or
economic system, not even by giving new laws, but by spreading through the world, first by means of the apostles, then by
the Christians who came after them, that special mentality
which is his spirit. The world is saved just in so far as it lives in
the spirit of Christ, and it is lost when it refuses that spirit.
Sometimes Christianity in general, and the Catholic Church
in particular, are reproached with having failed in their
mission of saving the world. The answer to this reproach is that
the Christian way of life cannot be forced on the world from
the outside: Jesus died for the very reason that he refused to
impose himself on us in the slightest way by force. We will be
saved if we accept freely what he has given us, but not otherwise.

It is well known that the programme and the purpose of our
specialized lay apostolate—Catholic Action—groups is to
spread the spirit of Christ in such a way as to penetrate the
whole of society. In this way, not only will individuals be
saved, but little by little a whole human community will be
built up, within which salvation will become easier because
each person will help the others along the right road by his
faithfulness to Christ's spirit. At the same time, the community
will be able to organize the various social institutions so that
they serve the same purpose. The problem is contained very
simply in this question: which is going to rule the world, the
spirit of Christ or the spirit of evil?

The study of the Gospels soon shows us that while Jesus made friends, disciples and apostles during his time on earth, and while he sometimes drew large crowds to listen to him, he also made enemies, who revealed themselves as soon as he began his preaching, and whose hate for him grew without ceasing. Their hostility came from the very fact that they refused to accept the spirit which Jesus came to spread among them. Odd though it may seem to our way of thinking, it must nevertheless be understood that these enemies of his were not sinners in the ordinary sense of the word. On no occasion do we find the notorious or the anti-social opposing him. On the contrary, he accepts their company, and when other people express their surprise, he answers: "It is those who are sick, not those who are in health, that have need of the physician. I have not come to call the just; I have come to call sinners to repentance" (Luke 5. 31–2).

The Devil

In that case, who are the enemies of Christ? There are two: the devil and the Pharisees. The first appears on the threshold of the Gospel preaching, and if he leaves Jesus when he is ordered to, it is only "until the time should come" (Luke 4. 13). At his return he will no longer be visible, but will act through the intermediary of individual men. They, not he, are responsible for the Passion and death of the Saviour, although they are acting under satanic influence. When the devil works in the open he is not so dangerous, but when he stirs men to act on his behalf he is very dangerous indeed.

All the same it is important to study the temptations he puts before the Messiah, because they still apply to us today, although in a slightly different form. In these three trials, as the Gospels describe them,[1] the purpose of the adversary is always the same: to make the apostolate of Christ deviate from the way marked out for him by the Father. Thus the Messiah himself, and after him the Church, would achieve results which were not desired by God, and everything would have failed in spite of its apparent success, which might even be taken for a sign of God's approval.

[1] We are following St Matthew's order (4. 1–11). In St Luke's version, the second and third temptations are interchanged.

It is not surprising that we are still threatened by this danger; Christ constantly has to re-live in his Mystical Body all that he lived when he was on earth. He did not come to surmount all the obstacles in the way of our progress towards the Father by removing them from our path for ever, but by living through them himself and showing us, by his example, how we can overcome them by our faithfulness to his love.

(1) "If thou art the Son of God, bid these stones turn into loaves of bread. He answered, It is written, Man cannot live by bread only; there is life for him in all the words which proceed from the mouth of God" (Mat. 4. 3–4). This is a subtle temptation, all the more so because it comes in a moment of lassitude, one of those moments when good and evil fight for our souls, and when we have to be able to make an extra effort in order to remain faithful. The devil suggests a miracle to change the stones into bread. After all, why not? Later on Jesus will perform many miracles. One more or less, here or there, what could it matter? In fact it matters a great deal, for to give in to this suggestion of the devil would be to put the Almighty at the service of the material wishes of one person, or, if you like, to turn the spirit of Jesus towards material considerations, which would lead him to neglect his spiritual mission, or else to perform it with diminished strength.

For ourselves, this temptation occurs frequently; for some people it is there all the time, often in the form of fears for the future, against which Jesus warned us in the Sermon on the Mount. "Do not fret, then, over to-morrow; leave to-morrow to fret over its own needs; for to-day, to-day's troubles are enough" (Mat. 6. 34). This is the trial which awaits the father of a family who wonders how he is to feed his growing number of children, or the parish priest who is concerned about his schools and his church building funds. Now, although material questions must be dealt with, and dealt with to the best of our ability, for negligence is against the spirit of Christian poverty, they must not be allowed to dominate our faculties to the exclusion of everything else, for this would lead to crippling our powers of action and of thought. Worse still, to follow this idea further, it would eventually lead to loss of faith, because as we build up a mental picture of the universe whose perspectives no longer coincide with those of God, and as we ask him only

F

for material things, so we gradually come to feel that he is inattentive, and we move farther and farther away from him and forget him.

In the apostolate, this leads to all sorts of problems which are not always easy to solve. Is it our duty to help the rich before we help the poor, or the other way round? But the Church should belong to everyone, because she is everyone's family. Should we give large sums of money to charity? Of course, but we should not forget that you do not convert people by showering them with earthly goods; extreme poverty is not the fundamental cause of unbelief. In the United States there are Communists who earn $100 a day and ride around in Cadillacs, whereas in every country in the world vice and irreligion attack all sorts of people who have no idea what extreme poverty is and who have no pity for those who do know it. Lastly, to go even further along the same lines, we may mention the incessantly recurring mirage that material assistance alone will solve all the world's problems.

Sometimes, to help us to protect ourselves against such serious dangers, it pleases Providence to allow us a success which seems at first absolutely impossible. Without a penny in his pocket, a certain priest will manage to establish several works of charity and to find the money to keep them going from day to day. Another one, in spite of abject poverty—or perhaps because of it—will draw people to him and achieve numbers of conversions where others before him have failed. These are signs which we should notice attentively. We should have no doubts about it: if our faith were greater, we should see these favours of Providence increase and multiply. "Watch and pray, that you may not enter into temptation; the spirit is willing enough, but the flesh is weak" (Mark 14. 38).

(2) "Next, the devil took him into the holy city, and there set him down on the pinnacle of the temple, saying to him, If thou art the Son of God, cast thyself down to earth; for it is written, He has given charge to his angels concerning thee, and they will hold thee up with their hands, lest thou shouldst chance to trip on a stone. Jesus said to him, But it is further written, Thou shalt not put the Lord thy God to the proof" (Mat. 4. 5–7).

In this temptation, Satan suggests to Christ that he should

THE SPIRIT OF CHRIST AND ITS ENEMIES 151

attract the crowds by a stunt worthy of a circus acrobat. As
far as we ourselves are concerned, this is equivalent to a
temptation which may seem out of date, but which happens to
have become curiously modern: it consists in a morbid taste
for the sensational, and an excessive desire for the supernatural. It was this cult of the miraculous that prompted the
Jewish crowds to be always crying out for "signs", and to say
of Christ crucified: "If he is the king of Israel, he has but to
come down from the cross, here and now, and we will believe
in him" (Mat. 27. 42). Now Jesus, every time he is faced with
demands for a sign, reacts strongly, sometimes even violently:
"The generation that asks for a sign is a wicked and unfaithful
generation; the only sign that will be given it is the sign of the
prophet Jonas. Jonas was three days and three nights in the
belly of the sea-beast, and the Son of Man will be three days
and three nights in the heart of the earth" (Mat. 12. 39–40).
He does not like it when people are attracted to him because
he performs miracles, but only when they come to him because,
like St Peter, they realize that his words "are the words of
eternal life" (John 6. 69).

In reality, experience shows us that the extraordinary and
the marvellous may dazzle people but they do not convert
them. It also shows us that whenever this desire is strongest
among the people, their religion is weakest. The success of
fortune-tellers runs parallel with the failure of priests.

There is another temptation which resembles this one: the
tendency to base our apostolate on power tactics, using force
to get people into the Church or to keep them there. This
tendency is almost always apparent in places where the Gospel
has penetrated sufficiently to form a solid Christian community.
After the multiplication of the loaves and fishes the crowd
showed signs of this tendency when they wanted to carry off
Jesus to make him their king (John 6. 15). On that occasion
he escaped from them to spend the night in prayer. The secret
of his behaviour, here as with the devil, is that he did not
come down to earth to testify to the almighty power of God, but
to his love. It would not have been difficult to make a display
of the divine power. One or two sensational miracles, accompanied by suitable strategic victories to drive the forces of the
Roman occupation beyond the frontiers, would have been

quite sufficient. But in that case there would have been no cross, no tomb, no resurrection on Easter Day, and everything would have deviated from the way set out by God.

We should always remember that our apostolate is not intended to be a form of propaganda. We are not supposed to impress people, but to bear witness, to teach, to develop religious knowledge, and to form true Christians by our patience and love. It is a humbler calling, and it commits us much more because we have to give of ourselves, and the results seem slower in coming. But really it is time saved, because anything which departs from the way of Christ is a waste of time and energy for the Church.

Human beings must not be manipulated as if they were material objects without souls. You cannot pour religion into them like tea into a cup. They should be handled with infinite tact and delicacy. Here again the behaviour of Jesus is most enlightening: he gives his message, he calls someone to him, but if the man does not want to come, he does not insist any further. When he is asked to leave the land of the Gerasenes he does not curse the men who reject him; he gets into a boat and crosses to the other side of the lake, and that is all (Luke 8. 37).

When he works a miracle it is always in the service of love, in order to relieve suffering, to cure illness, and to give instruction. Very often he avoids being seen by the crowds, and sometimes he insists on silence about what he has done. Nothing is ever spectacular or theatrical. One could almost believe that he wanted to leave us free to doubt, so much does he respect human souls and wish them to come to him in total liberty. The moment we stop imitating his behaviour in this way, we go wrong, and if we have some temporary success we are only preparing the most terrible reaction in those we have brought to religion by the wrong paths.

Very much the same situation occurs when, in a State or a society which is on good terms with the Church, she lets herself be drawn into worldly affairs or even into the struggle for power. On this point also Jesus makes himself perfectly clear; he always refused to take part in politics, and he even refused to help the two brothers divide their inheritance (Luke 12. 14). It is not surprising, therefore, that, as soon as we step outside our proper sphere and attempt to meddle in affairs which are beyond our competence, we obtain the most deplorable results. What a deliverance the loss of the Papal States meant to the Holy See! And how essential it is that all priests everywhere should be seen to be completely free of bondage to political parties or financial interests of every kind.

(3) "Once more, the devil took him to the top of an exceedingly high mountain, from which he shewed him all the kingdoms of the world and the glory of them, and said, I will give thee all these if thou wilt fall down and worship me. Then Jesus said to him, Away with thee, Satan; it is written, Thou shalt worship the Lord thy God, and serve none but him" (Mat. 4. 8–10).

If the first temptation was a subtle one, and the second makes us smile a little, this one startles us by its outrageousness: give homage to the devil indeed! What an idea! To understand its implications we should remember that this temptation comes very close to an old daydream of the Jews, that of the leadership of the entire world. In the Old Testament, the Kingdom of God was never separated from a certain amount of earthly power, nor from the idea of a universal triumph. We know, furthermore, that the apostles remained rooted in this conception until the day of Pentecost. It recurs in various forms at almost every point in history, either by affecting one particular person or else by taking hold of a whole section of the clergy, or even of a whole country. It reveals itself in a desire to succeed at any price, and in order to do so, to do Christ's work by any means whatever, even those of the devil, which is an indirect but indisputable means of giving homage to Satan. It involves a tendency to scheming, to double-dealing and cunning, to considering anything justifiable which leads to success or which makes money. In the matter of money-raising schemes, priests sometimes have to think twice before agreeing to ideas suggested by misguided parishioners. They should sometimes question seemingly propitious circumstances, too, for it is not so very long ago that people considered that every charity bazaar should end in a free-for-all dance, and we know personally of a cinema built out of charity funds, where unsuitable films are shown in order to "make money and so gradually to gain influence" [sic]. In other cases people are prepared to come to terms with error, and encourage conversions by compromising with doctrine. Of course none of this is Christian, and of course it is very easy to pass judgement on paper, sitting at one's desk in a peaceful study. But in the heat of action it is a different matter, and it is easy to slip into the most fatal compromise. The outstretched hand of the Communists and the vacillations caused by their tactics should be enough to show the extent of the danger. Above all, we should be clear as to what we stand for: "To drink the Lord's cup, and yet to drink the cup of evil spirits, to share the Lord's feast, and to share the feast of evil spirits, is impossible for you" (I Cor. 10. 21). And we may be sure that even from a practical point of view it is better for us to show that we are people of integrity, ready to be accused of inflexibility, than to embark upon schemes which we know in advance are doomed to failure.

The Pharisees

"Two men went up into the temple to pray; one was a Pharisee, the other a publican. The Pharisee stood upright, and made this prayer in his heart, I thank thee, God, that I am not like the rest of men, who steal and cheat and commit adultery, or like this publican here; for myself, I fast twice in the week, I give tithes of all that I possess. And the publican stood far off; he would not even lift up his eyes towards heaven; he only beat his breast, and said, God, be merciful to me; I am a sinner. I tell you, this man went back home higher in God's favour than the other; everyone who exalts himself will be humbled, and the man who humbles himself will be exalted" (Luke 18. 10–14).

It is impossible to discuss Pharisaism unless one realizes clearly the great scandal it constitutes in the Gospels. This is the scandal: the Pharisees were the virtuous and respectable Jewish people, the very ones who opposed Jesus more than anyone else and had him crucified. And yet they lived by the very same Scripture, Law and traditions of the Jewish people which were based on the hope and the ardent expectation of the Messiah. We should make no mistake about it, their virtues were very real ones. When the man who goes up to the temple to pray boasts of fasting conscientiously and of paying his taxes with scrupulous exactitude, he is telling the truth. Even more, these people generally respected the laws of marriage, and numbers of them lived in a certain poverty. And yet, with all these good qualities, all they receive from Jesus is harsh words. Anyone would think that he took a pleasure in goading them by choosing a sabbath day in each case, when he cured the paralysed man of Bethsaida and the man born blind. What had they done that was so terrible?

It is very simple—it is disturbing too, because it is so easy to fall into the same trap—they preferred the letter of the Law to Love itself. They were men of the Law, as they said to Pontius Pilate: "We have our own law, and by our law he ought to die" (John 19. 7). It was a good law, but they had taken it into their own possession: "We have a law", and they interpreted it in their own way by emptying it of all its content of love, and by observing it so rigorously that its observance verged upon the ridiculous. Thus, they attributed importance to the most unimportant things, and allowed important things to pass unnoticed. "Woe upon you, scribes and Pharisees, you hypocrites that will award to God his tithe, though it be of mint or dill or cummin, and have forgotten the weightier commandments of the law, justice, mercy, and honour; you did ill to forget one duty while you performed the other; you blind leaders, that have a strainer for the gnat, and then swallow the camel!" (Mat. 23. 23-4). And from this comes the appalling hypocrisy with which Jesus so violently reproached them. They created their own moral code alongside the code of true morality. We should beware of this, for it *always* happens when outward observance becomes rigid. Cramped in his pillory of formal observance, mankind must compensate for the restriction somehow, and he does so by turning in on himself instead of reaching out to God and his fellow men. The Pharisee in the parable, in the Douay version, "prayed thus within himself". Instead of asking God to give him his gifts, he prefers to gloat over what he believes are his own possessions. By doing this, he is literally barricaded and locked in within himself so that he becomes incapable of receiving anything whatever which might disturb his set habits of thinking. So that when the Messiah comes, even if he is obliged to admit that he accomplishes astounding miracles, there is no question of his becoming a disciple, and he is bound to find a pretext to get rid of him at any price. The trial of the man born blind (John 9) is characteristic: it is impossible to deny the miracle, so they manage to get round it by declaring Jesus a sinner for curing people on a Sabbath! Then again, when Lazarus is raised from the dead, they do not attempt to deny his resurrection; but they plan to kill him, and they cast a vote for the death of Jesus as well (John 12. 10 and 11. 47–52). There is no help for it; they will die with their sins upon them (cf. John 8. 24).

The final definition of this sin is that it is the sin of pride, and we will now give a brief analysis of pride based on the work of St Thomas Aquinas, who perceived four separate forms of it.[1]

(1) Imagining that some good thing one possesses, one possesses of oneself. This is a false idea, for "who is it that gives thee this pre-eminence? What powers hast thou, that did not come to thee by gift? And if they came to thee by gift, why dost thou boast of them, as if there were no gift in question?" (I Cor. 4. 7). But while it is quite easy to agree in theory with the words of the apostle, it is quite another matter to put them into practice. In order to do this, it would do us no harm to remind ourselves frequently of all our parents have done for us: given us life, seen to our education, fed and clothed us, and passed on to us their experience and family background; and then to think of all that other people have done for us and of what we still continue to receive from others; and finally, of all that God gives us. Perhaps then we shall be less full of self-importance! We should remember the words of the Magnificat: "My soul magnifies the Lord; my spirit has found joy in God, who is my Saviour, because he has looked graciously upon the lowliness of his handmaid. Behold, from this day forward all generations will count me blessed; because he who is mighty, he whose name is holy, has wrought for me his wonders" (Luke 1. 46–9). This is the language of true humility. Mary realizes the good which is within her, but she praises God because all good comes from him.

(2) Imagining that what one possesses is due to one's own merits. This is a more subtle error, but an error nevertheless, for God's gifts are given freely. When we come to think of it,

[1] *Summa Theologica*, IIª IIᵃᵉ, 162, 4.

were we given our baptism because we deserved it? Did
St Peter deserve to be head of the Church, St John to be "the
disciple whom Jesus loved" (John 21. 7), Saul, to become
Paul? On the other hand, if we have done a certain amount of
good and even if we live reasonably Christian lives, what we
give bears no comparison with what God gives to us: "Not
that I count these present sufferings as the measure of that
glory which is to be revealed in us" (Rom. 8. 18); "This light
and momentary affliction brings with it a reward multiplied
every way, loading us with everlasting glory" (II Cor. 4. 17);
"I will shew pity, he tells Moses, on those whom I pity; I will
shew mercy where I am merciful; the effect comes, then, from
God's mercy, not from man's will, or man's alacrity" (Rom.
9. 15–16).

(3) Boasting of possessing talents and virtues which in fact
one does not possess. This is a crude form of pride which is
nevertheless widespread, particularly in those who are lukewarm or half-hearted. It comprises the illusion of having
graces, talents and virtues, an illusion entertained by not a few
armchair politicians and public-house prophets. It is the error
of considering oneself superior to others because one observes
the commandments better than they do, while being unable
to see the beam which is in one's own eye (cf. Mat. 7. 3). Let
us beware: it is often hard to accept an objective criticism of
oneself; but humility and peace of mind are only to be obtained
at this price.

(4) While despising others, making believe one possesses
oneself what they possess. This double attitude clearly shows
the contradiction inherent in pride, for if other people are
worth so little, why envy their possessions or be jealous of their
success? It is quite irrational—but then, evil is basically
lacking in logic. In practice, this form of pride can be recognized
by the pang of resentment we feel when we hear someone else
being admired. This is an alarm signal which should not be
ignored, for it means that the evil has already taken hold of us.

We have just touched on one important aspect of the sin of
pride: that the proud man finds it difficult to see that he is
wrong, and without necessarily going to the lengths of obstinacy
of the Pharisees in the Gospels, he still responds with bad
grace when it is pointed out to him. To help us to realize that

we have something to learn in this domain, we will quote a few symptoms given by Frs Lebret and Monier in their "spiritual exercises":

> Being discouraged by difficulties or failures.
> Being subject to and nursing touchiness or hurt feelings.
> Always believing one is right.
> Always wanting to have the last word.
> Speaking sententiously.
> Giving one's opinion on subjects one knows nothing about.
> Refusing to pray, or to ask God for anything when one does pray.
> Refusing to look things in the face; being given to brooding, to shyness, to false pride.

The cure of the sin of pride is something which goes slowly and needs perseverance, for habits of mind are not changed quickly. It will be achieved first and foremost by the constant exercise of brotherly love, for this will open our eyes to a lot of things, and therein lies progress. But we should beware of spectacular displays of humility, for they have one disconcerting result, which is to prove that we do not possess the virtue of which we make such a parade!

Chapter 17

THE SPIRIT OF CHRIST:
THE LIFE AT NAZARETH,
TRUTH

For our sakes a child is born, to our race a son is given, whose shoulder will bear the sceptre of princely power. What name shall be given him? Peerless among counsellors, the mighty God, Father of the world to come, the Prince of peace—Is. 9. 6.

We have seen that Christ's aim is to save the world by the diffusion of a particular spirit. All those who wish to be his disciples, therefore, must become so filled with this spirit that they do as he would have done in the same circumstances. It has been revealed to us from the beginning of the Scriptures that man is made in the image and likeness of God. By developing this likeness in himself, therefore, man becomes what he was made to be. Already in the Old Testament we read: "Be ye holy, because I the Lord your God am holy" (Lev. 19. 2),[1] but since Jesus has revealed to us that his Father is also our Father, the commandment takes on new force and precision. "As God's favoured children, you must be like him. Order your lives in charity, upon the model of that charity which Christ shewed to us, when he gave himself up on our behalf" (Eph. 5. 1–2); "Follow my example, then, as I follow the example of Christ," said St Paul (I Cor. 11. 1). Jesus himself said: "I have been setting you an example, which will teach you in your turn to do what I have done for you" (John 13. 15); "You are to be perfect, as your heavenly Father is perfect" (Mat. 5. 48). Imitating Christ or imitating the Father comes to the same thing, for "he is the true likeness of the God we cannot see" (Col. 1. 15), and "whoever has seen me, has seen the Father" (John 14. 9). We must remember that one of the reasons for

[1] [Douay Version.—*Translator.*]

the incarnation was to reveal the Father to us, not simply by words but by showing us in physical form all that we could learn about him. The essence of our task in life, therefore, is to follow the example of Christ as perfectly as possible. We must be clear about this: following his example does not mean imitating the exterior and material circumstances of his life, except in the rare cases of a vocation like that of St Francis of Assisi or, nearer our own time, of Charles de Foucauld. Not everyone has a vocation to complete poverty, or a vocation to preach, still less a vocation to live in Nazareth, but we can all acquire the spirit of Jesus by examining as closely as possible the motives of his actions, and his way of living. This is what we have tried to do each time we have commented on a scene from the Gospels or on a parable. We shall now try to continue in the same way looking at the period of Christ's life before his public ministry, and at his attitude to truth.

Nazareth

St Luke's Gospel (3. 23) tells us that at the beginning of his public ministry Jesus had "reached the age of about thirty". By comparing secular events mentioned in the Gospel with other historical data, the figure thirty would appear to be a minimum. His period of preaching having lasted just over two years, one can see that Nazareth occupied an extremely large portion of his life, over nine-tenths, the period in Egypt having been probably quite short. The Gospels tell us nothing at all about the life in Nazareth, except that Jesus lived there with Mary and Joseph "and was subject to them" (Luke 2. 51),[1] and the rare allusions, later in the Gospels, to this period show us that, in fact, there was nothing to know because exteriorly their life was like everyone else's with no extraordinary happenings. Just one event stands out from the regular routine of daily life: the time when Jesus, aged twelve, stayed behind in the Temple at Jerusalem, talking with the elders while his parents believed him to be with the rest of the caravan. This very simplicity can teach us many things, for if we look at it closely, we see that it is very surprising.

(1) Having come on earth "to save his people from their

[1] [Douay Version.—*Translator.*]

sins" (Mat. 1. 21) and so that "the world might find salvation through him" (John 3. 17), Jesus seems to be in no hurry about starting his task. He will begin it at the hour his Father has chosen, and not before, and in the meantime he will carry out more humble tasks such as making furniture and scaffolding for houses. Humanly speaking he makes no preparations for the task ahead, he does not even go to school (John 7. 15). There will be a complete contrast between the authority he will show later and the self-effacement of his youth and early manhood. But this does not worry him in the least, the only thing that counts in his eyes is doing the will of his Father.

(2) If Jesus and Mary sanctified themselves for thirty years in a very ordinary way of life, it is not necessary for us to leave our ordinary way of life in order to become better Christians; what counts in God's eyes is not so much what we do as the spirit in which we do it. A very ordinary task carried out in obscurity takes on great value if it is full of love. Conversely, good deeds done to attract attention and praise lose all their value in the eyes of God. "Believe me, they have their reward already"; these words are repeated three times in the Sermon on the Mount (Mat. 6. 2, 5, 16) referring to those hypocrites who give alms, pray and fast for the pleasure of being admired.

Although this teaching is frequently repeated, we cling obstinately to the idea that the life of a saint must resemble an epic. Nothing could be further from the truth; the love that saves is not a triumphant and glorious love, it is a humble love that is willing to serve as Jesus served. The Holy Family were happy in the poverty of Nazareth because they loved each other dearly and served each other gladly. Their mutual love created an atmosphere of perfect happiness; one can imagine Mary reading the Scriptures to the child Jesus, and later listening to his commentaries on them when he grew to be a boy and then an adult. The Church should be a Nazareth on a world scale where men are happy to be together, and united because each is at the service of the others.

(3) This service will consist partly in giving alms and partaking in works of charity, but mainly in accomplishing the duties inherent in our state of life, as this takes up the greater

part of our active life.[1] If there is no spirit of service here, we might as well admit at once to being thoroughgoing egoists. This is a matter of the greatest importance. It makes a tremendous difference to a business when those who run it come to understand that they are not its proprietors in the absolute, Roman, sense of the word, but that the business is at the service of everyone who has any contact with it: those who work in it, from the managing director to the cleaners, the clients and the suppliers. If only everyone understood and practised this, social problems would solve themselves!

(4) In Nazareth the Holy Family were not, presumably, in dire material need. There is nothing to make us suppose that Joseph, and then Jesus, did not earn a satisfactory living. We know that they remained poor, however, and this is surprising, as a family of three, all of whom were healthy, intelligent and hard-working, would normally have been reasonably well off. Why was this not the case? Only one explanation is possible: it was because, when possible, they gave generously both of their goods and of their time. We may well imagine that when Jesus and Joseph were busy at their work, Mary went and helped her neighbours with their children, their various household tasks and the care of the sick.

(5) The Holy Family did not cut themselves off from the rest of the world; Jesus and Mary were willing to mix with all their neighbours, not just the respectable ones, but the sinners too, for there is no reason to suppose that the people of Nazareth were any better than other men. These contacts were not always pleasant, for Jesus "could read men's hearts" (John 2. 25) and Mary was certainly not lacking in intuition. In their relations with other men they did not have the comfort of ignorance, but such was the will of the Father. Christ never ceased this familiarity with the crowd: when the time came for his baptism by John, his precursor, Jesus took his place among all the others who were waiting to be baptized. We must remember that it is the Father's will that Jesus should always be in our midst, even when we are sinners.

(6) When the Father gave to Mary and Joseph the mission

---

[1] One must avoid the idea that the duties of one's state of life are simply one's professional duties. The father of a family still has other duties to perform after he has returned home from his work.

of bringing Jesus into the world, and then of bringing him up, he was giving them a responsibility that was literally superhuman. In addition, Palestine, in those days, was often a dangerous country: armed robbery was common, Roman soldiers were addicted to massacres and the Herods were cruel. It is, therefore, true to say that the life of the Saviour was in constant danger. Apart from the exceptional circumstances that followed the visit of the Magi, no other miraculous interventions appear to have taken place. God trusted those he had created. Mary and Joseph used their intelligence and remained calm and unafraid; they knew that if they made a mistake something or someone would put things straight again. But, as far as possible, God avoided giving any particular warnings, and when he did so, they were brief and to the point. In this way there developed between God and man relations of friendship and liberty which prefigured the atmosphere of the Church. There too, God allows men to act freely. Their initiative must be allowed free play, they are no longer slaves but collaborators, which means that they must not have the impression of being browbeaten by a strict and over-exigent authority, but of developing their personalities in a world of love.

Truth

When he was teaching, Jesus often used the phrase which he made famous: "Amen, amen, I say unto you", and in one of the crucial moments of his Passion, he said to Pontius Pilate: "What I was born for, what I came into the world for, is to bear witness of the truth. Whoever belongs to the truth, listens to my voice" (John 18. 37). The gravity of the occasion made this a particularly solemn pronouncement, but he had made many previous ones on the same subject. He spoke to the Samaritan woman of "true worshippers" who "will worship the Father in spirit and in truth" (John 4. 23), and to the Jews he said: "If you continue faithful to my word, you are my disciples in earnest; so you will come to know the truth, and the truth will set you free" (John 8. 31).

By giving us access to the truth the Saviour fulfils men's deepest desire. He shows the way to the ideal of great men in every age. There is probably no aspiration more noble than that of becoming true in all one's thoughts and deeds. This seems to be the characteristic which makes one feel most strongly the resemblance between God and man, and the extent to which man is made for God who is Truth. But as a result of original sin, men have fallen so low that there is no spontaneous agreement among them even on so fundamental a point. Consequently a certain amount of analysis of our ideas about truth is necessary.

Firstly, we would say that a man is true when he is sincere, in other words when he is in agreement with himself, when his thoughts are coherent and logical and his acts are in accordance with his thoughts. If we lack this form of truth we are either hypocrites or weaklings. Modern man is right to be demanding on this point, and to condemn all forms of duplicity.

But he is wrong when, because he values sincerity, he finishes by thinking it sufficient and saying, for example, that one can believe anything providing one believes it sincerely, and practise any religion if one practises it fully. If I state that two and two make five, I am wrong, and no amount of sincerity will make me right. Consequently one cannot neglect that other ingredient of the truth which is that thoughts and beliefs should correspond with the facts.

Truth cannot unite either with error or with half-truths. It is intransigent by nature and one cannot take liberties with it. In addition, if we deceive a man we do him immense harm because we distort his intelligence, the most noble part of his being. This helps us to understand why the Church is extremely severe on the subject of heresy, which is the separation of the intelligence from God, the rejection of Christ in himself or in the Mystical Body. However, this does not mean that we must confuse the love of truth with narrow-mindedness, which is a refusal to understand other ideas, or with sectarianism which is the love of one's personal points of view. When the intelligence is nourished with truth it feels free. If it feels deprived the chances are that it has been fed on error.

The whole-hearted seeking after truth and the courage to act on the truth as soon as it is found, these are what brings man closest to God, but they demand considerable sacrifices. The fullness of truth always includes facts which we find hard to admit, because their acceptance requires humility. It is not easy to admit our faults and the mistakes we have made; it is even harder to admit that at certain periods of our life we have lived according to false ideas, in a misguided intellectual system, or that we have taken refuge behind an array of sentiments that we would have been better off without. We cling to these things because they have become so incorporated into our beings that they seem to be a part of us. Man's intelligence is not a detached and independent faculty; it works in conjunction with the will, so that the feelings have a noticeable influence on its decisions. If we make the wrong choice, if we turn inwards towards ourselves instead of opening out towards God, we will slide into error, whereas if we ask Christ to irradiate all things with his light, then we shall reach the fullness of truth. "If you continue faithful to my word, . . . you will come to know the truth" (John 8. 31–2).

In practice, the Christian seeks not only to avoid what is untrue, but also to eliminate from his life all ambiguity and half-truths. He aims at developing a well-informed conscience, at speaking truthfully and accurately, and at having the courage of his convictions and honesty in all things. It is better that we should speak in too decisive a manner, for lack of experience, or that our morality should tend to be over-severe, rather than that we should become yes-men who never have an opinion of our own or never dare to express it. With God's grace the element of hardness will gradually disappear until the right balance is achieved, a balance which enables its possessor to speak with complete freedom to all men without either shocking or hurting them. Moreover, the refusal to compromise which comes from a love of truth does not have the same effect as that which comes from defending a system: it does not wound, and the fact that its motives are good is quickly recognized.

Humility is essentially a loyal acceptance of truth, combined with the will to act in accordance with that truth. It places us in our true position: that of creatures and children of God, of sinners, but sinners who have been redeemed and forgiven. Humility is, of course, a conviction of the mind; it has nothing in common with those exterior humiliations which we accept while at the same time we continue to cultivate our self-esteem. Those who are humble do not deny the talents they possess nor the virtues they manage to acquire, but they remember that their talents and their virtues come from God, and like Mary they "magnify the Lord who has wrought for them his wonders". They put their talents and their virtues to work for the glory of God and the salvation of their brothers, remembering what happens to the unprofitable servant (Mat. 25. 24–30). Humility is the virtue most necessary to those who are in command, men are only good leaders and only have the right to command when they lead others towards what is right and true in a spirit of service and not for personal gain. Humility gives the peace of mind which knows no discouragement because its strength is in God, no anxiety because the only answer Christ can give to its love is more love, no failure because its success lies in doing the will of the Father. "The prayer of the humble pierces the clouds, and he will not be consoled until it reaches the Lord. . . . And the Lord will not delay" (Ecclus. 35. 17, 18).[1]

[1] [Revised Standard Version.—*Translator.*]

Chapter 18

THE LAW OF SPIRITUAL
PRACTICES: PRAYER

*Nothing must make you anxious; in every need make your
requests known to God, praying and beseeching him, and giving
him thanks as well*—Phil. 4. 6.

The second law of divine life is the law of spiritual practices.
It is based on the simplest of principles: any life which is not
active is already a kind of death and leads to death itself.

Look at a pile of corn, stored in a barn after the harvest. At
first glance there is little to distinguish it from a heap of gravel,
and we have to examine the grains closely before we realize
that they have an organic structure. On the other hand, as
soon as they are put into the earth and begin to swell in its
moisture, there is no doubt whatever that they are living
things. In the barn their life was slowed down or suspended,
as the biologists say; when they begin to germinate out in the
fields, their life is active again. In his teaching, Jesus always
speaks of life as following the course proper to its nature: for
example the lilies of the field, the grain of mustard seed, the
sparrow. And so with us, divine life must find an expression, an
outlet in our actions, otherwise it will slow down or come to
a stop, like the grain of corn after the harvest. But what does
this mean exactly?

Since our baptism makes us God's children, our life is above
all a life of filial love. Filial love comprises two elements:
affection and obedience. Here we should be careful, for it is not
a question of separating these two elements, but of combining
them. This is one of the keys of spiritual equilibrium, and here
life in the human family gives us an idea of life in the family of
God.

For example, if we bring up a child by forcing him to obey,
without either giving or asking affection, we will turn him into

a hard and arrogant man, and probably a rebel as well. If on the other hand he is given affection without discipline, he will turn into a sentimental egoist, avid for marks of affection but incapable of making any great effort. To return to supernatural life, we may notice that this equilibrium we have mentioned is one of the pivots of the thinking of St John. Whether in the discourse after the Last Supper or in the First Epistle, Christ's favourite disciple keeps repeating that in order to love we must keep the commandments, which in their turn are commandments of love. Filial love should be spontaneous and freely given, and it is in this atmosphere of fulfilment that our dependence on God should be developed. In the apostolate, it is a waste of time trying to bring human souls to God by force. In order to achieve our spiritual growth, we have to make an effort, of course, in order to transform ourselves progressively, but we are not asked to go against our own nature. It is God who creates, and it is the devil who comes "to steal, to slaughter, to destroy" (John 10. 10). The variety of different personalities should reflect the many facets of God's glory. The Church has canonized an immense number of saints, and between them they represent almost every form of love for God imaginable.

For some four thousand years, God has been gradually taking the world back into his spiritual fatherhood, restoring what was destroyed by man's lack of love. This is accomplished in progressive stages which mark the rise of humanity.

The first man to be chosen was Abraham, a man full of faults, too tied to nature but still living by faith, that is to say, he had faith to the point of trusting in God completely, he "believed, hoping against hope; and thus became the father of many nations" (Rom. 4. 18). He is not only the man who marks the starting point of revelation, he is a prototype, for "the words, It was reckoned virtue in him, were not written of him only: they were written of us too. It will be reckoned virtue in us, if we believe in God as having raised our Lord Jesus Christ from the dead: handed over to death for our sins, and raised to life for our justification" (Rom. 4. 23–5). During all eternity, the basis of salvation is faith, and this continuity links the Old Testament with the New.

Abraham receives a very great reward from God: "to see the day of my coming", says Jesus (John 8. 56). So his readiness to answer God's call leads him to God's close friendship, and in him faith rises to the heights of mystic vision. The Jewish people are not capable of this fidelity on their own: Moses comes to give them a Law whose main purpose was to give existence to a community and whose commandments were of a social rather than a personal order. Of course, love is not absent from this law, but men are led towards love from the outside: a multitude of actions are prescribed, which are intended to lead the Israelite step by step into a climate where love can grow and develop. The gravest faults are highlighted and he is preserved from them, as far as this is possible, by all the social ramifications surrounding the law.

In the hands of doctors and scribes, the work of Moses deviates from its purpose. The arid legalism which leads people to prefer the letter of the law to its spirit, leads them to "fasten up packs too heavy to be borne, and lay them on men's shoulders" (Mat. 23. 4).

Then come the prophets, who vie with one another in protesting at this corruption of God's law:

A tender heart wins favour with me, not sacrifice;
God's acknowledging, not victim's destroying (Osee 6. 6).
Oh, but I am sick and tired of them, your solemn feasts;
incense that goes up from your assemblies I can breathe no
    longer! . . .
And like waters rolling in full tide, like a perennial stream,
right and justice shall abound (Amos 5. 21, 24).
Add prayer to prayer, I will not listen;
are not those hands stained with blood?
Wash yourselves clean,
spare me the sight of your busy wickedness,
of your wrong-doing take farewell.
Learn, rather, how to do good,
setting your hearts on justice,
righting the wrong, protecting the orphan,
giving the widow redress (Is. 1. 15–17).
Nay, son of Adam, what need to ask?
Best of all it is, and this above all the Lord demands of thee,
right thou shouldst do,
and truth love,
and carry thyself humbly in the presence of thy God
                                                    (Mich. 6. 8).

They all have the same mission, which is, in a manner of speaking, to teach the people to see the love that is in the law, and to observe the law out of love.

Jesus, in his turn, came both to "bring the law to perfection" (Mat. 5. 17) and to put an end to it. More exactly, he pushes to its utmost limits the observance of the commandments of love. The details of the law are rendered obsolete, they serve no purpose, and they even become an impediment in so far as they come between the heart of man and his God. All this is summed up in the words of the discourse after the Last Supper: "I have a new commandment to give you, that you are to love one another; that your love for one another is to be like the love I have borne you. The mark by which all men will know you for my disciples will be the love you bear one another" (John 13. 34-5); "This is my commandment, that you should love one another, as I have loved you" (John 15. 12).

Jesus is the prototype of the new man, who is commanded "to be perfect, as your heavenly Father is perfect" (Mat. 5. 48). He will create a new community, the Church, the true people of God, whose beginnings, as described by the Acts of the Apostles, show something of this state of perfection: "These occupied themselves continually with the apostles' teaching, their fellowship in the breaking of bread, and the fixed times of prayer. . . . There was one heart and soul in all the company of believers; none of them called any of his possessions his own, everything was shared in common. Great was the power with which the apostles testified to the resurrection of our Lord Jesus Christ, and great was the grace that rested on them all" (Acts 2. 42; 4. 32-3).

Then the initial enthusiasm fades, just as the spirit of the ancient patriarchs had weakened in Egypt. It faded notably when, after the conversion of Constantine, mass baptisms took place almost everywhere. More and more, degrees of fidelity became apparent among those who called themselves Christians. It happened in the Church as it happened about Jesus himself; there were the true disciples and there was the crowd. And then emerged the enormous numbers of semi-Christians, those who trail far behind and have to be dragged along by the rest like a heavy burden. All the same, the Church has one splendid achievement to its name, the large numbers of genuinely holy men and women who rise from her ranks at every moment in history. For confirmation of this we have only to realize that up to the present time there have been something like sixty million martyrs, and an even greater number of people, who, not having the opportunity of dying for Christ, have made an offering of their daily lives instead.

In recent times the Father has put a new desire into our hearts: that of seeing the fervour of the apostolic age restored to the whole community of the Church. St Thérèse of Lisieux came to us to remind us of the supremacy of love and charity over asceticism and all other virtues. Wherever one goes one senses that people are tired of mediocrity, individualism disgusts them, and they feel a need to live in community, sharing the same ideals; lay people are beginning to realize that sanctity is not the monopoly of priests and members of religious orders; the Church is making a considerable effort at renewing itself by simplifying the liturgy and bringing its internal discipline up to date. The time has come for Christ and his Mother to enter into possession of their kingdom; let us play our full part in this renewal which is bringing fresh life to the Church.

(1) *Practices of Obedience: Work*

A man's work is the sphere in which his natural life finds its normal expression—it becomes the expression of the divine life in him for the baptized person tries to carry out the will of God in everything he does. By doing this he develops his filial obedience to God. There is no reason for us to suppose that obedience is the monopoly of members of religious orders; it is required of all Christians, for Christ "accepted an obedience which brought him to death, death on a cross" (Phil. 2. 8), and we say in the prayer he taught us: "Thy will be done." This duty should be taken very seriously, for if we want our own will to be done instead of the will of the Father, we are on the wrong road. Usually we know what is God's will by taking stock of the circumstances and seeing how best we can apply the commandments of the Holy Scriptures and the Church to them. The basis of lay asceticism lies in this: to learn how to interpret circumstances so as to recognize God's will in them, and as soon as it is clear to us, to carry it out with all our hearts.

One mistake we should beware of: to want to obey God

without obeying other men is an error. God delegates his authority to his representatives: fathers of families, heads of State, directors of business concerns, pope, bishop, . . . each in his own sphere. Here are the words of St Paul on the subject: "Every soul must be submissive to its lawful superiors; authority comes from God only, and all authorities that hold sway are of his ordinance. Thus the man who opposes authority is a rebel against the ordinance of God" (Rom. 13. 1-2). Christian obedience finds its dignity in the fact that through his obedience to other men the Christian is obeying God, and he will only accept orders from another for as much as the other can claim to derive his authority from God. Under such conditions, the obedience which binds men together becomes the sacrament of unity, the master who gives the order being the witness that that unity exists, and the orders he gives, the outward, perceptible sign of the will of God.

Even so, obedience on its own is not sufficient to give a spiritual value to our work. We must also make an offering of it, that is to say, the voluntary gift of our work to the Father, so that he may take from it the glory he expects from it. Man's work does not concern himself alone; it is, if he goes about it in the right way, a participation in God's activity of creation. In bringing other men into the world, in giving them the essentials of life, in cultivating the earth so that it can support the largest possible number of God's children in the best possible conditions, man is continuing the work of God. Seen in this way, intellectual or manual labour takes on a great nobility; it recovers the value which the teachings of Holy Writ and the example of Jesus gave to it, but which it does not fail to lose when it gets bogged down in materialism.

(2) *Practices of Affection: Prayer*

When people talk about prayer, the first question they always ask is: "Why should prayer be necessary?" This necessity cannot come from God, for he has no need of anything, whether prayer or anything else. Therefore this necessity comes from us, and is based on the law of human sentiments: we have to *cultivate* those sentiments we wish to have, and *escape* from those we do not wish to have. This word "escape" contains the key to the struggle against all the evil thoughts which invade our minds. These thoughts can be of various kinds, for example thoughts against purity, charity or faith, but in every case they take on an obsessive form: mental images, ideas, fancies and anxieties which keep coming to us in spite of ourselves. That is why, if we attempt to get rid of them by force, by saying: "No, I don't want to!" we will only succeed in strengthening the obsession until it becomes uncontrollable. Our best plan is, therefore, to avoid thinking about it and give our minds something else to occupy them. This is a classic piece of spiritual advice, but all the same it is worth insisting on, for the anxious people to whom it applies have the greatest difficulty in believing it, as they are afraid that by acting in this way they are somehow joining forces with evil. But on the contrary, it is easier to rid oneself of a thought by despising it and refusing to bother with it, than by engaging in direct battle, which is doing it too great an honour. Moreover, one might at least have the grace to admit that a piece of advice which is given by every single one of the spiritual masters, so different from each other in other ways, might have some small chance of being right!

Christian life cannot exist without prayer. Affectionate love is one of its laws: "Thou shalt love the Lord thy God with the love of thy whole heart, and thy whole soul, and thy whole strength" (Deut. 6. 4), and if we do away with prayer in order to indulge in activity, even religious activity, we are being untrue to love.

Work is a way of praising God; we know that; but praising God in a general way is not prayer in the exact meaning of the word. And anyway our work, as soon as it is no longer inspired and strengthened by prayer, would soon cease to be directed towards the Father with all our affection. "Piety," said Pius XII, "just piety is the first, the great apostolate in the Church of Jesus Christ, and anyone who, for the sake of external activity, reduced his practice of it or held it in lesser consideration, would be showing little or no understanding of the essence, the nourishing marrow of Christianity; for this central core of Christ's religion is the union of the soul with God in a love of deeds and of obedience."[1] The man who

---

[1] *La Visita che* (Address to Salesian Cooperators, 12 September 1952). *Acta Apostolicae Sedis*, 44 (1952), p. 777.

wishes to live as a true disciple of Christ, therefore, must always take care to assure that, in the midst of his life—however busy it may be—there are what we may call "spiritual rest-places", which will enable him to recharge his whole activity with the trust, calm and love it will always require.

Christian life is based on the three theological virtues of faith, hope and charity, since these, and these alone lead to the direct union of the soul with God. Certainly, Jesus tells us to practise the moral virtues (see for example Mat. 10. 16), but he did not come to teach us these virtues. His mission was altogether different; he came to bring man a new dimension, so that through him the whole universe should be shot through and permeated by the divine presence and power.

The main purpose of prayer is to cultivate our feeling of love for God. We cultivate a sentiment, of course, by expressing it and by repeating this expression in the same form or in different forms, by exploring the depths of its various meanings, and finding its cause, its extent and its limits. We have to accomplish all this in the practice of religion, and we should keep this objective before us if we do not wish to depart from our purpose. The mistakes we make with regard to prayer, although they may appear to be subtle, all come from our failure to remember certain simple principles which we only have to bear in mind in order to stay on the right road.

There are two kinds of prayer: *collective* prayer, made by several people gathered together, and *private* prayer, said by each one on his own. Both are recommended to us by our Lord: "But when thou art praying, go into thy inner room and shut the door upon thyself, and so pray to thy Father in secret; and then thy Father, who sees what is done in secret, will reward thee" (Mat. 6. 6); and also: "And moreover I tell you, that if two of you agree over any request that you make on earth, it will be granted them by my Father who is in heaven. When two or three are gathered together in my name, I am there in the midst of them" (Mat. 18. 19). Therefore, there is no question of comparing the merits of these two kinds of prayer, or of devoting oneself so exclusively to one kind that one appears to have no use for the other; they must be combined, for each should be a complement to the other.

Collective prayer must naturally be expressed aloud in speech or song; it has to use prearranged forms if it is not to be a cacophony. That being so, the exterior framework matters a good deal. Great care should be taken over the music, the words should be spoken in unison, neither too quickly nor too slowly, and with correct phrasing. It is the care given to all these details that really fills people with a sense of the glory of God. Participation in this communal act of worship demands a certain unselfishness on our part, first of all in a general way, so that we are able to forget ourselves as individuals in order to become a part of the community, sometimes so that we can overcome old habits, and again, in some cases, when we have a special reason for not feeling particularly in harmony with the liturgy of the day; for example, a heart which is overflowing with human happiness hardly feels attuned to the ceremonies of Ash Wednesday! But this abnegation must be freely made, first because it represents an act of charity indispensable to the good of others, and then because we ourselves will reap great benefits from the effort we have made. We get out of collective prayer as much as we put into it.

Collective prayer is called "public" prayer when it is performed in the name of the Church by people consecrated and appointed to do so, for example, canons who recite the Office. We need not deal with this here because this book is written for lay people, but we should like to discuss certain questions concerned with collective prayer. Every human community should pray as a community. For example, let us take a Christian family: what is it that essentially distinguishes it from a non-Christian family? Precisely this existence of family prayers, for if a family does not pray together, it is not a Christian family.

When is the best time for family prayers? In general, once a day, at a time which does not interfere with important activities, such as older children's homework. Very often the best time is after the evening meal. Prayers should be presided over by the head of the family, but it is a good idea for everyone to take an active part, reading certain passages aloud, choosing a hymn, etc. These prayers should be neither too long nor too short, and they should be varied to harmonize with the liturgical cycle. Eccentric or too personal devotions should be avoided, and they should be kept to the main lines of thought suggested by the Church.

A man does not only belong to his family, he belongs to his parish as well. The parish calls its faithful together every Sunday, once, compulsorily, for Mass, and once, optionally, for an evening service. These services demand our whole-hearted participation, so that we may help the clergy to give them all their meaning and all their efficacy. Three hundred years ago it was considered normal for little-instructed people to say their rosary during Mass, which they attended in a purely passive way. Nowadays, when people are better-instructed and more alive to the communal significance of the Mass, the Church rightly asks that they should take a more active part in it.

Sunday raises another problem, whose seriousness it would be hard to exaggerate: it should be the day consecrated to God. Is it really so for all those who consider themselves good Christians? We feel that there is room for a certain amount of doubt on this subject. Do people seriously believe they have respected the Lord's Day when they have "just got in at the Creed", in the middle of a series of largely pagan pleasures, carried to such an excess that by no stretch of the imagination could they possibly be described as Christian? It is a very serious problem indeed, because a man expresses his whole personality in the way he uses his leisure and the way he relaxes from work. If Sunday is a pagan day, that means that our whole civilization has become pagan, whilst a Christian Sunday is the sign of a Christian society. It is also a serious problem because in this respect, in a country like ours, so much has still to be done. Do many people realize that in a great part of our countryside, for example, young people have absolutely no form of entertainment available to them on Sundays? Or that in many towns the only popular recreation available is the cinema, or television? We must at all costs shake off our lethargy and do something about this problem, as about so many others. For we should realize that it is not the priest's responsibility; he did not receive at his ordination the special grace of being an organizer of entertainments and outings. This is the layman's affair, and there is plenty of scope for him to exercise his talents.

As for private prayer, it is simply an intimate conversation with the Father, Jesus, Mary, or the saints. Saint Teresa puts it perfectly: "Mental prayer is nothing else, in my opinion, but being on terms of friendship with God, frequently conversing in secret with Him who, we know, loves us."[1] If we wish to succeed in this exercise, we must take care that love does not disappear from it. This is a thing that can happen very quickly if, instead of talking to God, we simply think about him. Personally, we believe that this error is often committed by consecrated men and women, for, although reflection on the Christian mysteries is the basis and starting point for many prayers, it is not yet prayer itself, which is an exercise of love and a search for the closest possible contact with God. If we forget this, we are liable to slide little by little into pharisaism.

It is a good plan, in the beginning, to stick to definite methods of prayer, for they constitute a useful guide which may save us from many mistakes. But we should be careful that we make use of the methods, and do not become slaves to them, for a time will come when they will have served their purpose and we shall no longer need their help to bring us close to God.

Here are some examples of different methods:

(a) Reading and meditation: You choose a book that is both serious and stimulating and you read a very short passage from it (two or three sentences). Then you think about what you have read, and see what you can learn from it that will help your spiritual life, and what petitions it may suggest to you. You detail these requests for a while. Then, when you feel you have drawn all the meaning from the passage, you go on with the next one, little by little, in the same way.

(b) The contemplation of a scene from the Gospels with the purpose of coming to know our Lord better and to love him more. This method is developed by St Ignatius in his *Spiritual Exercises* and is explained, with slightly different shades of meaning, by St Francis de Sales in his *Introduction to the Devout Life*.[2] It consists in studying all the details in the scene and analysing the words and gestures of all the characters who play a part in it; then one draws from this consideration the material

---

[1] *The Life of St Teresa of Jesus* . . . written by herself, Transl. by David Lewis, Chapter viii, 7, p. 51. London, 1962.
[2] Part II, Chapters 4 and following.

for a personal conversation with the Father, Jesus, Mary. . . .
So, little by little, the atmosphere of the Gospels becomes so
familiar that one's thoughts turn constantly to Jesus and to the
Father.

(c) The repetition of certain very simple thoughts which are
a part of Christian piety, for example: "I love you, my Lord"—
"Lord, forgive me"—"God, have mercy upon me"—"Help me,
Lord".

(d) In a way, the highest form of prayer is that in which
we gaze upon our Lord in silence, with our soul at peace in the
presence of its Beloved. Naturally it brings with it the danger
of distractions, but these can be avoided by concentrating on
a crucifix, or a picture, or else by some verbal prayer said
slowly at the same time.

(e) Another manner of praying is to use the liturgical
prayers found in the missal or the breviary. Here there are
immense riches which are easily available to everyone, since
nowadays there are excellent vernacular translations of all
these texts.

Gradually our souls should grow more and more contemplative. Now, a contemplative is someone who can see God in
nature and in the hearts of his fellow men; as he has realized
a perfect unity within himself, he is equally receptive both to
divine realities and to realities here on earth. He experiences
the beatitude of the "clean of heart" (Mat. 5. 8). We should not
imagine that this state is reserved for a few exceptional beings;
we are all called to it, since Jesus proposed the beatitudes to
all his disciples, and not just to the select group of the apostles.
The catechism of the Council of Trent speaks in the same
vein.[1] Therefore, we should not limit our ambitions with regard
to prayer; the Holy Trinity inhabits our souls, it is only our
lack of purity which prevents us from finding it and rejoicing
in its presence. It is always possible for us to be purified with
the help of grace; we only have to want it deeply and per-
sistently, and when we seriously try, we see that we do not
have to wait long to be rewarded.

[1] Part IV, "De Oratione", No. 362.

Chapter 19

THE LIFE OF PRAYER

Your heart is enough for me. Go, I am with you and do not say a word—Paul Claudel, *The Tidings Brought to Mary*, Act II, Sc. III.[1]

We have seen that our spiritual life needs to be practised, that the love of God within us calls for expression in work and prayer, which in their turn help our love to grow. But if we left it at that we should only have said a fraction of the truth, for we should only have reached the outer shell of reality. So we must go further, and this we shall attempt to do by saying a few words about the life of prayer.

Our prayer can only be the answer given by our love to the love of the Father, and so it must be a complete answer, for one cannot love with only a part of oneself; love takes hold of the entire man and leads him towards the one he loves. Therefore, it is not enough just to say prayers, we have to live a life of prayer—better still, our whole life must become a prayer. So we can reverse the usual procedure, and instead of saying that we pray to God to have our wishes granted, we can say that we pray so that God's wishes may be granted, by the way we live our lives in re-living the *fiat* of Jesus and of Mary. It is not for us to try to bend the will of God to accord with our own, but to follow the divine plan, to become part of it, which means becoming part of God, for his will is inseparable from himself.

When we have clearly seen what the will of God is, we can no longer say "No", for man is made for God, and he has a natural taste for the things of God. If this taste has diminished to the point where it seems to have disappeared altogether, it is because of our sins. But, as we gradually come closer to God, so the gift of wisdom is free to work within us, this wisdom which usually goes hand-in-hand with charity. And so this

[1] London, 1916.

"Yes" of ours is not a question of being simply resigned, it is a wave of love which lifts the whole being up to the Father. In fact this "Yes" completes our attachment to Christ and helps us to rise with him to the Father, because it is in him that the Father calls us.

To love means to take upon oneself the beloved's will and fulfil all his desires, even those he has not expressed. When a married couple really love each other, they anticipate each other's wishes. And so what were two separate wills unite to become one. This is what should happen to us, our will becoming the will of Jesus and of his Father. When one has reached this stage, anything can be endured for the other's sake: Jesus was only able to endure his agony in the garden because his will was entirely united to that of his Father: "What I do is always what pleases him" (John 8. 29). "As Christ comes into the world, he says, No sacrifice, no offering was thy demand; thou hast endowed me, instead, with a body. Thou hast not found any pleasure in burnt sacrifices, in sacrifices for sin. See then, I said, I am coming to fulfil what is written of me, where the book lies unrolled; to do thy will, O my God" (Heb. 10. 5-7).

The man who tries to do God's will all through his life eventually reaches a point where he prays with his whole being. It is as if he became a call to love, a magnet, so powerful that he attracts the Holy Spirit to his soul, just as Mary did long ago: "The Holy Spirit will come upon thee, and the power of the most High will overshadow thee" (Luke 1. 35). Because this man's life "is hidden away now with Christ in God" (Col. 3. 3) without his having left the world, we can say that in him God's will is established on earth, and uses him as a sort of spiritual lever. It does not matter whether such a person is enclosed in a Carmelite convent like St Thérèse of Lisieux or whether he dies in a concentration camp like Father Kolbe; his life is of incalculable value to millions of people. He, like Jesus, has become a living "witness" to the Father (Apoc. 1. 5; 3. 14) and he can really help in the redemption.

His prayer is a direct relationship with the Father, made up of silence, calm and meditation. With all his strength the man of prayer contemplates the will of God, and makes an effort of his whole being so that he, and others as well, can give it

their full obedience. Then, religion is achieved,[1] the miracle
has happened; he has fully encountered Christ's love; he
thinks, speaks, and acts "through him, and with him, and in
him".[2] He is filled with sanctity and joy, for he lives in the
closest contact with the Holy Trinity.

Indeed, if the love of the Father is within us, it is, says
St Paul, "poured out in our hearts by the Holy Spirit, whom we
have received" (Rom. 5. 5), and he adds: "Only, as before,
the Spirit comes to the aid of our weakness; when we do not
know what prayer to offer, to pray as we ought, the Spirit
himself intercedes for us, with groans beyond all utterance:
and God, who can read our hearts, knows well what the
Spirit's intent is; for indeed it is according to the mind of God
that he makes intercession for the saints" (ibid. 8. 26–7). This
leads us to a most moving discovery: we never have to pray
alone. We pray in Christ, under the influence of the Holy
Spirit, and with all our fellow men; that is why all the petitions
of the *Our Father* are made in the plural.

Because of this our prayers are sure to be answered, for,
taken up by the Church and by Christ, they become part of
that prayer of Jesus in which he says: "I know that thou hearest
me at all times" (John 11. 42). "When that is said, what
follows? Who can be our adversary, if God is on our side? He
did not even spare his own Son, but gave him up for us all; and
must not that gift be accompanied by the gift of all else?"
(Rom. 8. 31–2).

To pray means to contribute to the glory of the Father by an
exchange of *fiats*. We say "Yes" to God, he will reply "Yes"
to us. The Father's will is to fulfil his children's needs, and he
knows what these are: "Your heavenly Father knows well what
your needs are before you ask him" (Mat. 6. 8). So we need not
worry or feel that we have to give him the information![3] But
God's love looks for a point of contact with us. His desire is to
give, and he can only do so if we are, so to speak, on his wave-

---

[1] Religion probably comes from *religare*, to bind, and means the bond
between God and men.
[2] Canon of the Mass.
[3] "We need to pray to God, not in order to make known to Him our
needs or desires, but that we ourselves may be reminded of the necessity
of having recourse to God's help in these matters." *Summa Theologica*, II*
II*, 83, 2, ad 1.

G

length. What we have to do is always to be ready to receive the gift of God. Any prayer that remains unanswered is a prayer that somehow has met with an obstacle at our end. God's love makes its proposal all right, even risking our rejection and disdain. The Father begs us to give him our prayer.

The answer we make, if it is complete and sincere, goes straight to the Father's heart and touches him deeply, because by praying in this way we are entirely transformed into pure desire for his love. All we want is the beloved; he is everything we need. We must learn to let this desire for him grow within us. We should ask from God nothing but God, from Love nothing but Love. Does this mean that we are asking for everything? It does; so we will give everything we have in exchange.[1] "Consider not thyself as mean, neither pay heed to the crumbs which fall from thy Father's table. Go thou forth from them and glory in thy glory. Hide thee therein and rejoice, and thou shalt have the desires of thy heart."[2] Jesus gives us, he surrenders to us, his body, his blood, his soul, his divinity, everything: "If thou knewest what it is God gives" (John 4. 10). The Father gives so that I too shall give to him, for the joy of love is in exchange. In the *Our Father* we think of him first:

Hallowed be thy name;
thy kingdom come;
thy will be done,
on earth as it is in heaven (Mat. 6. 9–10),

before we ask for our daily bread and the forgiveness of our sins. And when the Father answers, he turns towards his beloved child and gives him the grace to live more completely as his son, "sharing the inheritance of Christ" (Rom. 8. 17).

The virginity of Mary is an example of a supremely effective prayer. Going against the popular opinion of her day, which held that the only fulfilment of woman was in marriage and childbearing, she was able to understand that God's love for human beings is so great that he can sometimes ask them that their body shall never be given to anyone else. Seen in this

---

[1] "Give all for all." *Imitation of Christ*, 3, 37, 5.
[2] *The Complete Works of St John of the Cross*, Vol. iii, "Spiritual Sentences and Maxims", p. 222. London, 1953.

way, virginity means a giving of the whole self to God whom
we love. There is a completeness and so a kind of purity about
this love which, because it wants to belong entirely to the
beloved, can never in any way be shared with any other.
Consecrated by a vow which assures its unchanging fidelity, it
becomes a kind of spiritual marriage with God.[1] Indeed, really
virgin souls have a very special power over the one to whom
they have unreservedly given themselves. We should, therefore,
ask Mary, to whom such great power has been given, to let us
share in the fruit of her virginity, so that every one of our
prayers, by increasing the life of Christ within us, will renew
and continue the mystery which began long ago with the
incarnation of the Son of God in her womb.

[1] Cf. Pius XII, Encyclical *Sacra Virginitas*, 25 March 1954. [Engl. tr. in
American Ecclesiastical Review, No. 131, July 1954; *Catholic Documents*, XV,
see pp. 26–7.]

Chapter 20

THE MYSTERY OF THE CROSS

This sign of the cross shall be in heaven when the Lord shall come to execute judgement—Roman Breviary, 14 September.

Jesus did not only come down from heaven to reveal the Father to us and to save the world,[1] he also came "to give his life as a ransom for the lives of many" (Mat. 20. 28). This gift of his life, in the midst of terrible sufferings, is the Mystery of the Cross, with its infinite wealth of meaning, for it is a sacrifice whose greatness is a compensation to God for the wrong done to him by men: "He suffered for your sakes, and left you his own example; you were to follow in his footsteps" (I Peter 2. 21); a proof of his love for the Father: "The world must be convinced that I love the Father" (John 14. 31), and of his love for us: "God has proved his love to us by laying down his life for our sakes" (I John 3. 16), and of supreme obedience: "He dispossessed himself, and took the nature of a slave, fashioned in the likeness of men, and presenting himself to us in human form; and then he lowered his own dignity, accepted an obedience which brought him to death, death on a cross" (Phil. 2. 7–8); all this is to be found in his Passion, and it has that infinite value, inexpressible in ordinary terms, which is conferred on everything he does by the fact that he is God.

In this book we prefer to contemplate this mystery rather than to analyse it from a purely theological point of view. In this way we shall approach it as closely as we can, and this will help us to understand it and encourage us to study it more deeply. There are two aspects in particular for us to consider:

An Aspect of Life and Death

"This my Father loves in me, that I am laying down my

[1] Cf. Chapter 10, "The Testimony of Christ".

life, to take it up again afterwards. Nobody can rob me of it; I lay it down of my own accord. I am free to lay it down, free to take it up again; that is the charge which my Father has given me" (John 10. 17–18).

This perspective is symbolized in the miracle of the raising of Lazarus from the dead, the most sensational miracle in all the Gospels (John 11. 1–44). The attitude of Jesus during this episode is somewhat surprising, and for this reason it is revealing. For "Jesus loved Martha, and her sister, and Lazarus" (v. 5), and when he was told: "Lord, he whom thou lovest lies here sick", in spite of the absolute trust in him shown by this solemn and poignant appeal, he did not seem to respond to it, but stayed on for two days in the place where he was. Then he said: "Let us go back into Judaea", not to Bethany, as if he had forgotten all about his friend. All the same he was indeed thinking of him, and he clearly said to his disciples: "Lazarus is dead. And for your sakes, I am glad I was not there; it will help you to believe." Therefore, his delay was deliberate, he intended his unfortunate friend to die; thus he anticipates what his Father does for him, a few days later: he seems to have abandoned him, just because he wants him, for the sake of his love, to go through death and the tomb so that he can rejoice in the glory of the Resurrection and the possession of a new life: "I love you, that is why I send you the cross. I love you, that is why I send you to the cross."[1]

Christianity is not and never will be a cheap consolation or a mere easy means of comfort; it is an ennoblement of man. It is not concerned with merely mending human life, but with raising it up to share in the life of God; this is what Jesus wants us to understand; he wants to inspire his disciples and his friends with such a trust in him that it will survive even death.

When he had nearly reached Bethany, he saw Martha coming to meet him, showing amazement at his behaviour and throwing reproaches in his face: "Lord, said Martha to Jesus, if thou hadst been here, my brother would not have died; and I know well that even now God will grant whatever thou wilt ask of him" (vv. 21–2). This is faith of a kind, and it is real faith, but it is not enough. Jesus does not need to ask his Father for anything, he has already received all he could wish for:

[1] Fr Livragne, manuscript notes.

"Just as the Father bids the dead rise up and gives them life, so the Son gives life to whomsoever he will" (John 5. 21). And so in the presence of the tomb, he does not ask God for anything, but thanks him for what he has received. But in order to make use of his supreme prerogative—the gift of life—and in such solemn circumstances, he demands a fully lucid faith in his divinity: "I am the resurrection and life; he who believes in me, though he is dead, will live on, and whoever has life, and has faith in me, to all eternity cannot die. Dost thou believe this?" These words underline the meaning of the miracle. Just as, before he restored sight to the man born blind, he had said: "As long as I am in the world, I am the world's light" (John 9. 5), now, at this moment, he proclaims: "I am the resurrection", before bringing the dead man back to life. It is not only a miracle, it is teaching in deed. Because of the gravity of what was to follow, and because he knew that the culminating point of the revelation of his Person had been reached, he was twice seen to sigh deeply. . . .

Like Martha, we all need to reach this total faith: "When a man is in Christ Jesus, there has been a new creation" (Gal. 6. 15), and we must accept this transformation even at the price of death. The Father only allows death in order to bring to life again, he only lays low in order to raise up again.

An Aspect of Suffering

"No man has ever gone up into heaven; but there is one who has come down from heaven, the Son of Man, who dwells in heaven. And this Son of Man must be lifted up, as the serpent was lifted up by Moses in the wilderness; so that those who believe in him may not perish, but have eternal life" (John 3. 13–15). This is why, at the beginning of his ministry, in the meeting with Nicodemus, Jesus speaks of the necessity of his suffering and enduring the cross (in the legal parlance of Rome, "to lift up" meant "to crucify"). Later he returned to the subject again, when speaking to the disciples of Emmaus: "Was it not to be expected that the Christ should undergo these sufferings, and so enter into his glory?" (Luke 24. 26). There is, therefore, no question of death pure and simple, but of the death of a man chastised, a death which will only come

after a whole series of unthinkable tortures and humiliations—
the Son of God between two thieves!

What credence for such news as ours?
Whom reaches it, this new revelation of the Lord's strength?
He will watch this servant of his appear among us,
unregarded as brushwood shoot,
as a plant in waterless soil;
no stateliness here, no majesty, no beauty,
as we gaze upon him, to win our hearts.
Nay, here is one despised, left out of all human reckoning;
bowed with misery, and no stranger to weakness;
how should we recognize that face?
How should we take any account of him, a man so despised?
Our weakness, and it was he who carried the weight of it,
our miseries, and it was he who bore them.
A leper, so we thought of him,
a man God had smitten and brought low;
and all the while it was for our sins he was wounded,
it was guilt of ours crushed him down;
on him the punishment fell that brought us peace,
by his bruises we were healed.
Strayed sheep all of us,
each following his own path;
and God laid on his shoulders our guilt,
the guilt of us all.
A victim? Yet he himself bows to the stroke;
no word comes from him.
Sheep led away to the slaughter-house,
lamb that stands dumb while it is shorn;
no word from him.
Imprisoned, brought to judgement, and carried off,
he, whose birth is beyond our knowing;
numbered among the living no more!
Be sure it is for my people's guilt I have smitten him.
Takes he leave of the rich, the godless, to win but a grave,
to win but the gift of death;
he, that wrong did never,
nor had treason on his lips! (Is. 53. 1-9).

Now Jesus is obliged to accept all this because "the world
must be convinced that I love the Father, and act only as the
Father has commanded me to act" (John 14. 31) and to give
those he was leaving behind him "the uttermost proof of his

love" (John 13. 1). This double love, for mankind and for his Father, was what led him to crucifixion and death.

Jesus is not only a God incarnate, he is also a crucified Messiah, and this is an essential part of his life on earth: "I have only reached this hour of trial that I might undergo it" (John 12. 27). His image and his message to the world would be seriously distorted if we attempted to remove the Passion from them; this has always been a temptation, and how strong it is in our present day! We are ready to accept the mystery of the incarnation, but refuse that of the redemption through the cross.

We shall now attempt to go more deeply into this disconcerting necessity of Christ's suffering. The first thing we notice is that if ever a prophet had everything in his favour in order to succeed, then Christ was the one:

When he spoke, says St Luke (4. 22), his hearers "were astonished at the gracious words which came from his mouth"; so then, people did like him instinctively.

"He taught them . . . like one who had authority," says St Matthew, after the Sermon on the Mount (7. 29) and this came, no doubt, not only because he used expressions such as: "Moses has said to you, and now I say", but also because his words had an eloquence and a ring of truth which convinced his hearers.

He worked many miracles, always for the benefit of those who heard him, and frequently as direct reinforcement of his teaching; for example, the episode of the man in St Luke who was palsied, the one they let down on his bed from the roof-top because of the crowds (5. 17–26). Jesus begins by forgiving him his sins, thus scandalizing the scribes and Pharisees as he did in the case of the poor sinful woman; his reply was: "Which command is more lightly given, to say, Thy sins are forgiven thee, or to say, Rise up and walk? And now, to convince you that the Son of Man has power to forgive sins while he is on earth (here he spoke to the palsied man), I tell thee, rise up, take thy bed with thee and go home." And as soon as he spoke these words the sick man was cured.

He prayed—at length: for three-quarters of the night after the first multiplication of loaves (Mark 6. 46ff.), and for a whole night before he made the choice of his apostles (Luke

6. 12ff), and again, at the raising of Lazarus: "Father, I thank thee for hearing my prayer. For myself, I know that thou hearest me at all times" (John 11. 41–2).

And in spite of all this, he did not succeed. He died abandoned by nearly everyone, attended only by his mother, one single disciple, and a few poor women. Not one of the people for whom he had wrought miracles came forward to attempt to save him in the tribunal of Pontius Pilate. The crowd followed him for a while, but displayed an inability to grasp what he was talking about which we find quite disturbing. After the cure of the palsied man, St Luke goes on to say: "Astonishment came over them all, and they praised God, full of awe; We have seen strange things, they said, today" (Luke 5. 26). Is this not heartbreaking? To reply to such a display of goodness and loving-kindness with nothing but open-mouthed amazement and fear, and to dismiss it with the kind of remark one might expect to hear after a circus performance! There was no question of their following this Christ with all their hearts. Worse still: at the moment he made them his most loving promise, that of the Eucharist, many disciples chose to leave him: "This is strange talk, who can be expected to listen to it?" (John 6. 61). Finishing his story of the public life of the Master, St John writes with infinite sadness: "Such great miracles he did in their presence, and still they did not believe in him" (John 12. 37).

But his death, by contrast, made way for the success of the Church: "Yes, if only I am lifted up from the earth, I will attract all men to myself" (John 12. 32). After Pentecost, the first sermons of St Peter reached the hearts of thousands of men and converted them (Acts 2. 41; 4. 4). Some thirty years later, Christian communities had been founded in about half the Mediterranean area, sufficiently well rooted to be able to face the beginnings of persecution: "Believe me when I tell you this; a grain of wheat must fall into the ground and die, or else it remains nothing more than a grain of wheat; but if it dies, then it yields rich fruit" (John 12. 24). "Jesus himself", says St Augustine, "was the grain of wheat which had to die so that it could multiply; he was put to death by the lack of faith among the Jews, and he is multiplied in the faith of many nations."[1]

---

[1] St Augustine, *Tractatus in Ioannem*, 59, 1.

G*

Furthermore, in spite of its painful nature, the mystery of the cross is beloved of Christ, and he will not allow us to separate him from it. Let us re-read the scene in the Gospel according to St Matthew (16. 16 ff.): Peter has just proclaimed his faith in his Master: "Thou art the Christ, the Son of the living God", to which Jesus replies: "Thou art Peter, and it is upon this rock that I will build my church; and the gates of hell shall not prevail against it; and I will give to thee the keys of the kingdom of heaven; and whatever thou shalt bind on earth shall be bound in heaven, and whatever thou shalt loose on earth shall be loosed in heaven." Then he goes on to speak of his future trials, of his death and resurrection, and Peter, no doubt full of pride at being promoted head of the Church, draws him aside: "Never, Lord, he said; no such thing shall befall thee," Jesus answers with incredible violence: "Back, Satan; thou art a stone in my path; for these thoughts of thine are man's, not God's." "Satan" means "adversary", and any man who tries to bar his way, attempting to force him off the road marked for him by his Father, is his adversary; particularly when the vital importance of the cross is at stake.

Nonetheless this mystery shocks people, and not only the Jews; the Gospels note that on several occasions when Jesus spoke of it, the disciples did not understand what he was talking about: "They could make nothing of all this; his meaning was hidden from them, so they could not understand what he said" (Luke 18. 34). No doubt they assumed that he was speaking metaphorically or was using hyperbole, to describe the trials he was to endure. What is so surprising about there being difficult times in the life of the Messiah? Did not David and all the great ones of Israel have difficult times as well? But it was quite impossible for the apostles to have any idea of the catastrophe of Calvary, where the whole life's work of Jesus seemed to collapse into the irreparable and total failure of death without glory, accepted without a struggle and even without any resistance at all, added to his abandonment by all his disciples during his agony in the garden: "And now all his disciples abandoned him, and fled" (Mat. 26. 56). Peter fails his Master twice; first when he does not understand him in the scene we have been discussing, and secondly by denying him at the critical moment.

And we in our turn are shocked, because now we are the ones who have to live the mystery of the cross, and really live it, for suffering is part of every human destiny. Whenever suffering comes our way, our reaction is always to take flight, literally if we can; if not, by mentally shutting our eyes to it.

Camus describes this attitude very well in his book *The Plague*: the doctor is called to the bedside of a sick girl; in front of her mother, he turns back the sheet; the symptoms of the scourge are so appallingly evident that there is no need for him to give a diagnosis. And yet outside the room the mother has just said: "Oh, I do hope it's not the fever everyone's talking about."[1]

When serious suffering descends upon us it always presents a problem and a mystery; these are an inseparable part of it. Even if we have thought about it seriously, trying to be realistic about it, it makes no difference; for the day it actually happens, we are still faced with the same difficulty, which will have to be solved anew by prayer, by love, and by the contemplation of the sufferings of Christ. Only when we reach the summit of mystical union can we attain complete serenity. To understand this, we shall now examine Jesus' attitude to pain and sorrow.

First of all, with regard to his own suffering, Jesus did not live in any state of rarefied detachment; therefore, even the highest degree of sanctity will give us no immunity to human pain and anguish, otherwise the Saviour would not have been able to pronounce the beatitude of those who mourn.

About a year before it took place, thinking of his Passion, he exclaimed: "There is a baptism I must needs be baptized with, and how impatient am I for its accomplishment!" (Luke 12.50). In these words we sense his anguish, and at the same time his impatience[2] to grapple with the decisive moment.

But a few days before it actually happens, on the day of his triumphal entry into Jerusalem, his tone changes: "And now my soul is distressed. What am I to say? I will say, Father, save me from undergoing this hour of trial; and yet, I have only reached this hour of trial that I might undergo it. Father, make

[1] Albert Camus, *The Plague*, Part 2, 2 (end). [Engl. tr. by Stuart Gilbert, p. 76. Harmondsworth, 1960 (later reprints).]
[2] According to Fr Lebreton, *Tu Solus Sanctus*, footnote p. 35, the Greek expression used by the evangelist implies an ardent and anxious desire.

thy name known" (John 12. 27–8). All trace of impatience has gone, and all that is left is his distress, which is only overcome with difficulty by his desire to submit to his Father's will. In the end, at the very moment that the suffering breaks upon him, he cries out in agony: "Father, if it pleases thee, take away this chalice from before me; only as thy will is, not as mine is" (Luke 22. 42). Jesus only just has the strength to cling to his Father's wishes. At this moment he shows that he is a true man like ourselves; not remote or distant, but sharing all our human sorrows: "It is not as if our high priest was incapable of feeling for us in our humiliations; he has been through every trial, fashioned as we are, only sinless" (Hebrews 4. 15).

With regard to the suffering of others, Jesus has only one attitude, that of compassion and healing. It is, in fact, one of the most noticeable traits of his character, that he responds so swiftly to the calls of sorrow and suffering, even if he has to perform a miracle to do so. People have only to come to him with their illnesses and infirmities and, providing they have faith, he cures them at once, usually at the moment of asking, and in some cases without even waiting to be asked. Considering the way that he behaved, it is as if he could not bear to see a man in suffering, and yet people say that Christianity likes to make people suffer! Does not the Master in fact order the disciples he sends out before him to the places he is to visit, to "heal those who are sick" (Luke 10. 9), and does not the Church begin all her missionary work by building hospitals and orphanages?

But the question still remains, and people ask how the Father, so good and kind that "instead of passing judgement on any man himself, [he] has left all judgement to the Son" (John 5. 22), how the same Father who forgives the prodigal son, could have chosen the sufferings of his own child as a redemption of our sin? Certainly not because of any mysterious joy in watching others suffering; but we may suggest three possible reasons:

(1) In every kind of sin there is some form of self-gratification: the obvious pleasure of the senses, and the more subtle intellectual pleasure like that which caused the downfall of Renan, and nearly that—so they say—of St Jerome; but in every case it is still self-gratification. If we admit that repara-

tion must be made for sin, not only in the sense that we must re-direct our headstrong wills and make our peace with the Father, but also in the sense that the damage done must be made good—if we admit this, then there is only one thing possible for us to do: to replace the excess of selfish pleasure by an excess of suffering, in order to restore the balance. With this in mind we may care to meditate upon the words of St Thomas Aquinas: "Christ willed to deliver the human race from sins not merely by His power, but also according to justice. And therefore He did not simply weigh what great virtue His suffering would have from union with the Godhead, but also how much, according to His human nature, His pain would avail for so great a satisfaction."[1]

(2) If we accept suffering in a spirit of love and without rebelling against it, it will, in the end, detach us from ourselves; in this way suffering evokes in the person it visits an attitude which is the very opposite of sin.

(3) The acceptance of suffering at the hands of those we love is a proof of our love, perhaps also a mysterious necessity, for are there not moments in all our lives when we feel like saying, with Claudel's hero: "We are too happy, and the others not happy enough. . . . I am weary of being happy"?[2]

Now let us take a look at the sufferings of the Passion: we cannot go through them all, but we will take the beginning and the end:

In the beginning there is the agony, the struggle between the human will of Jesus which recoils from suffering, and the will of the Father which he has to accept and which requires that he should endure the trial of the cross. It is a conflict between his love for sinful humanity—a love so powerful that he is closely united to all his unfortunate brethren and shares with them the fate they have deserved: St Paul says that "for our sake [God] made him to be sin" (II Cor. 5. 21)[3]—and that other love, the love which binds him to the Father, who is Holiness and Justice. He sees himself before the divine tribunal, entirely alone and covered with the stain of our sins; he sees the heavenly court turning away from him in horror; he feels himself trampled in "the wine-press of God's anger" (Apoc.

---

[1] *Summa Theologica*, III[a], 46, 6, ad 6.
[2] *The Tidings Brought to Mary*, Act I, Scene 1. [Engl. tr., pp. 33, 35.]
[3] [Revised Standard Version.—*Translator*.]

14. 19), and the conflict becomes so violent that "his sweat fell to the ground like thick drops of blood" (Luke 22. 44); and so an angel—was it perhaps Gabriel, the "Might of God"?—had to be sent down to give him courage. The King of Angels is sustained by one of his subjects, the Son of God by one of God's creatures; it was as if the Father himself refused to intervene directly.

Passing over all the intermediate stages, we arrive at the foot of the cross, where Jesus is dying. His body is stretched to its limits; it has to be, otherwise the convulsions of pain would tear his hands and feet from the nails which hold him. Every compulsive jerk of his body pulls on his wounds and increases the pain of them; he is seized with cramp in his arms and legs and all his muscles, those of the trunk as well, so that no part of him is spared. This body is now one single living wound: the furrows left by the flagellation, the weight of the cross and its lacerations have raised blood from nearly the whole surface of his flesh. He is covered with dust. He is shaken with extremes of burning fever; pouring sweat and glacial chill; he is overcome by an abominable feeling of vertigo: with the feeling of falling, first forwards, then backwards. But his wounds hold him up. His head has suffered the ravages of the crown of thorns. Their points have worked their way under the skin, right against the skull. He is almost sightless but his eyes register the spasms of pain. From his lips comes a continuous moaning sound, intermingled with occasional sobs of pain; and Mary, standing beneath him, hears his groans and notices —with what anguish—that they are growing fainter and fainter, showing the approach of death. Then come his last words: "Woman, this is thy son", and to John: "This is thy mother"; the pardon of the good thief: "I promise thee, this day thou shalt be with me in Paradise". Then: "My God, my God, why hast thou forsaken me?"—"I am thirsty"—"It is achieved"—"Father, into thy hands I commend my spirit"; and suddenly lifting his head, Jesus gives a great cry terrible to hear, a cry that tore the veil of the temple down the middle, made the earth tremble, and brought the dead from their graves. Then his head drops forward again, it is over; he has given up his spirit.[1]

[1] We have followed the order of M. J. Lagrange, o.p., in *The Gospel of Jesus Christ*, Vol. ii, pp. 267–73. London, 1938.

He had served his time of humanity;
He was leaving the prison for the home of glory;
He was returning to his father's house. . . .
Like a tired traveller at the last hours of his journey,
He saw his home. . . .
He was like a son at the last hours of his day;
His father was waiting for him to embrace him at last;
An eternal kiss would lave his unsullied side;
A fatherly kiss would lave his unsullied brow;
An eternal kiss from his father would lave his smarting
  wounds,
Would refresh his smarting wounds,
And his head, and his side, and his feet, and his hands. . . .
A fatherly kiss would descend on his brow. . . .
The task was over and the work was done.
He had served his time of humanity.
The angels awaited him to celebrate his day.[1]

Now the phase of suffering humanity is over for Jesus; soon will come that of honourable burial, then the day after, the resurrection in joy and glory, and soon the ascension and his coronation for an eternal reign. The defeat and degradation of the cross lasted for one day, but his victory is without flaw and without end

All the same, even if he has accomplished his task, if "Christ, now he has risen from the dead, cannot die any more" (Rom. 6. 9), now it is the turn of his Mystical Body to go through the same experience; each one of us must, like St Paul, "help to pay off the debt which the afflictions of Christ still leave to be paid, for the sake of his body, the Church" (Col. 1. 24). We are all of us called to follow him in everything, and therefore to be hung on the cross with him.

Suffering has never ceased to be redeeming, from the time he endured it and consecrated it by his torture and death; going further than that we may say that at any given moment the greater the sufferings the world offers up, the greater and the fuller the redemption that is bestowed on it. We say "offers up" deliberately, for what redeems us is not suffering as such, but suffering for love's sake. Nowadays, if we remark on the

[1] Charles Péguy, *The Mystery of the Charity of Joan of Arc.* [Translated by Julian Green, London, 1950, pp. 94-6.]

increase and development of spiritual life within the Church, it can mostly certainly be attributed to the enormous mass of suffering offered up all over the world by innumerable martyrs and voluntary penitents, and by all those legions of people who, in one way or another, give their lives for the Kingdom of God: "Powerful is suffering when it is as voluntary as sin,"[1] says Violaine. And this is what will always be the final explanation of Christianity as well as its highest justification: united to the Passion of Jesus, suffering acquires an incomparable efficacy in attracting graces from God and in adding to the growth of the Mystical Body. Suffering can always be of use, for even that of small children who are too young to make a conscious gift of it is offered up by their parents and by the Church; all that is necessary is not to say "No", and not even the smallest particle of it will be wasted.

We should add that the personal perfection of each individual soul necessitates the journey along the same painful way. Ever since original sin, we cannot be united to God without suffering, for purity cannot unite itself with what is impure without first transforming it, and that cannot happen without suffering. But by accepting it, we make ourselves very pleasing to the Father, who responds by giving us more abundant graces.

When someone consents to pass through long and difficult trials, when he says "Yes" with love in his heart, then, little by little, like Jesus, he becomes a victim offered for the salvation of the world; then everything is changed for him, and he can say, again with Violaine: "Where I am, there is patience, not sorrow. The world's grief is great."[2] And then at last, in the depths of his shattered being, he finds a new meaning in the incarnation, an increased awareness of the world's needs, and a new compassion for his fellow men. This is the sign of good suffering: that it does not embitter a man, but opens his heart to other people and to life.

Sufferings which are not offered up and cannot be—those of sin—have no redeeming power; they have no other significance for the unhappy creature who experiences them, than that they are a foretaste of the hell he is preparing for himself.

For us, there is a bad suffering, or rather a bad way of using

---

[1] *The Tidings Brought to Mary*, Act III, Scene III. [Engl. tr., p. 112.]
[2] *The Tidings Brought to Mary*, Act IV, Scene III. [Engl. tr., p. 135.]

good suffering: everything which shuts us up within ourselves and becomes a matter of pride; and there is a good suffering: all voluntary penance and all trials sent to us which are accepted with love. There is also an excellent suffering: that which increases our desire to unite ourselves with Christ for the redemption of our fellow men.

"The whole life of Christ was a cross and a martyrdom."[1] So if one day we are visited by suffering, we should not feel sorry for ourselves; the Father is treating us exactly as he treated his own beloved Son.

[1] *Imitation of Christ*, 2, 12, 7.

Chapter 21

BROTHERLY LOVE

*How can the man who has no love have any knowledge of God,
since God is love?*—1 John 4. 8.

Brotherly love is the natural consequence of all that we have
been discussing in the preceding chapters. It is one of the
marks of the spirit of Christ, it is an exercise of our love for the
Father, it is the expression and the incarnation of our spiritual
life, and it is one of the means of making us abandon our self-
centredness and act accordingly.

The first Christians referred to each other as "brothers"
spontaneously, the Acts of the Apostles tell us that "there was
one heart and soul in all the company of believers" (Acts 4. 32).
Later on, when the pagans saw the communities which were
formed by the disciples of Jesus, they exclaimed: "See how they
love one another."[1] In this way the early Christians accomplished the words of the Master: "The mark by which all men
will know you for my disciples will be the love you bear one
another" (John 13. 35).

On account of the misconceptions and serious errors of our
time, we must at once add that brotherly love is not the whole
of Christianity, nor even the most important element; the love
of God occupies first place, as the Church has constantly
reminded us. Pius XII in 1947 wrote: "The ideal of the
Christian life is the close and uninterrupted union of everyone
with God."[2]

But although brotherly love is not the whole of Christianity,

---

[1] Tertullian, *Apologeticus*, 39. It is interesting to remember that these
famous words expressed no admiration for the Christians. On the contrary
the pagans were mocking the Christians for what seemed to them a sign
of weakness. This is enough to show us the progress that Christianity and
its morality brought to the world.

[2] Pius XII, Encyclical *Mediator Dei*. [Engl. tr., *Christian Worship*, C.T.S.,
1947, p. 57, No. 146.]

it is an indispensable part of it, because it forms the logical outcome of all the rest. It is also the most visible part, it is so noticeable that one finishes by judging the rest by it alone. This is not a false criterion, it is based on a perfectly true principle: where there is no brotherly love there is no real filial love either. "If a man boasts of loving God, while he hates his own brother, he is a liar. He has seen his brother, and has no love for him; what love can he have for the God he has never seen?" (I John 4. 20).

The apostles did not consider that brotherly love replaced the other virtues, but that it contained them and gave them form and consistency: "After all, the whole of the law is summed up in one phrase: Thou shalt love thy neighbour as thyself" (Gal. 5. 14), and: "Do not let anybody have a claim upon you, except the claim that binds us to love one another. The man who loves his neighbour has done all that the law demands. (All the commandments, Thou shalt not commit adultery, Thou shalt not murder, Thou shalt not steal, Thou shalt not bear false witness, Thou shalt not covet, and the rest, are resumed in this one saying, Thou shalt love thy neighbour as thyself.) Love of our neighbour refrains from doing harm of any kind: that is why it fulfils all the demands of the law" (Rom. 13. 8–10). And St John says: "It is the man who loves his brother that lives in light; no fear of stumbling haunts him" (I John 2. 10). Let us remember also the famous passage from the First Epistle to the Corinthians: "Charity is patient, is kind; charity feels no envy; charity is never perverse or proud, never insolent; does not claim its rights, cannot be provoked, does not brood over an injury; takes no pleasure in wrong-doing, but rejoices at the victory of truth; sustains, believes, hopes, endures, to the last" (13. 4–7).

Many people find it difficult to understand how it is that all the other virtues can be contained in charity. The reason is that, as we have said before, sin always has repercussions on society, and sooner or later it affects our neighbour. Clearly therefore, perfect charity, by allowing nothing that could in any way harm others, removes all evil from our hearts. Of course this result is only achieved by that perfect charity which reigns so completely in a man that it inspires every one of his actions; it would be naïve to think that one is exempt from sin because one has been particularly generous in giving alms or because one is normally kind and helpful. However, brotherly love that is not "in word, nor in tongue, but in deed, and in truth" (I John 3. 18) will "persuade our hearts. For if our heart reprehend us, God is greater than our heart, and knoweth all things" (ibid. 19–20).[1] St John shows us here that our love for others is a clear symptom of the state of our souls, and that it can reassure us if we become worried on this subject. We feel that this is a principle which should be much more widely used in the direction of souls who are tormented by scruples or by spiritual trials.

"Love is the only thing that distinguishes the children of God from the children of the devil. They may all sign themselves with the sign of the cross of Christ; they may all answer, Amen; they may all sing, Alleluia; they may all be baptized, come to church, build up the walls of the basilicas; the only thing that distinguishes the children of God from the children of the devil is love. They that have love are born of God, they that have not love, are not born of God. A striking sign, a striking distinction! You may have what you like: if this one thing is missing, all the rest is of no avail; but if you lack all the rest and have nothing but love, you have fulfilled the law."[2]

Brotherly love stems from our love for the Father, just as, in a human family, the love between brothers and sisters comes from their common love for their parents. "Beloved, let us love one another; love springs from God; no one can love without being born of God, and knowing God. Beloved, if God has shewn such love to us, we too must love one another" (I John 4. 7 & 11).

Filial love that is really genuine automatically leads to brotherly love, which explains why, as soon as there are a number of men who love the Father, a community is formed, and if this fails to happen, one can be certain that their apparent piety is an illusion. Jesus, whose whole being is filled with filial love, gives himself as a model for brotherly love: "I have a new commandment to give you, that you are to love one another; that your love for one another is to be like the love I have borne you" (John 13. 34). The host in our tabernacles

---

[1] [Douay Version.—*Translator*.]
[2] St Augustine, *Tractatus in Epistolam Ioannis*, 5, 7.

is there to *give* us Christ, not to *show* him to us; all we see in the host is a piece of white unleavened bread. It is in Christians that Christ wants to appear, in all of us who are members of his Mystical Body, prolongations of his being as the branches are of the vine. His desire will be fulfilled if we show in all our actions that we do not consider ourselves as isolated beings but as individuals who are organically attached to one another, and among whom there is a mutual love strong enough to form a living community.

In the world of today where so many people have reverted to pagan values, and become blasé and indifferent to values other than these, an isolated individual is often unable to convert those about him, but when they see a community in which the members have learnt to love one another, they are deeply moved and astonished to find at last what they have been looking for, often without admitting it even to themselves. By contrast, where Christians do not live in charity and help one another, but quarrel among themselves, their numbers inevitably decrease. This is not surprising; men who are honest dislike living in a society that does not practise what it preaches, that stresses the duty of loving one's neighbour and does nothing about it that requires any effort.

Brotherly love comes from the heart, like all other forms of love, "from a sincere heart loving one another earnestly" (I Peter 1. 22).[1] It brings men together, it unites them and causes them to raise their hearts together to their Father in heaven. Here again, as in a previous chapter,[2] we find that need which love creates of carrying the one it loves on with it and out towards another.

From these quotations, it is easy to understand why the apostles placed such emphasis on brotherly love, why they were so demanding in this matter, and why they regarded with such horror anything that could affect the unity that was found in each of these Christian communities. In connection with their emphasis on this point, it is astonishing but true that in the early days of the Church when preaching, spreading the message of Christ and the salvation of all men were clearly the main preoccupations, *not once* in the writings that have

---

[1] [Douay Version.—*Translator.*]
[2] Chapter 13, "The Laws of Human Love: The Law of Extension."

survived do we find a question like: "How many converts have you made?", but they speak constantly of the atmosphere that prevailed within the young communities. From this we can suppose that they considered that if the atmosphere was one of charity, the growth of the communities would take care of itself. At the end of one of the idyllic pictures of the Church in Jerusalem that the Acts of the Apostles have left to us, we find this significant reflection: "And each day the Lord added to their fellowship others that were to be saved" (Acts 2. 47).

In the matter of charity not only did the Apostles place great emphasis on it, but they were extremely demanding: "If anything is meant by encouragement in Christ, by loving sympathy, by common fellowship in the spirit, by feelings of tenderness and pity, fill up my cup of happiness by thinking with the same mind, cherishing the same bond of charity, soul knit to soul in a common unity of thought. You must never act in a spirit of factiousness, or of ambition; each of you must have the humility to think others better men than himself, and study the welfare of others, not his own. Yours is to be the same mind which Christ Jesus shewed. His nature is, from the first, divine, and yet he did not see, in the rank of Godhead, a prize to be coveted" (Phil. 2. 1–6). This is indeed an exacting programme! We are asked to value union so highly that, beyond all our differences in character, we will succeed in finding a common point of view. This is not an easy task for a husband and wife, and St Paul is speaking of an entire community! He is not speaking in one of those bursts of enthusiasm to which impetuous men are prone, he returns to the subject frequently, and he is right: we have all experienced the way in which "discussing our ideas" can cause serious rifts among those who have so much in common. Jesus himself goes much further in his discourse after the Last Supper: "That they too may be one in us, as thou, Father, art in me, and I in thee" (John 17. 21). He gives us as our model the union that is between him and his Father and which makes them live "each in the other". If we look at our own lives in the light of these texts, we will probably understand why the numbers of those converted to the Church today are so small.

When Paul hears of the divisions among the Christians in Corinth, he reacts vigorously: "I entreat you, brethren, as you love the name of our Lord Jesus Christ, use, all of you, the same language. There must be no divisions among you; you must be restored to unity of mind and purpose. The account I have of you, my brethren, from Chloe's household, is that there are dissensions among you; each of you, I mean, has a cry of his own, I am for Paul, I am for Apollo, I am for Cephas, I am for Christ. What, has Christ been divided up? Was it Paul that was crucified for you? Was it in Paul's name that you were baptized? Thank God I did not baptize any of you except Crispus and Gaius; so that no one can say it was in my name you were baptized. (Yes, and I did baptize the household of Stephanas; I do not know that I baptized anyone else.)" (I Cor. i. 10–16).

Later, he writes: "And here is a warning I have for you. I can give you no praise for holding your assemblies in a way that does harm, not good. From the first, when you meet in church, there are divisions among you; so I hear, and in some measure believe it. Parties there must needs be among you, so that those who are true metal may be distinguished from the rest. And when you assemble together, there is no opportunity to eat a supper of the Lord; each comer hastens to eat the supper he has brought for himself, so that one man goes hungry, while another has drunk deep. Have you no homes to eat and drink in, that you should shew contempt to God's church, and shame the poor? Praise you? There is no room for praise here" (I Cor. ii. 17–22).

The chief obstacle to union within Christian communities is that tendency that men and women have of becoming walled up in some kind of closed circle. This sort of mentality must be vigorously eliminated in our parishes and Catholic societies, and we must be perpetually on the alert against it, as it is a spiritual ground-ivy that springs up at great speed wherever the smallest piece of root remains. These days many people feel the desire to group together as Christians, which is good to the extent that the groups remain open, and in contact with the rest of the community.

One group that needs restoring to its former vigour is the parish, the family of Christians gathered round the parish priest who is their spiritual father. The role of the laity in the parish is not new: St Pius X considered that it was essential to have a group of lay people, in every parish, who really lived the Gospel and were ready to spread it to others.[1] We should like to add that these people should aim at giving the priest all the support he needs in his work among the mass of ordinary people committed to his pastoral care. More and more the laity are beginning to understand that the complete moral isolation of the priest, his life year in year out among people whose attitude is one of unvarying and total lack of interest, are not precisely conducive to the general health of a priest's soul. What hope can there be of seeing priestly vocations germinate and thrive in places utterly insensitive to anything even remotely like an affectionate understanding on the priest's part?

It is now time to be more specific and to look more closely at the doctrine of Christ. We will take his teaching from the Sermon on the Mount in St Matthew's Gospel, and two parables in St Luke. One point is made quite clear: "And I tell you, that if your justice does not give fuller measure than the justice of the scribes and the Pharisees, you shall not enter into the kingdom of heaven" (Mat. 5. 20). A Christian who knows for certain that "God is love" and that he is God's son, will never imagine that sanctity is a mere matter of carrying out a set of legal observances, even if he were to do so with great care and good will; his sanctity must come from trying to behave as God's son, a thing which is demanding but which frees him from the legalistic mentality, alas, too prevalent in times gone by. He must try to answer all the demands of love, however great they may be.

(1) "You have heard that it was said to the men of old, Thou shalt do no murder; if a man commits murder, he must answer for it before the court of justice. But I tell you that any man who is angry with his brother must answer for it before the court of justice, and any man who says Raca to his brother must answer for it before the Council; and any man who says to his brother, Thou fool,[2] must answer for it in hell fire. If

---

[1] Cf. *L'Ami du Clergé*, 20 January 1931, which gives an account of a remarkable conversation between the Holy Father and a group of cardinals.

[2] [In the French, "fool" is rendered as "*renégat*", i.e. "renegade." This translation explains the author's subsequent commentary.—*Translator*.]

thou art bringing thy gift, then, before the altar, and rememberest there that thy brother has some ground of complaint against thee, leave thy gift lying there before the altar, and go home; be reconciled with thy brother first, and then come back to offer thy gift. If any man has a claim against thee, come to terms there and then, while thou art walking in the road with him; or else it may be that the claimant will hand thee over to the judge, and the judge to the officer, and so thou wilt be cast into prison. Believe me, thou shalt not be set at liberty until thou hast paid the last farthing" (ibid. 21-6). This first commandment concerns those attitudes which destroy unity—which explains why the tone is so uncompromising. The man who is angry with his brother is damaging unity and deserves a punishment, as the text implies by citing him "before the court of justice"; the man who is guilty of insulting another man gravely deserves to be brought before a higher tribunal which can pronounce a heavier sentence; and finally, the man who accuses another of having abandoned the community deserves to be excommunicated himself and so "answer for it in hell fire". It goes without saying that both the insults and the anger are taken to be fully intentional.

If unity is destroyed it must be re-established without delay—"before bringing thy gift before the altar", as Jesus said. We must remember that the Mass is the gathering together of Christians round their priest to offer themselves to the Father in union with the body of Christ. This gathering becomes hypocritical if those it brings together are in fact divided by persistent quarrels. We should not allow such hypocrisy, and still less should we ever go to communion with a grudge in our heart: this is a sacrament of "common union", and to receive it without accepting its spirit is to commit that "falsehood against the sacrament" of which Thomas Aquinas speaks.[1] The duty of reconciliation inculcated by Jesus cannot be taken lightly, to do so is to weaken the links of the Christian community and prepare the way for its disintegration.

We all know that it is never easy to settle a quarrel; it takes a great deal of goodwill on both sides, such as only an atmosphere of genuine prayer can produce; and certain practical rules must be observed. For example, we must avoid asking

---

[1] *Summa Theologica*, III*, 80, 4, resp.

ourselves whether we were 95% wrong, or only 5%; we must act as though the fault was ours and take the initiative in ending the quarrel and, if necessary, in apologizing. We must stop wondering *who* was wrong or *who* was right, and look together for *what* is right. Above all we must follow the procedure that Jesus himself advised in the Gospels: "If thy brother does thee wrong, go at once and tax him with it, as a private matter between thee and him; and so, if he will listen to thee, thou hast won thy brother. If he will not listen to thee, take with thee one or two more, that the whole matter may be certified by the voice of two or three witnesses. If he will not listen to them, then speak of it to the church; and if he will not even listen to the church, then count him all one with the heathen and the publican" (Mat. 18. 15–17).

To take him before the Church as a first step would show a distinct lack of enterprise, and might give the matter an importance that it did not deserve. Therefore, we must start by a personal and friendly effort; only if this does not succeed will we ask the help of our friends, and finally, if necessary, of the Church in the person of the priest. If all this is still unsuccessful, the man who refuses to be reconciled must be excluded from the community, as must those who are such bad Christians that they are causes of scandal to those around them. Paul, in certain cases, has no hesitation on the subject: "Why, there are reports of incontinence among you, and such incontinence as is not practised even among the heathen; a man taking to himself his father's wife. And you, it seems, have been contumacious over it, instead of deploring it, and expelling the man who has been guilty of such a deed from your company. For myself, though I am not with you in person, I am with you in spirit; and, so present with you, I have already passed sentence on the man who has acted thus. Call an assembly, at which I will be present in spirit, with all the power of our Lord Jesus Christ, and so, in the name of our Lord Jesus Christ, hand over the person named to Satan, for the overthrow of his corrupt nature, so that his spirit may find salvation in the day of our Lord Jesus Christ. This good conceit of yourselves is ill grounded. Have you never been told that a little leaven is enough to leaven the whole batch? Rid yourselves of the leaven which remains over, so that you may be a new mixture, still uncontaminated as you are. Has not Christ been sacrificed for us, our paschal victim? Let us keep the feast, then, not with the leaven of yesterday, that was all vice and mischief, but with unleavened bread, with purity and honesty of intent. . . . Banish, then, the offender from your company" (I Cor. 5. 1–8, 13). There are certain evils which threaten the life of the Church, and unless we exclude these evils, and the men who spread them, from the community, it will be weakened and the message of love we have to preach will be diminished.

(2) "You have heard that it was said, Thou shalt not commit adultery. But I tell you that he who casts his eyes on a woman so as to lust after her has already committed adultery with her in his heart. If thy right eye is the occasion of thy falling into sin, pluck it out and cast it away from thee; better to lose one part of thy body than to have the whole cast into hell. And if thy right hand is an occasion of falling, cut it off and cast it away from thee; better to lose one of thy limbs than to have thy whole body cast into hell. It was said, too, Whoever will put away his wife must first give her a writ of separation. But I tell you that the man who puts away his wife (setting aside the matter of unfaithfulness) makes an adulteress of her, and whoever marries her after she has been put away, commits adultery" (Mat. 5. 27–32). This second commandment deals with faithfulness in marriage, which is the basis of the family. Problems in this connection are generally treated these days as problems of chastity, but they are equally matters of charity. It is not possible to live in charity if one does not start by respecting the ties that are made by nature and strengthened by the sacrament of marriage. How can a man who is not capable of being faithful to his wife claim that his behaviour towards society in general is all that it should be? We all know the consequences of adultery and divorce, especially when they become commonplace in society: the unhappiness caused to the innocent party, frequently the breaking up of another family, financial difficulties, invariably trouble in bringing up the children, and finally the problems of children in broken homes who may be unwanted and even maltreated by their own parents.

We can be grateful to Jesus for the firmness of his principles, and we must cultivate in our hearts that awareness of the feelings of others which he asks of us. The Christian home should remain a stronghold of love and as such it is one of the best gifts that our Lord has given to the world. But often our homes are not a complete success because we are not willing to give ourselves completely. We must, therefore, ask ourselves what there might be in our own family that would prevent any one of us from making that whole-hearted gift of self, and then we must ask our Lord's help to put things right, confident that he will never refuse it.

(3) "Again, you have heard that it was said to the men of old, Thou shalt not perjure thyself; thou shalt perform what thou hast sworn in the sight of the Lord. But I tell you that you should not bind yourselves by any oath at all; not by heaven, for heaven is God's throne; nor by earth, for earth is the footstool under his feet; nor by Jerusalem, for it is the city of the great king. And thou shalt not swear by thy own head, for thou hast no power to turn a single hair of it white or black. Let your word be Yes for Yes, and No for No; whatever goes beyond this, comes of evil" (Mat. 5. 33–7). How is this commandment, which appears to be concerned entirely with our relations with God, connected with the love of our neighbour? Because it helps us to create an atmosphere of frankness and mutual confidence that is essential if we are to live as brothers. Swearing is both the seed and the fruit of discord, and love cannot thrive in an atmosphere of mistrust and boorish indifference to the feelings of others. Conversely, it is where our ties are closest that mutual respect must be greatest. There is no happiness in a marriage where husband and wife no longer respect each other or in a family where parents and children have no consideration for one another's rights.

(4) Let us leave St Matthew for a moment and pass on to St Luke to study the parable of Lazarus and the rich man (16. 19–31): "There was a rich man once, that was clothed in purple and lawn, and feasted sumptuously every day. And there was a beggar, called Lazarus, who lay at his gate, covered with sores, wishing that he could be fed with the crumbs which fell from the rich man's table, but none was ready to give them to him; the very dogs came and licked his sores. Time went on; the beggar died, and was carried by the angels to Abraham's

bosom; the rich man died too, and found his grave in hell. And there, in his suffering, he lifted up his eyes, and saw Abraham far off, and Lazarus in his bosom. And he said, with a loud cry, Father Abraham, take pity on me; send Lazarus to dip the tip of his finger in water, and cool my tongue; I am tormented in this flame. But Abraham said, My son, remember that thou didst receive thy good fortune in thy life-time, and Lazarus, no less, his ill fortune; now he is in comfort, thou in torment. And, besides all this, there is a great gulf fixed between us and you, so that there is no passing from our side of it to you, no crossing over to us from yours. Whereupon he said, Then, father, I pray thee send him to my own father's house; for I have five brethren; let him give these a warning, so that they may not come, in their turn, into this place of suffering. Abraham said to him, They have Moses and the prophets; let them listen to these. They will not do that, father Abraham, said he; but if a messenger comes to them from the dead, they will repent. But he answered him, If they do not listen to Moses and the prophets, they will be unbelieving still, though one should rise from the dead."

The thing which strikes us about this parable is the severity of the rich man's punishment. His sufferings are terrible—so terrible that he begs for a drop of water on his tongue—and irremediable: one by one his pleas are rejected without a word of pity in a style that, in its tranquil unconcern, sends shivers down our back. We would do well to consider, therefore, exactly what he had done wrong. Had he led too opulent a life? But this is not a crime in itself, especially as there is nothing in the Gospel to indicate that his behaviour was debauched or even mildly scandalous. Did he refuse to give alms to Lazarus? Certainly not; had he done so Lazarus would never have stayed at his gate. So where did his sin lie? It must undoubtedly have lain in the fact that he never realized that the man was in need. It was not enough to give alms occasionally, he should have brought the poor man into his house, given him enough to eat and taken care of him until he was in good health, found him a job and generally set him on his feet again, which is quite different from an occasional handout.

Compare the rich man's indifference with the understanding goodness of the Samaritan (Luke 10. 25–37). We can see how, one after the other, he thinks of all the needs of the robbers' victim: he binds up his wounds, he brings him to the inn and he pays for his lodging until he has recovered. The conclusion is obvious: the role of the Christian is to discover the needs of his neighbour, and then do all he can to help him. This is not easy, as the needs of those around us are many and varied: there are the needs of the body and those of the heart. Can we in all honesty say that we create about us an atmosphere that brings out the best in people, and encourages their personalities to develop? If this is not yet true of us, we are not living in charity. Love is very demanding: the mother will look for and anticipate the needs of her child; Jesus came on earth and experienced our needs for himself; now it is our turn: "Do to other men all that you would have them do to you; that is the law and the prophets" (Mat. 7. 12).

(5) We now come to what can be called the paradoxical commandments of the Sermon on the Mount: "You have heard that it was said, An eye for an eye and a tooth for a tooth. But I tell you that you should not offer resistance to injury; if a man strikes thee on thy right cheek, turn the other cheek also towards him; if he is ready to go to law with thee over thy coat, let him have it and thy cloak with it; if he compels thee to attend him on a mile's journey, go two miles with him of thy own accord. Give to him who asks, and if a man would borrow from thee, do not turn away" (Mat. 5. 38–42). To be asked not to retaliate is hard enough, and here is Jesus asking us to turn the other cheek! This seems like an acceptance, if not an encouragement, of evil. If we think about it we shall see the logic of this advice: if we really wish to preserve the oneness of the community, if we value it, it is worth putting up with a lot to prevent its destruction. But why should we tolerate something that is wrong? The reason is easy to see: we should do so in order to kill the resentment that springs up in our hearts, and which will certainly flourish if we do nothing about it. Jesus advises us to attack as the best method of defence, and if the examples he gives us are not ones that occur in our daily lives, it is not hard to think of others which do! When we are criticized, our whole attitude must show that we are willing to receive further criticism also; or when someone returns a book to us with inkstains on it, we must be willing to lend him another one.

Must we apply this commandment in all circumstances? Of course not; it is given for the benefit of the community and does not apply where it is subversive or harmful to our neighbour. Christianity, therefore, does not oblige us to allow burglars free rein, or to give up the right to defend ourselves in court. Deciding where the commandment holds good, and where it does not, is a question of applying common sense, not simply that of the natural man, but that of the Christian who is penetrated through and through by the grace and the light of Christ.

(6) "You have heard that it was said, Thou shalt love thy neighbour and hate thy enemy. But I tell you, Love your enemies, do good to those who hate you, pray for those who persecute and insult you, that so you may be true sons of your Father in heaven, who makes his sun rise on the evil and equally on the good, his rain fall on the just and equally on the unjust. If you love those who love you, what title have you to a reward? Will not the publicans do as much? If you greet none but your brethren, what are you doing more than others? Will not the very heathen do as much? But you are to be perfect, as your heavenly Father is perfect" (Mat. 5. 43–8). The law of Moses did not say: "Hate thy enemy", and the phrase appears in the Gospels chiefly for literary effect. But it does draw our attention to an important fact: namely that the Old Testament did not open up any distant vistas to the law of the universality of love. Jesus invites us to look with love on those who are not yet, or who are no longer, our brothers. In this way the community will be able to grow, and it is natural that its members will want to invite those around them to become part of the community in their turn. The Good Samaritan helped the man who had fallen among thieves without worrying whether or not he was a Jew—the Jews were enemies of the Samaritans—and because of his kindness, two men who might have been hostile to each other became bound by ties of friendship. The Good Samaritan "made a neighbour". This is what the practising Christian does when he looks around and sees what needs to be done, and then helps his brother from a heart that is filled with love.

We can see how perfectly balanced is this precept which marks the summit of charity. There is no question of preferring our enemies to our friends, or of doing them special favours, but equally we should never refuse them our goodwill or our help when they need it, just as the Father does not refuse the unjust the sun and the rain that they need for the harvest. Still less are we asked to collaborate with them in wrong-doing.

In order to love fully we must be clear about our priorities. Those nearest to us come first. It is only too easy to be full of sympathy over a tragedy that has happened at the other side of the world, and about which there is really very little we can do; it is only too human to be charming and full of good works where those outside the home are concerned and to reserve one's ill-humour for one's family. In the Gospels Jesus always gives as examples situations where people find themselves in direct contact with something that needs to be done. It is not that we should narrow our horizons: he himself desires "that all men should be saved, and be led to recognize the truth" (I Tim. 2. 4), but we must not take refuge from facts in dreams to cushion our laziness; we must keep ourselves in the healthy atmosphere of reality.

Charity, therefore, will make us look kindlily on all men, even those who wish us ill. We shall be for the sinner, but remain opposed to sin, for the Communist but against his doctrines, for the Freemason but against Freemasonry.[1] We must oppose false doctrines, but not the men who preach them, otherwise we shall be guilty of sectarianism.

Finally, when a sinner comes to regret his past, we must welcome him into the community with understanding and trust. It is a terrible thing when Christians no longer believe in conversions. Our Master did, and he trusted the repentant converts, as we can see by the way he behaved to St Peter after the future head of the Church had denied that he ever knew him. In spite of this lapse—and what a lapse!—Jesus, after his resurrection, gave back to Peter those powers which he had so richly deserved to lose. A community which no longer believes that a man can have a change of heart clearly has an atrophied faith and is sinking fast into a religion of mere routine. We must not forget that Jesus has called us to be "perfect, as our heavenly Father is perfect", to follow him and set no limits to our love.

[1] [The Freemasonry in France and many other countries which is known to be actively anti-religious.—*Translator*.]

Chapter 22

THE LAW OF NOURISHMENT

In order that our spiritual life may be sustained and increased, it is not enough for it to be put into practice in ground that has been cleared for it, and then left to grow of its own accord. It will need continual nourishment.

This supply of nourishment comes from the sacrament of the Eucharist. We must, therefore, study the use of this sacrament, and this will lead us to the problem of organizing our own personal spiritual life.

It is nearly sixty years since St Pius X, by his decree *Sacra Tridentina Synodus*,[1] reopened the tabernacles and recalled the unchanging teaching of the Church on Holy Communion. And yet it must be admitted that, in spite of so much that has been achieved in this domain, Christian public opinion does not appear to have realized to the full the meaning of this sacrament. So let us try to understand what the Holy Father and the Church are saying to us.

As we look at the host, raised above our heads by the priest at Holy Mass, our hearts are filled with two thoughts at the same time:

(1) This host really contains the Body of Christ. I will bow down and worship my Lord, present in it for love of me.

(2) This host is a sacrament established for the good of my soul. I will go and receive this sacrament.

Both are excellent thoughts, both are recommended by the Church, no doubt about that. But the question is, which is the more important?

If we open the Gospels, we see that on two separate occasions, Jesus speaks of the Eucharist, the first time to promise it, the second time to give it, and each time he does so he associates it with food.

---

[1] Decree of the Congregation of the Council, 20 December 1905. *Acta Sanctae Sedis*, 38 (1905-6), pp. 401 ff.

In Galilee, Jesus found himself standing before a crowd which had followed him and listened to his teaching. These people were hungry, and to give them something to eat he multiplied the loaves, and then, seeing they were carried away by their enthusiasm after this miracle, he went away alone up on to the hillside (John 6. 15). That night he rejoined his disciples as they were rowing their boat across the stormy sea. And the next day he once more spoke to the crowd which had come to find him again at Capharnaum: "You should not work to earn food which perishes in the using. Work to earn food which affords, continually, eternal life, such food as the Son of Man will give you; God, the Father, has authorized him" (John 6. 27).

The crowd replied mentioning the "bread out of heaven" given by Moses; they were suddenly not satisfied with the multiplication of ordinary bread, they wanted something more. But when Jesus spoke to them of a kind of bread that would give them eternal life, they did not understand him, any more than he had been understood by Nicodemus or the Samaritan woman. Men were willing to come to him, but they refused to believe in him, and they "complained among themselves" when he said he was the bread which had come down from heaven. Knowing they were complaining, instead of toning down the paradoxical nature of what he was saying, he insisted upon it, laying particular emphasis on its most disquieting aspects: "My flesh is real food, my blood is real drink" (ibid. 56). He went so far that in the end they were thoroughly upset, and "after this, many of his disciples went back to their old ways, and walked no more in his company" (ibid. 67).

All this happened in a context of food, nourishment and eating; it is a question of faith and food, never of respect.

When the time came to carry out his promise Jesus called his disciples together. In what circumstances? Those of the paschal *meal* at which a lamb had to be killed and eaten. This was not eating in a purely spiritual, and even less in a purely symbolic or mythical sense, but in a real and physical one. It was in the middle of this meal that the Master offered his followers the bread which is his body and the wine which is his blood. What did he say? He said: "Take, eat, this is my body. . . . Drink, all of you, of this; for this is my blood", and he gave the bread and the wine to each of them in turn (Mat. 26. 26, 27). Here again, there is no question of worship or respect, everything is seen from the point of view of the *use* of the sacrament.

So our question is answered: Jesus instituted the Eucharist not primarily in order that his presence in the sacrament should be the object of our adoration and respect, but in order to give us nourishment.

It is not surprising, therefore, that Jansenism, which insisted on the respect due to the Real Presence to such an extent that "very few people were considered worthy of receiving the Holy Eucharist every day",[1] achieved just one thing, which was to make people close their minds and harden their hearts to love. At the present time in France, there are whole dioceses where the faith has practically disappeared, dating from the time when there happened to be a Jansenist bishop. So when Christ speaks of love, the last thing we should do is to click our heels, and stand to attention! Instead, we should run to his embrace like the little children in the Gospel.

Food gives life, and with life comes the strength which shows itself in action and growth. An undernourished population becomes weak, an easy prey to every kind of disease, and the death-rate increases rapidly, as we can see only too well in so many underdeveloped countries. A vigorous and healthy population can grow and take action, and it is the same with the Church: lack of the Eucharist produces weakness and death for her; abundance of divine food makes her grow. Soon after the action of St Pius X concerning the Eucharist, we had the missionary action of Pius XI, who set up as many missionary dioceses in the eighteen years of his reign as had been founded over a number of centuries before him. We should not forget that every time we receive Holy Communion we are helping in the growth of the Church, and every time we do not receive it we are refusing this help and slowing down its rate of growth, so we should realize that our responsibility is far more than a merely personal one.

How often should we take this heavenly bread? St Pius X leaves us in no doubt about it: daily communion is normal and desirable for every Christian. And if it is difficult for some

[1] *Sacra Tridentina Synodus.*

H*

people to achieve this, then at least they should receive communion weekly, and this is certainly possible for almost everyone since the relaxation of the rules of fasting. Therefore, we should have no hesitation in taking advantage of the new rules, for if the Church has allowed such a change in regulations that have lasted for more than a thousand years, she does not do so lightly or without good reason, and so we should take the path she is inviting us to follow.

Here we may answer a question which may occur to some people: if frequent communion is desirable and to be recommended, why does the Church tell us we are only obliged to take communion once a year, at Easter time? This, we believe, is really very simple: the law of nourishment does not really contain any commands, properly speaking. You cannot order someone to eat; it is for the individual to know when he needs food and to satisfy his hunger; therefore, when we are ordered to "do our Easter duties" it has quite a different meaning: it means our reconciliation with the Father and our return to Christian charity, from which we have cut ourselves off by our sins. Over and above its value as spiritual food, this communion has therefore a value as reconciliation; it puts a seal on our reunion with our brothers in Christ, and of course, we may assume that it leads to a return to spiritual health, and will be followed by a normal intake of spiritual food.

Lastly, we may note in passing a fact of which many people seem to be unaware, namely, that when one is in danger of death, the reception of Holy Communion becomes an *obligation* (can. 864, §1).

"The desire of Jesus Christ and the Church that all the faithful should approach the sacred banquet every day is founded above all on the following consideration: that the faithful, joined to God through the sacrament, may receive in it strength to calm their passions, to wash out the stain of their daily slight sins and to forestall the danger of those more serious sins to which human weakness is exposed. It is not chiefly in order that this may give honour and worship to the Lord, nor in order that the reception may be some sort of payment or reward for the virtues of the communicants."[1]

[1] *Sacra Tridentina Synodus.*

Chapter 23

ORGANIZING ONE'S SPIRITUAL
LIFE

This title may seem to be a contradiction to what we have said previously about the need of freedom for our souls. But the contradiction is only apparent; in fact, if constraint kills love so does spiritual bohemianism, as it inevitably ends in laziness, and love needs effort to make it grow. In addition, what we must organize is not, and can never be, love itself but the acts which express it and enable it to grow. Finally, we can and must be adaptable as well as organized: rules are meant to free us from our own laziness, not to be tiresome strait-jackets.

As this book is addressed mainly to lay people, it is not possible to outline a programme that would be applicable to everyone. Some people are more called to prayer and have more opportunity for it than others whose lives are particularly crowded or busy. We shall, therefore, suggest a programme that would be suitable for a girl who works about eight hours a day, in an office for example, and has various things to do about the house when she goes home. She is not overworked, but neither has she a great deal of spare time, and so she can be taken as average in this context. We would suggest for her, apart from short night and morning prayers, the following:

(1) Communion as often as she can, if possible every day. If necessary, she should not hesitate to go to church simply for long enough to receive communion in a properly recollected spirit; it is not obligatory to be present for the whole of Mass in order to receive communion, and by asking too much there is a danger of obtaining nothing.

(2) About a quarter of an hour of spiritual reading every day. This exercise can be considered as the basis for all the others. If we never read, our stock of ideas is not renewed or enriched, and a fatal boredom sets in. We should choose books

that really teach us something and give us food for thought, and reserve the easier and more familiar books for the days when we are too tired to concentrate on new ideas. We should not hurry but really assimilate what we are reading in a spirit of prayer. It is better to read a little well than a lot carelessly.

(3) The rosary, also daily. Although there are not many people today, and certainly not many young women, who say the rosary regularly, it remains one of the devotions most encouraged by the Church. In the rosary God's own greeting that the angel brought to Mary rises up to her again in heaven. The practice of saying the rosary gradually took form in the Middle Ages. Known as "the layfolk's breviary" it grew up around the great abbeys and was the layman's way of sharing in the collective prayer of the Church. Normally when we are saying the rosary we think not about the words of the *Ave Maria* but about the different mysteries, either the traditional ones, or others if preferred. In this way the rosary should not present any great difficulties to the average Christian. There is the added advantage that one can easily say the rosary on the way to and from work, and in this way it does not take up any extra time in an overcrowded day.

This is a modest programme, but we believe it is sufficient to sustain a genuine spiritual life, and it goes without saying that one should try to supplement it whenever possible. If time can be found, a visit to the Blessed Sacrament can be included, and this will gradually lead to the practice of meditation.

Chapter 24

CONFESSION

Confession is, after the Eucharist, the sacrament most frequently used in the Christian life, and it is worth going into at some length because the penitent takes such an active part in it, and also because we make so many practical errors with regard to it.

First of all, let us take a glance at the attitude of Jesus to the sinners he meets in the Gospels. This attitude is not always the same.

(1) Anyone who admits he is a sinner is received without a word of reproach; he is forgiven at once, and almost, one might say, without formalities. This is the case of the sinful woman in St Luke's Gospel, and of the good thief, and the same note is struck in the parable of the prodigal son.

(2) When a sinner comes to him without thinking of his sins, Jesus reminds him of them, and here we think of the palsied man lowered from the roof, in the Gospel of St Luke (Chapter 5); elsewhere he brings the sinner to realize his sin, as he does for the Samaritan woman at Jacob's well (John 4).

(3) When a sinner is too full of vanity to realize his sin, Jesus is severe. To the Pharisees for example he uses very harsh words indeed: "You belong to earth, I to heaven" (John 8. 23); "You belong to your father, that is, the devil, and are eager to gratify the appetites which are your father's" (ibid. 44). In this way he tries to break open the "whited sepulchre" to reach the rottenness within and reveal it to them.

The priest should model his attitude on that of Christ; he should be very understanding with those who confess their sins, he should not allow those who are insufficiently aware of their sins to remain ignorant of them, neither should he tolerate the self-conceit which denies sin, but he must point it out so that the unfortunate soul of the sinner may be rid of it. Sometimes it is necessary to lance an abscess. The treatment is pleasant neither to give nor to receive, but this is the only way to drain away certain kinds of purulent matter.

The unhappy sinners who turn to Jesus are drawn to him by two qualities: his goodness which forgives their sins, and his holiness which refuses any dealings with evil. And so it is in our own time: the penitent hopes to find in his confessor the same combination of these two virtues. The priest, the channel through which forgiveness flows, should be able to reproduce the charity of Christ to the sinner, a charity full of kindness and understanding. As Christ's minister he must do everything he can to lead the soul entrusted to him away from evil; he must also put him on the road to recovery, and know how to ask of him a really serious effort, albeit one in proportion to his abilities.

Far from being an inhuman and intolerable burden, confession fulfils one of the most fundamental needs in the heart of man: to unburden our guilt, to hear the words of pardon, and to know for certain that we are forgiven, because of the outward and visible sign of the sacrament; all this gives us the peace of mind we need. On the level of human relationships, we can see the deepening of understanding which occurs in a family where the son confesses to his father if he has done something wrong. All the more reason, then, for this to be so when we turn to our Father in heaven, who, through the medium of the priest, lets the sense of his spiritual fatherhood fill our hearts with love and trust. The confessor tries not to apply the moral laws ruthlessly, but to look at each sinner with new eyes so as to see him as God sees him. For his part, the penitent must not be satisfied with just being within the letter of the law, but he should make use of his confession to learn to know himself and to become fully responsible for his own behaviour. He should not, under the guise of obedience, be dependent on the priest for every decision he makes; he should learn to achieve full spiritual maturity.

At this point we should like to tackle two problems which the Christian meets in the course of his life.

(1) *The Problem of Eliminating Serious Sins*

If we want to achieve this, the first condition is that we should realize that such sins are a very real possibility in any

Christian life, even if it is usually an irreproachable one. This is the attitude of true humility, and it brings with it another attitude. This is, that if we are faced with the fact of having committed a serious sin, we will feel regret and remorse, but we will not panic.

This, unfortunately, is not always what we find. It fairly often happens that people completely lose their heads at the thought that they have committed a mortal sin; it is hard to say whether through exaggerated self-esteem or as a result of an upbringing which taught them to be afraid of God, but in any case this terror seems to be curiously allied with a total absence of any true and sincere regret for what they have done. This has tragic consequences: first they try by every means they can find to persuade themselves that the sin they have committed is not, in fact, a sin; they deliberately silence their conscience, they are afraid to go and see a priest, and they start on the road of dubious or sacrilegious confessions and communions. In the end they are convinced that there is no way out and they are condemned by their own foolishness to live in a terrible despair. This lasts until some exceptional circumstance, like a retreat or a pilgrimage, leads them back to the confessional, where the abscess can be pierced and they can re-emerge whole and joyful again. Frankly, it would have been better if they had never got to such a point in the first place.

Again, we should not use one sin to fight another, for example achieving the virtue of chastity by the sin of pride. This is not merely an imaginary danger—we only have to think of Port-Royal, the breeding-ground of Jansenism.

From a practical point of view then, as soon as we are threatened by any consuming temptation, we should not of course neglect the measures of mental hygiene or the indications already given by us in other chapters of this book. But to these we should not forget to add prayer, a prayer in which, remembering all the love Jesus showed us by coming down on earth, we ask him to come into our hearts, among our perverse and wicked thoughts, just as, long ago, he lived among the sinners of Israel, and to live on in us so that by the strength of his love he may remove every obstacle that threatens to separate us from him.

If we should fall in spite of this prayer, we should not allow discouragement to overwhelm us; as soon as we can, we should pick ourselves up by making an act of perfect contrition, and then by making a sincere confession; then, valiantly, we can take up our struggle again, constantly repeating to Jesus the same prayer for help. We may be quite certain that the answer will not be long in coming. We should remember that what is known as perfect contrition is not a contrition that is free from any flaw, but one elicited by the will for motives which in themselves are perfect, such as the Father's love, the sufferings of Jesus, the purity of the Holy Spirit who lives in our soul. That being so, this contrition can always be attained when we really wish it. After that, our sins are forgiven, the son has confessed to his Father and feels free once more to enjoy his love, and all that is left to be done is to ask pardon of the Mystical Body of Christ, which will make official our regained state of peace by the gesture of absolution in the sacrament of penance, and will then allow us to receive the sacrament of communion again.

(2) *The Confession of Venial Sins*

This is the second problem for which we have to find a solution. It concerns all devout people who go frequently to confession and often say that their confessions are monotonous to the point of nausea because "I always seem to have exactly the same things to confess", and they are perfectly aware that the priest, on the other side of the grille, would not disagree with them. How are we to avoid this unfortunate state of affairs for both sides, and how can we derive real benefit from these confessions which we so easily imagine as leading to nothing but dreary routine?

In all Christians there are a certain number of what might be described as chronic faults, because they apply to shortcomings of which we never rid ourselves entirely. Such, for example, are the neglect of prayer and of the duties of our state of life, minor offences against charity, and small lies. We know that such sins are called *venial* because their triviality assures them immediate forgiveness, or rather, their very triviality makes it impossible for us to imagine they could in any way estrange us from God.

As a result of this, there is one supremely important consequence of which we should make use: namely that we are not compelled to declare these shortcomings. To go even further, their declaration can be a handicap to us, however paradoxical that may seem. In fact, if we really intend to bring up every little lapse due to our weaknesses, we will finish by finding "a little something" which applies to every one of God's commandments and every deadly sin, and in the end we shall have told the priest so much, that neither he nor we ourselves can see the wood for the trees.

Therefore, we must do what all schools of spirituality advise us to do, although many people inclined to scruples have difficulty in resigning themselves to it; that is to say, we must make a choice from among our sins and only mention certain ones. But how are we to choose?

As a beginning we may observe that there are three different categories of sins:

(a) Sins which have been entirely intentional, such as premeditated lying and malicious gossip, or deliberate greed.

(b) Serious negligence, for example of our prayer or of the duties of our state of life. The point is not whether we have done everything well, whether we have prayed without giving in to distractions or done some admirable piece of work, but whether we have been lazy or lacking in determination to make the most of our intelligence and strength.

(c) Sins which the Holy Ghost reveals to us: for example, a child who is an habitual liar and who one day is suddenly seized with horror at the idea of lying, will admit that this awakening is a warning from God, and it will encourage him to take up the fight against this fault of his, so that for quite some time he will take great care to mention everything he has said which he knows to be untrue. Little by little, as he begins to make some improvement, his confessions of lying will decrease, and at last they will only consist of the mention of one or two lapses and a summing up of the results he has obtained by his efforts.

Whatever the point we may have reached, it is most important to rid our confessions of the vague terms which seem to please some people, but which in fact mean absolutely nothing. Sometimes, what we say in this way is so watered-down that, as St Francis de Sales once remarked: "The greatest saints could say as much." What purpose do we imagine this serves, and to be quite frank, how do we expect it to be a basis for a sincere regret and a firm resolution to do better? And when we are faced with more serious sins, let us not be foolishly ashamed to admit the number of times we have committed them. Here again, when we answer—alas, only too frequently—: "Oh well, Father, not very often, you know", exactly what is he supposed to know? Does this show any trust in God's mercy?

How often should we go to confession, if we do not often commit mortal sins? Priests are required by Canon Law to make frequent confessions (can. 125) and members of religious orders weekly ones (can. 595). Lay people should go to confession not more often than once a fortnight, not less often than once a month. In all, about twenty confessions in the whole year.

Before we go to confession, we should make a thorough examination of conscience, while realizing that this serves little purpose if our soul is not turned towards God; for if it is not, those who are given to negligence will not see their faults, and will imagine that they have nothing to confess, in spite of an existence which is singularly lacking in love for God.

There is no use in our trying to "feel" repentant, for repentance is not a matter of emotion but of will; what we have to feel instead is our trust in God's forgiveness.

Lastly, it would be a good thing for us to remember the words which the priest says at every confession, which absolve us "from every bond of excommunication and of interdict". This is a vestige from a former time, when confession was less frequent than today, and only made in the case of very serious sins which cut off the sinner from the Church. All the same, this phrase is not without significance for us today, for every sin we commit is a sin against the charity of Christ and therefore tends to separate us from the "communion" or "common union" of our fellow Christians. Confession gives us back this element of union which sin made us lose, and therefore it is not only of value to the individual, but to the whole community.

Chapter 25

IN THE CHURCH

He too is that head whose body is the Church—Col. 1. 18.

Man's salvation is essentially a personal thing, as Ezechiel tells us (Chapters 18 and 33), because each soul is called to a direct relationship with God. But this salvation takes place within a community: in the Old Testament it was the chosen people of God, in the New Testament it is the Church.

Each of these communities has its origin in one man; Israel was the posterity of Abraham, a posterity of the flesh but miraculously given in the first place, and then purified by the rejection of Esau. The ties between Jesus and the Church are at once richer and more intimate. He himself describes the relationship like this: "I am the true vine, and it is my Father who tends it. The branch that yields no fruit in me, he cuts away; the branch that does yield fruit, he trims clean, so that it may yield more fruit. You, through the message I have preached to you, are clean already; you have only to live on in me, and I will live on in you. The branch that does not live on in the vine can yield no fruit of itself; no more can you, if you do not live on in me. I am the vine, you are its branches; if a man lives on in me, and I in him, then he will yield abundant fruit; separated from me, you have no power to do anything. If a man does not live on in me, he can only be like the branch that is cast off and withers away; such a branch is picked up and thrown into the fire, to burn there" (John 15. 1–6).

This shows us clearly that with him we form a single organism in which life is transmitted like the sap in a growing plant. St Paul, who gives us numerous variations on the idea of a body of which Christ is the head, expresses exactly the same thought. He also uses the image of a marriage, notably in the famous passage from Ephesians: "The man is the head to which the woman's body is united, just as Christ is the head of the Church, he, the Saviour on whom the safety of his body depends; and women must owe obedience at all points to their husbands, as the Church does to Christ. You who are husbands must shew love to your wives, as Christ shewed love to the Church when he gave himself up on its behalf. He would hallow it, purify it by bathing it in the water to which his word gave life; he would summon it into his own presence, the Church in all its beauty, no stain, no wrinkle, no such disfigurement; it was to be holy, it was to be spotless. And that is how husband ought to love wife, as if she were his own body; in loving his wife, a man is but loving himself. It is unheard of, that a man should bear ill-will to his own flesh and blood; no, he keeps it fed and warmed; and so it is with Christ and his Church; we are limbs of his body; flesh and bone, we belong to him. That is why a man will leave his father and mother and will cling to his wife, and the two will become one flesh. Yes, those words are a high mystery, and I am applying them here to Christ and his Church" (Eph. 5. 23–32). Here again St Paul is developing an idea we find in the Gospels, where John the Baptist says of the Messiah: "The bride is for the bridegroom" (John 3. 29), and in the Apocalypse: "Come with me, . . . and I will shew thee that bride, whose bridegroom is the Lamb" (21. 9). These two perspectives enable us to see what the Church represents for a follower of Christ.

(1) In a human family, both the husband and the wife share in giving life to the child, and from the time the child is born it is the wife who looks after him and sees that he grows strong and healthy. In the same way, the divine life is not given to us without the cooperation of the Church, for she is the guardian and the administrator of the sacrament of baptism, it is she who decides on the rites which accompany it and the people to whom it should be given or refused. This divine life which is given will then be strengthened, nourished or renewed when necessary by other sacraments, which are, of course, also acts of the Church. This should be enough to show that belonging to the Church is not a secondary consideration but one of the first importance.

It is for this reason that a Catholic is willing to suffer sometimes as a result of being in the Church, for example when his faults or his errors are corrected, or when members of the hierarchy or the laity make harsh judgements and sometimes cause him troubles that he has not deserved. He will not, on this account, conclude that he should leave the Church, because he knows that such a step would be fatal and cause sufferings quite out of proportion to any he may have to bear within the Church. We should add that our presence within the Church is a permanent one, it continues in heaven where those who enjoy in common the vision of the Father and of Christ are no longer isolated individuals, but persons grouped together in the Mystical Body.

(2) A mother passes on to the children the will of their father. Similarly the Church has authority to guide the faithful during the time of their pilgrimage on earth, teaching them, in the first place, the commandments of Christ, as he instructed: "All authority in heaven and on earth, he said, has been given to me; you, therefore, must go out, making disciples of all nations, and baptizing them in the name of the Father, and of the Son, and of the Holy Ghost, teaching them to observe all the commandments which I have given you" (Mat. 28. 18–20), and also preserving the natural moral law because, as we have said previously, it is not possible for divine life to take root in a natural order that is perverted.

(3) A wife remains lovingly faithful to the thoughts and wishes of her husband. Thus the Church remains loyal to the deposit of faith; it is through her that we know the Holy Scriptures, and the dogmas they contain. A Catholic knows that when he reads the Bible he is not doing so in an atmosphere of unattached exegesis but in one of Christian tradition, and in respectful obedience to this he finds all he needs to help him to interpret it correctly.

(4) All the cells in the body share the same life and react on one another. So, too, the actions of every Christian, whether he wishes it or not, affect the whole Church. This is why the dead branch of the vine or the gangrenous limb must be cut off and separated from the Body.

(5) The cells of the body do not all have the same importance, or the same function. In the Church, also, there will be different vocations and, as established by Christ, there will be a hierarchy of persons chosen to order the life of the Body and to lead the other members.

(6) When it is said that the Church is an "intermediary" between ourselves and God, we should on no account imagine this to mean that it forms some kind of barrier between men's souls and God. In fact the reverse is true. Everything in the Church is designed to produce direct contact between each soul and the three Persons of the Blessed Trinity. It would probably be better to say that the Church is a living community in which we meet our Lord.

(7) The Church is holy in all its parts, because the Holy Spirit lives in all its members. Even obvious sinners share in this holiness to some extent but their sins make it less visible, and this underlines our responsibility for living in such a way that the holiness of the Church becomes clearer and more transparent.

(8) The Church is essentially Catholic, that is to say it is able to welcome within it all nations and all races, to be large enough for all legitimate diversities, to receive within itself and give new life to all that is good and noble and beautiful, at any time, and in any place. For it is God's "will that all men should be saved, and be led to recognize the truth" (I Tim. 2. 4), and God, as we have so often said, never destroys but transforms and enriches.

Now let us stand back and look at the Church in relation to the whole of mankind. We shall see a moving sight, a whole procession of men and women, from the time of the Gospels to our own day, who have succeeded, in spite of their human weaknesses and failings, not only in raising themselves up to God, but in giving a new dimension to the moral evolution of mankind. This will help us to realize the incomparable gift that Christ has conferred upon us by making us members of his Mystical Body. The Church is unique in that she has never compromised on moral standards or on dogma, and has thus enabled us to live as sons of God, in spite of the world, the flesh and the devil. If we should hesitate to put our hand to the plough (Luke 9. 62) we should remember all the saints who have gone before us and who have shown us the magnificent results that can be achieved when men cooperate with God; they will not fail us and we must not fail them. We must think too of all those around us today who are looking for a meaning to life—and how are they to find God except through us who know him and love him?—and above all we must remember that it is in his Mystical Body that Christ comes to mankind. Finally we have the words of our Lord himself: "The harvest is plentiful enough, but the labourers are few; you must ask the Lord to whom the harvest belongs to send labourers out for the harvesting" (Luke 10. 2). And so we must pray with all our hearts that wherever he chooses to place us, we may always be counted among the number of his labourers.